CHILDREN and ANIMALS

CHILDREN and ANIMALS

Exploring the Roots of Kindness and Cruelty

Frank R. Ascione, Ph.D.

Purdue University Press / West Lafayette, Indiana

The writing of this book was sponsored by The Kenneth A. Scott Charitable Trust and American Humane

Printed in the United States of America

Library of Congress Cataloging-in-Publication Data

Ascione, Frank R.
Children and animals : exploring the roots of kindness and cruelty / Frank R. Ascione.
p. cm.
Includes bibliographical references and index.
ISBN 1-55753-377-6 (hardcover) -- ISBN 1-55753-383-0 (pbk.) 1. Animal welfare--Psychological aspects. 2. Cruelty. 3. Violence in children. 4. Conduct disorders in children. I. Title.

HV4708.A833 2004
155.4'1825--dc22

2004013476

CONTENTS

For Debbie

". . . and when all the pretty blossom had fallen
from our branches
we found that we were one tree not two."

From Louis de Bernières, *Corelli's Mandolin* (New York: Vintage International, 1994)

Support for this publication came from:

The American Humane Association

Founded in 1877, the American Humane Association is the nation's only organization dedicated to protecting both children and animals. Through a network of child and animal welfare and protection agencies and individuals, American Humane develops policies, legislation, curriculum, and trainings to protect children and animals from abuse, neglect, and exploitation. The nonprofit membership organization, headquartered in Denver, raises awareness about The Link® between animal abuse and other forms of violence, as well as the benefits derived from the human and animal bond. American Humane's regional office in Los Angeles is the authority behind the "No Animals Were Harmed..."™ End Credit Disclaimer on TV and film productions, and American Humane's office in Washington, DC, is an advocate for child- and animal-friendly legislation at the state and federal levels. Visit www.americanhumane.org to learn more.

The Kenneth A. Scott Charitable Trust, A KeyBank Trust

The Kenneth A. Scott Charitable Trust, A KeyBank Trust, promotes prevention of cruelty and humane treatment for companion animals, wildlife, and other animals. Most grants are made in Ohio, the Great Lakes region, or to national organizations for projects of national scope or significance in the protection of animals.

PREFACE

THE PATHS THAT CONVERGED to lead me to write this book were lined with ideas, people, and opportunities I could not have anticipated encountering when I became a student of developmental psychology in the late 1960s and early 1970s. During my studies, I was fortunate to have guides and mentors who affirmed, challenged, and sometimes redirected my efforts. I recall with great fondness the chance to work with Charles Ferster at Georgetown University and Jay Birnbrauer and John Burchard at The University of North Carolina at Chapel Hill. Each, in their own way, supported the development of my interest in how children are socialized - how they come to acquire and express the values most societies hold dear and see as critical to enhancing the human condition.

Some of my early research excursions into this general area were truly naïve and forgettable. But I continued to have an abiding interest in the factors that facilitated or impeded children's development of prosocial attitudes and behaviors - kindness, caring, altruism, and nurturance. Most often, these attitudes and behaviors were directed by children at other human beings but there were occasional studies that examined children's relations with nonhuman animals. These latter studies were few and far between and, at the time, I did not encounter any developmental colleagues with an interest in child-animal relations.

The 1980s saw my first collaboration with the Humane Society of the United States (HSUS), an organization that had developed one of the most carefully crafted educational curricula to teach elementary school children kindness, caring, and respect for the nonhuman creatures with whom we share this world, a field referred to as "humane education." Together with a group of colleagues at Utah State University, I spent a number of years evaluating HSUS's educational curriculum in schools in Connecticut, California, and Utah. This was an excellent opportunity to translate theoretical principles and research questions about the socialization process into a real-world setting with the potentially practical benefit of teaching children the value of their kindness toward and caring for vulnerable creatures in our environment. Much of this early work was supported by the Delta Society. However, neither my graduate studies nor my professional work in this area prepared me for the challenge I would encounter in 1990, a challenge provided by Phil Arkow.

Some of the questions I had addressed in my research included examining the mechanisms by which children learn kindness and caring, including the models provided by parents and other caregivers, peers, and various forms of media. The research also addressed how children's empathy toward animals developed and the relation of such empathy to empathy for other human beings. And yet, I soon learned how narrow my approach to this area had been. Phil Arkow, a well-respected professional in animal welfare, was familiar with my humane education research. We were both attending a professional meeting and he approached me with the following question: "Frank, you've been studying kids' kindness toward animals for quite a while now. What do you know about children who are cruel to animals?" My inadequate yet honest answer to Phil was, "Nothing!" It was literally at that moment I realized that throughout my undergraduate and graduate training and years of professional work, I could not recall any developmental psychologists who had addressed the topic of children's cruelty toward animals or the circumstances that might promote such abusive behavior toward nonhuman animals. And so began my exploration of the sometimes malevolent relation children may have with animals.

Beacons along this journey included clinical and forensic studies by pioneers in this area such as Fernando Tapia and Alan Felthous. But I quickly realized that mainstream developmental psychology had ignored this topic - it could not be found in the index or listing of topics in child psychology or human development textbooks and was absent from the major journals published in the field. Personal contacts with like-minded developmental psychologists proved more helpful. Phil Arkow's simple yet penetrating question was accompanied by the affirmation of scholars like Gail Melson and the late Aline Kidd who were pioneers, in their own right, in the study of the child-animal bond. Andrew Rowan, then editor of *Anthrozoös,* encouraged me to write a review of the topic of childhood cruelty to animals, a review eventually published in that journal in 1993. Andrew continued to be very supportive of my work in this area and his words of encouragement were valued and appreciated.

At this point, my work also benefited from the financial support of HSUS, the Delta Society, the American Society for the Prevention of Cruelty to Animals, the Massachusetts Society for the Prevention of Cruelty to Animals, the American Humane Association, and the Geraldine R. Dodge Foundation. Funding from HSUS and collaboration with my colleague Randy Lockwood, a vice president at HSUS, resulted in Randy and I editing the first academically-oriented book on animal cruelty (1998. *Cruelty to Animals and Interpersonal Violence: Readings in Research and Application.* West Lafayette, IN: Purdue University Press).

Supportive colleagues at the American Humane Association (now, American Humane) included Diane Hollums, Carol Moulton, Mike Kaufmann, Lynn Anderson, Suzanne Barnard, and Bob F. X. Hart. Their affirmation helped make my professional explorations a less lonely process. I must also thank John Richters, who was affiliated with the National Institute of Mental Health, for encouraging me to continue my examination of animal abuse as a possible sign of childhood psychopathology.

Another source of kind words and financial support was the Latham Foundation. Hugh H. Tebault II, Hugh H. Tebault III, and Judy Johns created many opportunities for disseminating information about the cruelty issue through the Foundation's publication, *The Latham Letter,* and by underwriting my attendance and presentations at a number of national conferences. The Latham Foundation also made possible my collaboration with Phil Arkow on the book *Child Abuse, Domestic Violence, and Animal Abuse: Linking the Circles of Compassion for Prevention and Intervention* (1999. West Lafayette, IN: Purdue University Press), the first collection of original, interdisciplinary essays on the topic of animal abuse.

On many occasions, I benefited from the clinical insights provided by my friend and colleague, Barbara Boat. Her expertise in intervention with children who were victims of maltreatment introduced me to the importance of attending to animal abuse in clinical cases. We have shared the podium at a number of conferences and I admire her continuing efforts on behalf of children who are abused.

Camilla Pagani and Franco Robustelli, psychologists at the National Research Council in Rome, Italy, have helped introduce me to the international scope of the problem of animal abuse. Their passion, hospitality, and care are dear to my heart and I look forward to our continued collaboration in this field. A number of other professionals and organizations facilitated sharing the messages of this book with international audiences. For these opportunities, I thank Dennis Turner (Switzerland) and others affiliated with the International Association of Human-Animal Interaction Organizations, Nienke Endenburg (the Netherlands) and the International Society for Anthrozoology, Nina Natelson (Israel) and Concern for Helping Animals in Israel, Lena Olsson (Sweden) and Svenska Kennelklubben, Françoise Sion (Belgium) and Ethologia, Anthony Podberscek (United Kingdom) and the University of Cambridge, Kayoko Tominaga (Kobe, Japan) and KNOTS, and Chizuko Yamaguchi and Keiko Yamazaki (Tokyo, Japan), and the Japan Animal Welfare Society. A special word of thanks to John Cornwall, general manager of Delta Society Australia, for coordinating, with a number of agencies, my visits to Sydney, Melbourne, Brisbane, and Mackay to deliver the Inaugural Bob Kibble Memorial Lecture in July of 2004. In addition to the wonderful companionship and fellowship provided by Mathilde Kearny-Kibble, my wife and I benefited from the support and affirmation of Eleonora Gullone, Judy Johnson, Michael Beatty, and many other animal and child welfare and domestic violence advocates who made us feel at home in a new land. Efforts to reduce animal abuse have now become a clearly global mission.

William Friedrich, a giant in the study of child maltreatment, especially sexual abuse, has been remarkably generous over the years. A busy clinician, author, and researcher, he still made time for an unfamiliar psychologist from Utah who kept asking for data about cruelty to animals. I am delighted that, after years of correspondence and dialogue, he and I were finally able to co-author a research paper on this topic.

I thank Tom Bacher, Margaret Hunt, Donna Vanleer, and the Purdue University Press "crew" for shepherding this book to publication. I have valued their advice and professionalism in facilitating this book project and appreciated our collaboration on two of my earlier co-edited books.

As a full-time faculty member at Utah State University, it would have been especially challenging to complete this book without some release from my usual teaching activities. Were it not for financial support from the Kenneth A. Scott Charitable Trust and American Humane, this book would likely have remained a dream. I extend my special appreciation to Richard Obermanns of the Scott Trust for believing in my vision for this book and to Suzanne Barnard and Lynn Anderson for encouraging American Humane to also lend its support.

A number of dedicated and competent undergraduate and graduate students assisted me with countless hours of searching through the Utah State University library stacks, ordering articles from interlibrary loan, and engaging in thoughtful dialogue surrounding the topics discussed in this book. For their valued assistance, I thank Claudia Weber, Teresa Thompson, David Wood, Tracy Cecchini, John Heath, Mika Maruyama, Jordan Williams, and the late Shane Bland.

For more than a decade, this work has introduced me to a world of people passionate in their caring for children and animals. Closer to home and for many more years, I have been fortunate to be cared for by my companion and wife, Debbie, and our three children, Matthew, Catherine, and David. Their patience with my devotion to my work has been a model of humaneness. Sharing this journey with them has made it all the more worthwhile.

—Frank R. Ascione

FOREWORD

FOR THOSE OF US who have spent our lives on its front lines, the protection of children is the only "holy war" worthy of the name. To us, the great mystery of life is not why some abused children grow up to become abusive adults, but why so many *don't.*

A cop's world view might vary radically from a caseworker's; a prosecutor's "solution" could be distinctly different than a therapist's; the academic's data might be contradicted by the anecdotal experience of the field investigator. But we all share this core belief: abusiveness is not genetically encoded. It has a genesis, a *discoverable* taproot. And we all agree that if "prevention" is ever to exist as anything more than a grant writer's buzzword, we have to keep digging.

But, while it is universally agreed that interpersonal violence is the greatest single threat to human civilization, there is nothing resembling a consensus on its etiology. Part of the problem is that people tend to superimpose their personal belief systems over any information presented to them. For example, announcement of a decline in the number of reports of child sexual abuse cases guarantees an instant onslaught of dueling interpretations.

Depending on the expert being consulted, such data "proves" that:

(a) the "tidal wave of false allegations" is finally ebbing; or
(b) "prevention" efforts are finally bearing fruit; or
(c) viewing child abuse as a crime (rather than a "family dysfunction") and prosecuting it accordingly has deterred some perpetrators; or
(d) reduced funding for child protective services has resulted in fewer existing cases being discovered; or
(e) something else.

For the abused child, none of this agenda-driven interpretation matters. And, for the society into which that abused child will eventually be absorbed—or, in some cases, disgorged—none of it helps.

But every few decades, a seminal work emerges. A dispatch from the front lines that combines innovative research, critical thought, and penetrating analysis so compellingly that it causes a cultural shift. C. Henry Kempe's *The Battered Child Syndrome* is a classic example.

A legitimate descendant of that groundbreaking line is Frank Ascione's *Children and Animals: Exploring the Roots of Kindness and Cruelty.* Its message will reverberate through politics, policy, and practice for generations to come.

To understand the significance of Ascione's work, we need to take a look—a hard look—at the predators who walk among us. Whom do we fear the most? The serial killer? The sadistic rapist? The arsonist who giggles at the flames he created? The pedophile who tortures children for pleasure, and markets the memorialization of his unspeakable acts for profit? Their crimes may vary radically, but the perpetrators are all members of the same tribe, one we now call "sociopaths." And what is the foundational characteristic of every sociopath? A profound, pervasive, fundamental *lack of empathy.* The sociopath attends to only his own needs, and feels only his own pain. If the pain of others interferes with his needs, it is casually ignored. And if the pain of others *becomes* his need, it is relentlessly pursued.

Despite enormous (and sometimes almost worshipful) media attention, we know very little about such creatures. We "profile" them endlessly, but we have never been able to *predict* them.

Few believe we can "treat" such predators. All agree we must incapacitate them. But what if we were granted the opportunity to *interdict* them? To actually alter the course of their development so that, when they reach full bloom, they are not toxic to others?

This stunning new work—the crown jewel in a career Frank Ascione has devoted to demonstrating the importance of understanding animal abuse in a developmental context—now offers us just such an unprecedented opportunity.

This book reveals what interactions between children and animals tell us about ourselves. Its premise is brilliantly direct: we have a window of opportunity—childhood—within which to redirect the production of sociopaths. The antidote is the development of empathy. And observation and analysis of children's interaction with animals is the key to that door.

Ascione persuasively argues that a society which carefully records acts of vandalism by youth—and considers such to have both symptomatic probity and predictive value—should do no less with acts of cruelty to animals. The correlations between animal abuse in the household and domestic violence are inescapable. And the link between animal abuse *by* children and the concurrent abuse *of* those same children by their "caretakers" is indisputable. Ascione's evidence is so overwhelming that I believe this book conclusively makes the case for sharing of reports between child protective and animal protective agencies.

As a lawyer, I am confident I now have the evidence to argue successfully that any report of animal abuse is sufficient probable cause to trigger a child protective investigation of the home in which it occurred. As a citizen, I intend to lobby for such changes in the law to be enacted.

But while those changes would enable detection of ongoing cases of child abuse, they would not prevent any child from initially being abused. Ascione's work is unique in that it *does* offer the opportunity to engage in true "primary prevention."

He points out that empathy isn't administered as an injection; it is learned over time. The young child who throws a rock at a flock of pigeons isn't so much endangering a bird as he is giving us the chance to intervene at the crossroads: We can teach empathy, or we can encourage cruelty.

The classic "triad" known to all criminal investigators—enuresis, fire-setting, and animal abuse—has never been especially convincing to me. My own experience is that it is the caregiver's *reaction* to the bed-wetting that determines the outcome. A loving, supportive environment takes the child right out of the "triad." But a punitive, humiliating response impels him toward the other path.

The abuse of animals, especially chronic, escalating abuse, is a "gateway" indicator. Whether committed in the home environment of a child, or committed directly by the child, it never occurs in a vacuum. It never fails to tell us it is time to act. But, first, we must to learn to listen.

The sociopath may lack empathy, but he (or she) is an expert at exploiting it in others. Any domestic violence professional knows of women who remained with abusers because of threats to harm a beloved pet. Any CPS caseworker can tell you about cases in which a child abuser also hurt—or killed—the victim's pet. Any sex crimes detective can tell you that child molesters know a puppy or a kitten is a far more effective lure than candy.

I've had protection dogs all my adult life. This doesn't mean *vicious* dogs, it means *trained* dogs. Professional trainers have a disparaging term for so-called "guard dogs" that mindlessly attack anything that approaches: "fear-biters." Typically, such animals have been "trained" by repeated beatings and other forms of maltreatment. It's time that we reached that same understanding about children.

Animal abuse is now one of the diagnostic criteria for Conduct Disorder in children. That's a beginning, but it barely scratches the surface. Pets reside in the households of the overwhelming majority of Americans. As Ascione so clearly illustrates, they offer not only the opportunity to teach empathy, they serve as early warning systems for the child protective profession, if only we learn to recognize the signposts.

The abuse of animals should be a mandatory portion of all interviewing and data-collection concerning "at-risk" children, because, as this book demonstrates with such striking clarity, it has the potential to tell us so much.

Animal abuse and children—as perpetrators or as witnesses—may be the Rosetta stone to predatory psychopathology. All of us concerned with public safety have been sailors on a vast, uncharted sea. Now, Frank Ascione has given us a new, and extraordinarily promising, navigational instrument.

Children and Animals: Exploring the Roots of Kindness and Cruelty should be required reading for everyone involved in child protection and law enforcement. It should be part of the training curriculum in schools of social work and in police academies. And it will be appreciated by every citizen who is willing to invest the time and trouble it takes to make our policymakers do the right thing.

I don't write well enough to adequately express the importance of this book. Fortunately, I don't have to: it speaks for itself. And it will inform and empower everyone who gives it the chance to do so.

—Andrew Vachss

CHAPTER 1

Children and animals: Joined by wonder, connected in pain

> **W**e need another and a wiser and perhaps a more mystical concept of animals. Remote from universal nature, and living by complicated artifice, man in civilization surveys the creature through the glass of his knowledge and sees thereby a feather magnified and the whole image in distortion. We patronize them for their incompleteness, for their tragic fate of having taken form so far below ourselves. And therein we err, and greatly err. For the animal shall not be measured by man. In a world older and more complete than ours they move finished and complete, gifted with extensions of the senses we have lost or never attained, living by voices we will never hear. They are not brethren, they are not underlings; they are other nations, caught with ourselves in the net of life and time, fellow prisoners of the splendour and travail of the earth.
>
> —Henry Beston, *The Outermost House*

As you reflect on Beston's (1928/1992, pp. 24–25) reverent view of animals and the close connection between their spirits and our own, contrast his words with the following headlines culled from daily newspapers and magazines:

- "To kill a sweet, furry beast. Who is killing bunnies all over Japan?" (*Newsweek*, September 22, 1997)

- "Authorities seek boys who tortured, killed cat." (*San Diego Union-Tribune,* November 6, 1995)
- "Teens charged with torturing and killing dogs, pups." (*Milwaukee Journal-Sentinel,* March 19, 1999)
- "Boy sentenced for disfiguring dog. A 13-year-old boy convicted of cutting the eyes out of a dog . . ." (*Herald Journal,* January 4, 2001)
- "Police investigating animal cruelty allegation. A teenage boy has been accused of torturing his puppy before drowning the animal and burying it next to his driveway." (Ogden *Standard-Examiner,* July 23, 1996)
- "Nevada spree leaves six animals dead. Four wild horses and two wild burros have been shot to death . . ." (*Salt Lake Tribune,* January 7, 2000)
- "Man arrested after dog tossed off cliff." (Newport, Oregon, *Register-Guardian,* August 17, 1997)
- "Teen accused of pet torture. Novato suspect described as 'budding young sociopath.'" (Marin *Independent Journal,* November 29, 1995)
- "Boy, 13, laughs at law after dog kill." (*Boston Herald,* June 3, 1994)

This terrible litany only highlights a few of the cases where humans' relationships with animals have been distorted and become examples of malevolence and cruelty. The perpetrators of such inhumane treatment are often children and adolescents but adults sometimes join their ranks. How common are these incidents? What motivates human maltreatment of animals, often animals we call pets or companions and whom we consider to be family members? Are there cultural, societal, neighborhood, and family contexts that contribute to cruelty to animals? How early in a child's life does cruelty to animals emerge? Is it always a sign of future interpersonal violence? Are there ways of preventing such cruelty? Can we intervene effectively with children who already have a history of abuse and violence?

Children and Animals: Exploring the Roots of Kindness and Cruelty is an offspring of my longstanding desire to bring to the layperson our current scientific and professional wisdom about the relation between the maltreatment of animals and interpersonal violence directed toward other human beings. It was written for parents, teachers, counselors, clergy, animal welfare professionals, foster parents, mental health professionals, youth workers, law enforcement professionals, and any one else whose work or interest crosses into the lives of children and adolescents. Although animal abuse has been an acknowledged problem for centuries, it is only within the past few decades that scientific research has provided evidence that the maltreatment of animals often overlaps with violence toward people. Interpersonal violence is manifest in many—too many—forms. The ways that our young people are affected by bullying or assaults in a schoolyard, child abuse in homes, violence between adult intimate partners, community violence in our streets and neighborhoods, and even the context of war are now the subject of concerted research efforts. And very often, the association of these forms of violence with cruelty to animals has been found.

Given the considerable research that now exists on this topic, I judged that it was important to present our current knowledge and understanding of the phenomenon to adults whose lives touch those of children and adolescents. Nearly all of the research is published in scientific journals and periodicals that laypersons are unlikely to access on a routine basis. Yet the questions this research addresses are of considerable importance to each of us as citizens, care givers, and community members.

> "Cruelty to animals" is such an ambiguous term. What do you mean by that?
>
> Isn't animal abuse just a phase that all kids, especially boys, go through in early childhood?
>
> Cruelty to animals is mainly a problem for preschoolers, isn't it?
>
> Does animal abuse in early childhood always lead to violence against people at later stages of development?
>
> We have such a significant problem with child abuse in our society, doesn't paying attention to animal abuse divert our attention from "real" problems?
>
> Isn't animal abuse already considered a serious crime, one we can track in national records of criminal activity?
>
> There are more shelters for animals in our country than shelters for women who are battered. Doesn't focusing on animal abuse distract us from dealing with the challenges of serious family violence?
>
> Cruelty to animals is only an issue for those radical animal rights people. Isn't cruelty *to people* where we need to concentrate our resources?
>
> Aren't psychologists and psychiatrists already trained to address animal abuse with clients who show this problem?
>
> Cruelty to animals is mainly an issue for animal lovers and veterinarians. Don't vets have to report animal abuse to the police?
>
> A child who abuses an animal just hasn't received the right education and training. There aren't any other reasons underlying animal abuse, are there?

I wish I could tell you, the reader, that decades of research in developmental psychology and family science have yielded definitive answers to questions like these.

But, unfortunately, that is not the case. At the end of the nineteenth and beginning of the twentieth centuries, there were a few research studies that examined children's relations with animals, but the topic never took hold with the majority of child psychologists and other professionals who focus on developmental issues until the end of the twentieth century and beginning of the twenty-first.

As an example of the neglect of this topic, a wonderful and fascinating book was published in 2000 entitled *From Neurons to Neighborhoods: The Science of Early Childhood Development* (Shonkoff and Phillips 2000). This detailed overview of our current understanding of children's early development and the contextual factors that can enhance or inhibit that development contains topics ranging from the development of the brain to the role of neighborhood and community factors in the prevalence of school failure or youth violence.

But nowhere in the index is there an entry for "pets," "companion animals," or even "animals." There are listings for "fathers," "mothers," "parents," "siblings," "friends and peers," and "grandparents," but pets, whom many of us consider to be family members, are conspicuous by their absence. Even though, as you will see or already know, pets are terribly important to children, my own profession—with some rare exceptions—has yet to treat relations with pets and other animals as legitimate areas of scientific focus. In our exploration of significant topics for study in human development, perhaps my colleagues and I should have heeded the words of the late Willie Morris, author and editor of *Harper's,* when he wrote in *My Dog Skip* about his boyhood pet dog:

> . . . I retain the sad-sweet reflection of being an only child and having a loyal and loving dog, for in the struggles of life, of the dangers, toils, and snares of my childhood hymns, loyalty and love are the best things of all, and the most lasting, and that is what Old Skip taught me that I carry with me now. (1996, p. 91)

Reflect, too, on the words of Sam Keen (Shepard 1996, p. 3):

> Forests are enchanted enough without elves or hobbits. Did you ever see a ruby-throated hummingbird?

Psychology actually has a long history of interest in the study of animals, in part, to understand animals in their own right but also to assess the differences and similarities between humans and animal species. This last endeavor is even given the formal label of "comparative psychology." Developmental psychology has also focused on animals especially because their development and life course are usually more rapid than those of humans. We know a great deal about children's development, the factors that enhance or impede it, from careful study of animals. This research includes topics such as the course of prenatal development and substances that distort that process, the importance of a stimulating early environment on the developing brain, the role of patterned light in promoting the development of vision, the need for appropriate social stimulation in the early years, and the role of peers in social development, to mention just a few. But human-animal *interactions and reciprocal influences* remain neglected topics. Perhaps developmental psychologists should pay greater attention to fellow scientists in biology and ecology who study the "geography of childhood," noting how children are enriched by experiences in nature, both inanimate and animate, by living in landscapes and among the creatures that inhabit them (Kahn and Kellert 1994).

Glimmers of scientific interest. Developmental psychology and related disciplines have virtually ignored studying the positive role that pets and other animals may play in the lives of children. This is also true if we examine the unfortunate cases where children are unkind, abusive, and violent toward animals. There are some notable exceptions and these come from the field of sociology.

In 1944, James H.S. Bossard published an article entitled "The Mental Hygiene of Owning a Dog" in which he proposed that "domestic animals play an important role in family life and in the mental health of its members, with particular reference to the children in the family" (Bossard 1944, p. 408). Focusing specifically on pet dogs, he suggested the following benefits of their presence in human homes:

- dogs provide an outlet for our affection and need for companionship
- dogs express affection appropriate to our individual needs
- the affection between dogs and humans is deep and continues over time
- caring for a dog teaches responsibility, especially to children
- having a puppy is a good model for toilet training a child
- dogs can assist in educating children about sex differences and sexuality
- anger can be taken out on a dog and if a child is feeling impotent, control of a dog can be satisfying (it's not clear if Bossard was *recommending* this!)
- dogs illustrate how basic physical processes are normal to all animals, human and nonhuman
- dogs can facilitate contact with other human beings

Despite the positive response this article received (it was reprinted in four veterinary journals, 125,000 (!) copies were reprinted for animal welfare organizations, and it generated 1,033 letters from interested readers), six years later Bossard lamented, "The role of domestic animals as household pets, their importance as a factor in family relations in general and in mental hygiene in particular, seems to be strangely neglected in the serious literature in these respective fields" (Bossard 1950,

p. 385). Bossard and co-author Eleanor Boll would include this information about pets and the family in their textbook, *The Sociology of Child Development* (Bossard and Boll 1966). But as late as 1960, they wrote, "The role of the domestic pet in family life and child development has been neglected for the most part by serious students, despite their obvious importance" (qtd. in Albert and Bulcroft 1988). Their statement was still valid when, in 1988, Alexa Albert and Kris Bulcroft published "Pets, families, and the life course" in the *Journal of Marriage and the Family*, a major journal of family sociology.

Albert and Bulcroft conducted telephone surveys with 320 pet owners in Rhode Island and compared their responses with those of 116 people who did not currently own pets. They found that pet ownership was highest for families with elementary school-aged children or with adolescents. As suggested by Bossard, 94% of these parents believed that pets served important roles for their children, including teaching responsibility and providing their children with companionship. Furthermore, 87% of the pet owners considered their pets to be part of the family. More recently, Daniel Eckstein developed a self-assessment questionnaire that families could use to gauge the role of pets in the home including the degree to which pets are considered family members, how much dominance and control owners exert over pets, and the degree of mutual affection between family members and pets (Eckstein 2000).

A few years earlier, Jack C. Horn and Jeff Meer reported the results of a survey conducted with more than 13,000 readers of the magazine *Psychology Today* (Horn and Meer 1984). They reported that 89% of the respondents had pets when they were children even though not all were current pet owners. Nearly everyone, 97%, believed it was good for children to have pets. And the reasons cited for this overwhelming support of providing children with pets, according to Horn and Meer, were that pets provided pleasure and companionship as well as opportunities for learning gentleness and responsibility. Throughout the article are numerous examples of how pets enriched the lives of their human owners—from providing a respite from a troubled marital relationship to increasing the fun and laughter shared by family members.

Pets also bring significant responsibilities to their humans caretakers and many parents are aware that there are "costs" and concerns when the family circle is widened to include animals. In a study of 10-year-old children whose families included pet dogs, Alaisdair Macdonald reported that many of the children's parents had considered a number of concerns that might accompany acquiring a pet dog. These included the effect of the loss or death of the dog on human family members, the danger of the dog annoying neighbors, the possibility the dog might injure the child or be mistreated by the child, and possible damage to others' property (Macdonald 1981). And children, themselves, acknowledge that having pets brings challenges as well as great joy (Bryant 1990).

We usually consider the human benefits of having pets to be primarily emotional and psychological in nature. But a number of studies have even demonstrated a relation between pet ownership and physical health, though most of these studies have been conducted with adults and the nature and reliability of this relation is still being explored (Allen 2003; Friedman and Thomas 1998; Headey 1999; Parslow and Jorm 2003; Ownby, Johnson, and Peterson 2002).

Another example of the reemergence of sociological interest in pets was the volume edited by Marvin B. Sussman in 1985, *Pets and the Family* (Sussman 1985). This excellent compilation of articles previously published in *Marriage and Family Review* illustrates the coming of age of pets as a legitimate topic of current sociological thought. And it included articles with a developmental emphasis and a focus on the importance of childhood cruelty to animals as a diagnostic sign.

As I will describe later, the topic of young people and animal abuse has also been a relatively neglected area of inquiry, especially in the field of developmental psychology. This, too, is surprising since throughout the past three centuries, philosophers and other students of the human condition have called our attention to the phenomenon as one worthy of study.

Animal welfare and human welfare. One of the first published treatments of the relation between animal abuse and human violence was provided by the British animal welfare advocate, Lewis Gompertz, who, in 1824, wrote "*Moral inquiries on the situation of man and of brutes . . . on the crime of committing cruelty on brutes.*" That same year, Gompertz helped found what would later become the Royal Society for the Prevention of Cruelty to Animals (RSPCA) (Gompertz 1997). In his book, he lamented the "ill treatment" that apprentices received from their masters and the ways husbands treated their wives, alluding to child maltreatment and domestic violence. His comment illustrates how human and animal welfare were viewed as related concerns even by the earliest animal welfare advocates.

In the United States, an organization modeled on and parallel to the RSPCA was the American Society for the Prevention of Cruelty to Animals (ASPCA), founded in 1866 by the well-known New Yorker Henry Bergh. In 1868, a similar organization was founded by George T. Angell of Boston and named the Massachusetts Society for the Prevention of Cruelty to Animals (MSPCA). Examples of laws related to the issue of cruelty to animals predated these organizations and could actually be found as early as 1640 in the Massachusetts Body of Liberties as well as state laws passed in New York in 1829 and Massachusetts in 1834 (Shultz 1924/1968).

Although the focus of the ASPCA was on the welfare of animals (e.g., how work horses, common on New York streets, were treated, the manner of transporting animals used for food), two events foreshadowed the emerging collaboration of animal welfare and human welfare organizations that is again becoming common in the twenty-first century.

The case of Emily Thompson. In 1871, a woman petitioned ASPCA President Bergh to intervene on behalf of an orphaned 8-year-old girl named Emily Thompson, who was being physically abused by her foster mother. As noted by E. A. Shelman and S. Lazoritz (2000), Bergh sent investigators to the child's home, verifying her injuries, and recording the testimony of neighbors who witnessed the abuse. A court ordered her removed from her home, tried and convicted the foster mother, but suspended the sentence when Emily recanted her testimony about her victimization. Remember, this child was an orphan and still regarded her foster mother as her only living and available caretaker. Emily was returned to this abusive caretaker, much to the displeasure of Bergh and the ASPCA. This early attempt by an animal welfare agency to reach out to help a human child seemed a failure. Fortunately, publicity about this trial brought forth Emily's grandmother, who had presumed Emily was dead. Child and grandmother were reunited, validating Bergh's willingness to widen the scope of his benevolent animal welfare agency's efforts.

The case of Mary Ellen Wilson. Approximately three years after the Emily Thompson case, Henry Bergh and the ASPCA became involved with another child at risk. Lela B. Costin (1991) suggests that Bergh may have been reluctant, at first, to again address a specifically human welfare issue. His agency's focus, after all, was the welfare of nonhuman animals. This also highlights the limits of the effectiveness of child welfare agencies, in that historical period, that could have been enlisted to remove and aid children who were victims of abuse in their own homes.

In 1874, Etta Wheeler, a church worker who assisted the impoverished families in New York's Hell's Kitchen, was approached by an ailing woman who lived near Francis and Mary Connolly, a couple who had taken Mary Ellen from a foundling home under the presumption that she was Francis Connolly's illegitimate child (Shelman and Lazoritz 2000). The Connolly's neighbor told Wheeler that Mary Ellen, who was then 9 years old but looked like a 5-year-old, was often left locked alone in her tenement apartment and was the victim of cruel beatings by her foster mother. Mary Ellen's cries and screams could be heard throughout the apartment building. Other tenants confirmed these observations. According to Shelman and Lazoritz (2000), neither a clergyman nor the police judged they could intervene since this child's abuse was occurring behind closed doors. Had Mary Ellen been similarly abused in public, the perpetrators could have been charged with assault. But our country did not yet have provisions for removing a child from a severely abusive home in cases where the abuse was not directly witnessed. And there was also the opinion that how parents "disciplined" their children was a family matter that did not warrant state intervention.

Wheeler visited the Connolly's apartment on the pretext of asking about the welfare of their ill neighbor. Mrs. Connolly and Mary Ellen were at home and Wheeler noted a rawhide whip and marks on Mary Ellen's frail body that appeared to be injuries such a whip would produce. Wheeler left the apartment distressed and in a quandary about how to protect this vulnerable child.

Perhaps because of her awareness of the Emily Thompson case as well as Henry Bergh's public prominence in New York City, Wheeler visited him, described the neighbors' reports about Mary Ellen as well as her own observations, and implored him to help. As the story is told, Wheeler suggested to Bergh that this child deserved protection since she was at least a member of the animal kingdom, the object of Bergh's benevolent efforts (Costin 1991). Bergh did agree to help but as a private individual and not under the official auspices of the ASPCA. Elbridge Gerry, the ASPCA's attorney was consulted and he sent an investigator to the Connolly's building, gaining access by posing as a census taker. The investigator reported Mary Ellen's condition to Gerry and Bergh at which point Gerry convinced a judge to order her removal. On April 9, 1874, the police rescued Mary Ellen and her foster mother was later charged with and convicted of assault; Francis Connolly was nowhere to be found.

Mary Ellen was placed in a foster care institution and was eventually adopted by Etta Wheeler's sister. Mary Ellen later married a widower with three children, adopted an orphaned child, and she and her husband had two children of their own (Stevens and Eide 1990). Respected throughout her adult life by her family and community, Mary Ellen died at the age of 92 on October 30, 1956.

The Mary Ellen Wilson case teaches us that, in some instances, it does literally take an entire community to guarantee the safety and well being of a child. The dying neighbor who reported Mary Ellen's abuse, Etta Wheeler and her uncompromising commitment to find help for this child, Henry Bergh and his resourceful lawyer Elbridge Gerry, of the ASPCA, who investigated and confirmed that this abused child was at risk, the judge who granted the order to remove Mary Ellen from her abusive home, the law enforcement officer who implemented the order, the media representatives who highlighted this child's plight, and the adoptive family that finally provided Mary Ellen with nurturance instead of neglect and abuse—it was the collaborative efforts of these individual citizens that finally made a difference in the life of this vulnerable child. And Mary Ellen's life, as well as recent research, dispels the myth that every abused child grows up to become an abusive adult (Lazoritz 1989).

In addition to the rich legacy Mary Ellen left to our understanding of the evolution of collaboration between those concerned with the welfare of children and of animals, her discovery and rescue in 1874 led directly to the founding of the New York Society for the Prevention of Cruelty to Children. The founders were Henry Bergh, Elbridge Gerry, and John Wright, a wealthy and widely respected New York businessman and child advocate. That same year, a national organization, the American Humane Association (AHA; now renamed American Humane or AH), was formed with the principle goals of "the prevention and suppression of cruelty, especially of cruelty to children and animals" (Shultz 1924/1968, p. 49). You may be most familiar with the AH's continuing efforts to supervise and ensure the welfare of animals in the production of films—the organization's approval of the care and treatment of real animals used in filming appears at the end of the credits. The AH remains the only national organization in the United State to address both child and animal welfare in their policy development, research, training, and public education efforts.

By 1910, there were 247 state or local humane societies that included the welfare of both animals and children within the scope of their efforts (Shultz 1924/1968). The seeds of efforts to treat the needs of vulnerable children and the needs of animals as interrelated issues had taken root. It would take nearly a century before the flowers of these early efforts would begin to appear.

Children and animals

The importance of animals in the lives of children is hardly news to parents, teachers, and others whose lives touch young people. Visits to zoos, family pets, watching neighborhood wildlife, the popularity of the cable channel *Animal Planet*™ and films with animal themes, the books with animal characters read to children and later read by them, the distress caused by the sight of an injured stray animal—these and many other examples attest to the importance attributed by our culture to animals and their place in young people's lives. During the writing of this chapter (February 22, 2001), I conducted a search at Amazon.com's™ website and found 32,000 listings for "animals," 7,976 for "pets," and 22,707 entries for the search combinations "pets and children" and "animals and children"! And yet, those who study child and adolescent development have devoted remarkably little attention to exploring the ways that the lives of animals and young people intersect, complement, and enhance each other.

Fostering positive relations between human beings and the animals in their world has always been one of the main goals of animal welfare agencies. The benefit to animals is obvious. But these same agencies also promoted the philosophy that the more humane treatment of animals would lead people to treat each other with greater civility, respect, and kindness. And the best way to implement this philosophy was judged to be through a focus on teaching children these humane principles.

Humane education. Societies for preventing cruelty to animals have historically focused on the education of young people as one of the most fruitful ways of enhancing the welfare of animals. These efforts to teach children the kind, compassionate, and responsible treatment of animals have taken many forms but are usually grouped together under the title "humane education." Shultz (1924/1968) describes how, in the beginning of the twentieth century, a number of states actually passed laws mandating or recommending the incorporation of humane education into the school curriculum, a trend supported by the American Humane Association (AHA). In 1915, AHA endorsed a proposal that all states include humane education in their school systems' curricula and by 1922, 20 states had done so (Shultz 1924/1968, p. 137). The Illinois law, passed in 1909, was considered to be a model and the language of the law made clear the presumed connection between humane education and the reduction of juvenile crime:

> . . . it shall be the duty of every teacher of a public school in this State to teach to the pupils thereof, honesty, kindness, justice and moral courage for the purpose of lessening crime and raising the standard of good citizenship . . . not less than one-half hour of each week during the whole of each term of school shall be devoted to teaching the pupils thereof kindness and justice to and humane treatment and protection of birds and animals, and the important part they fulfill in the economy of nature. (Shultz 1924/1968, p. 305)

Shultz notes that, despite the best of intentions in promulgating such laws, their implementation was not always insured. He describes how some school officials and teachers may have resented such edicts and, even when teachers were supportive of humane education, the lack of text material and outlines for lesson plans were obstacles to effective instruction.

The importance of stories. One method of trying to promote humane values in children has been through animal-themed literature. One of the early U. S. examples of this approach was Sarah Eddy's (1899) *Friends and Helpers*, in which children could read about various pet, farm, and wild animals, their characteristics, and their appropriate treatment. Numerous examples were included of the devastating effects of cruelty on animals and the child's role in preventing animal mistreatment. As Eddy wrote, "When young people learn to respect the rights of animals and to think about the causes of pain and suffering, they will apply these thoughts to their everyday life. They will learn to respect each other's rights, and crime of all kinds will be diminished" (p. 228). The last chapter of the book was directed to teachers and urged them to include humane education in their classrooms.

This genre continued in the twentieth century with books like Virginia Parkinson's *Kindness to Pets, Starring Spotty the Pup* (1943/1961), Helen Griffiths' *Just a Dog* (1975), and Phyllis Reynolds Naylor's Newbery Medal award winning *Shiloh* (1992).

Eddy's book also encouraged children to form groups referred to as "Bands of Mercy" whose motto was "I will try to be kind to all living creatures and will try to protect them from cruel usage" (Eddy 1899, p. 227). These Bands of Mercy, established in 1875 in England and 1882 in the U.S. (Finch 1989), were sponsored under the auspices of the Massachusetts Society for the Prevention of Cruelty to Animals (MSPCA) and encouraged by its president, George Angell, whom we will meet again in a later section of this book. By 1923, there were reported to be 4,000,000 members of 140,000 Bands of Mercy across the United States! Some religious denominations and the Boy Scout and Girl Scout programs also joined in promoting the benevolent treatment of animals (Shultz 1924/1968).

Angell also founded the American Humane Education Society to promote its programs in schools and homes across the country. There was even a proposal to include humane education and cruelty to animals issues at Stanford University in 1910. At this point in history, one humane society, in Chattanooga, Tennessee, included the issue of protecting children and women, as well as animals, as part of its humane education efforts.

Humane education continues today and includes programs like Operation Outreach-USA, which is a literacy-based approach, reprinting and making more accessible easily read versions of classics like *Black Beauty* and *Beautiful Joe* (Sewell 1965; Golden 1992).

The Latham Foundation, established in 1918, has always maintained a focus on humane education, especially through televised and other visual media. Today, it includes an advisory council on the prevention of child and animal abuse and continues its humane education efforts through a quarterly magazine, *The Latham Letter,* as well as sponsoring and publishing books on the topic.

Another elementary school approach was developed by the Humane Society of the United States (Savesky and Malcarne 1981). This program included humane education in a curriculum-blended approach. That is, it would not be treated as a separate subject (one *more* thing for teachers to address!) but rather incorporated animal welfare topics into existing subject areas already in the curriculum. Pet overpopulation would be addressed in mathematics lessons, human effects on animal habitats in geography, the effects of pollution on wildlife in health, etc.

It is unfortunate that these humane education efforts are rarely funded at anything close to the levels provided for "substance abuse resistance" or more general anti-violence education and prevention programs. And evaluation of the effects of humane education continues to be a difficult and challenging undertaking (Ascione 1997; Cavanaugh, Kaufmann, and Moulton 1998; Unti and DeRosa 2003). There are a number of reasons why progress has been slow in this area. First, there is no universally accepted humane education curriculum and no standard test to assess changes in children's knowledge about and attitudes toward animals. Second, much of the research has focused on middle- and upper-class children with little attention to the effects of such programs on children from less advantaged environments or children who may specifically be at risk for abusing animals. Third, it is rare for those who implement humane education programs to document the extent and quality of the instruction that actually takes place. Fourth, and perhaps most important, humane education programs seldom measure the effects of these interventions on children's *actual behavior toward animals.* As we have learned from the evaluation of school-based substance abuse prevention programs in the U.S. (for example, D.A.R.E.), programs that *appear* to be appropriate and effective may yield negligible or no positive change (Ascione 1997).

Given the long history of animal welfare programs and the devotion of professionals who work in this field to educating society, especially our young, about the care and welfare of animals, I next examine the science and research that addresses children, animals, and the varied nature of their relationships.

CHAPTER 2

The scientific study of children and animals

> To the young child, there is no gap between his soul and that of animals. (Hall 1904, p. 220)

In the late 1800s and early 1900s, children and animals were the subject of a series of psychological analyses conducted and encouraged by the father of developmental psychology in the United States, G. Stanley Hall. Writing at the end of the nineteenth and early part of the twentieth centuries, Hall and his associates published a number of scientific papers on children's knowledge, behavior, and attitudes toward animals. He became well known for the development of the questionnaire method of assessing children's knowledge and understanding of a variety of concepts. Hall had studied in Europe, where, in 1870, the Pedagogical Society of Berlin, Germany, published a report on "the contents of children's minds on entering school at the age of six years" (Hall 1972, pp. 68–74). Perhaps, one of the first precursors of notorious IQ tests, the purpose of the report was to prepare teachers for the level of knowledge and understanding possessed by children entering school. Since the children entering Berlin schools were judged to have a different understanding of their world than children reared in rural environments, questions about animals were included among the many concepts assessed.

Among the fascinating findings of this study were that 6, 028 of 10, 000 (60%) children could identify a butterfly but only 2,466 (25%) could identify a rabbit. The study recommended, in part, trips to zoos for these city children as a remedy for conceptual deficits like this one. Hall conducted a study of his own, modeled on the Berlin research but with children entering primary schools in Boston, which he published in the U.S. in 1883 (Hall 1883). Butterflies were correctly identified by 79.5% of children but only 27% could identify squirrels. Most of the questions he asked were about farm or wild animals. Later research would focus on pets, specifically the domestic dog and cat. A century later, Stephen R. Kellert found similar deficits in children's knowledge of animals (1984).

As public education became more common, there were some who lamented that the real-world lessons children learned as they explored their physical environment were being traded for the more formal and vicarious lessons of the classroom. Perhaps this was what led C. F. Hodge (1900) and others to encourage nature study as an essential component of a child's education. A contemporary of Hodge, C. Guillet, even suggested classroom pets as an adjunct to nature study in the field so that children's "interest in the wonders and beauty of nature may be made ever keener, more intelligent and more reverent" (Guillet 1904, p. 91).

Over 100 years ago, the issue of animal abuse in childhood was also deemed worthy of attention. In an earlier paper, Hodge (1899) wrote, "a child of even two or three is capable of some degree of appreciation of the sufferings of an animal" (pp. 544–545), a clear reference to the emergence of empathy in the developing child. In these toddler years, some children might experience pleasure in the movement and sounds made by an animal in pain. Helping children move past this inappropriate and immature response to animal suffering, suggested Hodge, was most successfully accomplished by parents teaching children appropriate ways of treating a pet kitten or puppy. So, early on, we see a reference to humane education as a way of curtailing or preventing the mistreatment of animals by children, a suggestion also made by the philosopher John Locke centuries earlier (see chapter 4).

A look at this early literature in child psychology will be instructive since so much information was gathered from the words of children themselves. And many of their insights still ring true in our own time.

Using a questionnaire developed by Hall in 1885, W. Frederick Burk studied children's ideas about teasing and bullying (Burk 1897). Included in his report are the following incidents: "Clifford (5) ties a string around his dog's neck and jerks it. When the dog whines he laughs" (p. 337); two cases of child murder, one by a 10-year-old boy in England, the other by a 9-year-old girl in Mississippi—the latter child was allegedly exposed to a grandfather who enjoyed killing cats (p. 341); children who fear certain animals are taunted by peers' threats to force contact with these animals (p. 353); sibling emotional abuse in which a "brother enjoyed pretending to choke his sister's cat or to give it to the dog" (p. 354).

The "faults of children" was the topic of a paper by Norman Triplett published in 1903. Young people from fourth grade to freshman in high school were asked to write essays that would "tell about the meanest boy or girl you ever knew and why you thought he or she was mean" (p. 225). Nearly 1 in 10 of the 309 essays mentioned cruelty to animals as the basis for defining "meanness" in peers. As Triplett writes, "Children who are fond of animals become much wrought up over the heartless acts of those who are still in the cruelty stage of life" (1903, p. 231). The children described animal abuse that ranged from pulling feathers out of live chickens to tying up a cat or dog and stoning it to death. It is of interest to note that neither teachers nor parents included examples of animal abuse in *their* reports of children's faults. For teachers, this may be due to lack of opportunities to observe children with animals and for parents, perhaps they judge that such behavior is normative or trivial, or, like teachers, may not be aware of their children's behavior away from home. Recognizing that parents may not always be aware of the lives their children lead when away from home and other aspects of parental supervision will be addressed later when I discuss the assessment of animal abuse.

Today, we see a renewed interest in "character education" and teaching virtues, an interest that was no doubt sparked by the terrible increases in youth violence we witnessed in the last two decades of the twentieth century. Our attention to the moral and spiritual development of our children seems to wax and wane over the course of our young history as a nation.

An early example of a book devoted to this subject was Mary Pilkington's *Biography for Boys; or Characteristic Histories Calculated to Impress the Youthful Mind with an Admiration of Virtuous Principles, and a Detestation of Vicious Ones* (1809). Included in her examples of "vicious" principles was the case of a young boy who killed another child's rabbit (Pickering 1993). Contemporary observers of violence in the development of children continue to highlight animal abuse as an indicator of development that has gone astray. For example, Myriam Miedzian (1991) describes a parenting curriculum for high school students designed to provide them with appropriate and nurturing child rearing and discipline skills. She describes some of the "tough questions" the students posed to their adult mentors using the following examples: "my cousin keeps pulling my cat's tail? My cat hides, now she's a nervous wreck"; "How can you not be negative if a kid keeps knocking a cage with a bird in it?" (p. 128). It is clear that these young people consider animal maltreatment a significant behavior problem and issue of discipline. One study of over 600 adolescents confirmed that these young people consider abuse and neglect as harmful to both children and pets (Roscoe, Haney, and Peterson 1986).

But not every adult mentor provides thoughtful guidance. Miedzian also describes a high school football coach who would encourage his players to kick around a live chicken spray painted gold to represent the opposing team's colors (p. 192). Some adults need humane education! And, as observed by Jonathan Kellerman (1999), "Boys will be boys, but violent boys will be dangerous" (p. 115).

Developmental psychology and psychotherapy. I have already mentioned that my own profession of developmental psychology has been slow to treat animals as a significant element of the landscape of children's lives and as important components of family life. Despite the early interest of G. Stanley Hall and his colleagues a century ago, the relation between children and animals has since languished as a topic of scientific inquiry, receiving only sporadic attention by a researcher, here and there, for most of the twentieth century. And the more specific topic of cruelty to animals perpetrated by young people has not fared much better. However, there are some exceptions to this relatively bleak characterization. Some of these exceptions are inspiring but others are more troublesome. Let me begin with the latter.

John Watson, the father of behavioral psychology, is perhaps best known for his famous study of Little Albert, conducted with his colleague Rosalie Raynor (1920). You may recall from a course in introductory psychology that Watson was interested in demonstrating that new stimuli evoking existing emotions could be learned through conditioning. The infant Albert was initially shown a variety of objects and animals, including a rat, toward which he displayed no fear. After this baseline was established, Albert was presented with a live rat at the same time that a metal bar was struck with a hammer behind the child's head. Albert was, of course, startled and frightened and that fear was evident the next time the rat was presented alone. Watson and Raynor were successful in creating a fear of this animal that had not been present before. Thankfully, later researchers would demonstrate that similar conditioning techniques (Cover Jones 1924) and the use of positive models for imitation (Bandura, Grusec, and Menlove 1967) could be used to reduce or eliminate children's existing fears of certain animals.

Another study I'm actually ashamed to report on as a psychologist is one conducted in 1972. You may recall the famous series of studies by Stanley Milgram on obedience to authority (1975). The remarkable finding of this research was that "average" adults were willing to give what they believed were increasingly painful electric shocks to another adult solely for the purpose of satisfying an "experimenter's" need for the data. Unbeknownst to the participants, the people supposedly receiving the shocks were actually the experimenter's confederates and were not being shocked at all. This kind of blind obedience to authority was also found when children were asked to deliver shocks to other children (Shanab and Yahya 1977).

Not satisfied that the "victims" in Milgram's research were sufficiently convincing, C. L. Sheridan and R. G. King, Jr. (1972) studied a group of 13 male and 13 female undergraduates, likely to be in their late adolescence. Instead of employing a human confederate pretending to be shocked, Sheridan and King substituted a live puppy who actually received the shocks, which were painful enough to cause howling and yelping. The authors found obedience levels just as high as in the original Milgram research. But how this study ever received approval from a research ethics review committee is beyond me!

Thankfully, there are more benevolent examples of developmental psychologists' interest in and use of animals in research with children. Roger G. Barker and Herbert F. Wright's classic study, *Midwest and Its Children: The Psychological Ecology of an American Town* (1954), provided a model for understanding children by observing them in their natural contexts. Observations of three of the children studied in one intensive analysis demonstrated that people, furniture (!), and pets were the most stable objects of their behavioral interactions, with dogs being the most preferred animal for two of the children. Referring to animals as children's "associates," Barker and Wright found that children mentioned their own pets, those of neighbors, strays, and even insects as "objects" of their attention. However, they did not elaborate on the role or meaning of these animals in the lives of the children.

In a study of the factors that may lead children to help someone in distress, J. M. Sprafkin, R. M. Leibert, and R. W. Poulos (1975) showed one group of children a filmed Lassie episode in which Lassie's owner, Jeff, rescued a puppy. Children exposed to this episode were more likely to help puppies they thought were in distress (but who were actually in no danger) than children who had not viewed the episode. And M. R. Yarrow, P. N. Scott, and C. Z. Waxler, in their classic study of how preschool-aged children learn concern for others (1973), included a number of actual opportunities for children to help animals (e.g., assisting a kitten entangled in yard, moving food back within the reach of a hungry mouse) as an assessment of their prosocial behavior. Children's reactions to more serious forms of animal distress were measured using three-dimensional dioramas with toy, not real, animals. I will return to the benevolent actions of children helping animals in need when I discuss the importance of empathy in chapter 6.

Brenda K. Bryant was one of the first developmentalists to publish information about children and pets in a mainstream developmental psychology periodical (1985). In her categorization of sources of interpersonal support, she included peers, parents, grandparents, and pets. As she noted, "a pet can be a confidant, a source of humor, a nonjudgmental companion, a source of shared daily activities and responsibilities, and a constantly available companion" (p. 7). Her intensive study of 7- and 10-year-olds revealed that children's intimate conversations with their pets were related to a measure of empathy, with older children considering pets their "special friends."

Pets and children: The important foundation laid by Boris Levinson

The psychologist who must be credited with the first comprehensive attempt to address developmental factors in children's relations with animals was Boris Levinson. Levinson published two seminal books on the topic, one in 1969, *Pet-Oriented Child Psychotherapy* and *Pets and Human Development* published in 1972. Although the relative handful of researchers interested in children and animals and the human-animal bond relied heavily on these books as resources, the rest of the profession of developmental psychology allowed these volumes to gather dust on the shelves of university libraries.

A case of bad timing? I would like to explore with you the rich content and almost unlimited ideas for research and application that Levinson provided in these books. But first, let me speculate on why Levinson's work might not have received the attention it deserved during his own lifetime.

Levinson's books were published at a time when developmental psychology as an academic discipline was undergoing change, especially in its theoretical models and areas of emphasis. This was the period of the "cognitive" revolution in developmental psychology. After decades of dominance by behavioral and social learning approaches (how children become socialized, especially through the processes of modeling and imitation), cognitive development and the growth of children's minds took center stage. The ideas of Jean Piaget, the famous Swiss developmental psychologist, became the center of attention for scientists in the U.S. The development of perception in infancy, the growth of language in the preschool years, how children think about moral dilemmas, and similar topics were prominent. Of course, social development was not forgotten. There was a raft of research on the development of attachments in infancy, peer relations in older children, the development of emotional self-regulation, aggression, empathy, and prosocial behavior. But the emphasis in all these areas of study was on relations between human beings. Animal partners simply did not appear in the developmental literature. As Levinson observed, "Scientific investigation into the significance and use of pets for both children and adults has been very sparse. L. Carmichael's compendious 'Manual of Child Psychology,' for example, nowhere even mentions the word 'pet' " (1954, p. 220).

I believe that this change in emphasis in developmental psychology, as exciting and productive as it was, was not fertile ground for the messages Levinson shared. It would take decades for developmental psychology to begin to show openness to his ideas. And I believe this, too, is related to a more recent change in developmental approaches—a greater emphasis on the *ecology* of children's psychological development. This ecological approach considers the importance of all the varied contexts in which children develop, from the intimacy of their family relationships to schools, church, neighborhood, society, and culture. This change, together with the rents in the fabric of peace—child maltreatment, community violence, assaults between intimate partners, violence between peers, countries devastated by war—have illustrated how animal welfare may be implicated. Some children may look to animals as sources of support in these stressful times but others may manifest their distress by attacking animals who are even more vulnerable than the children themselves. I don't think my speculations exhaust all the possibilities, but I think these reasons, in part, suggest why Levinson's messages initially fell on, not deaf but at least distracted ears and why they should be heeded even more by contemporary students of human development.

The legacy of Boris Levinson. Levinson's 1972 book, *Pets and Human Development*, is, I believe, the first comprehensive attempt to address human-animal relations across the life span. I will focus here on his chapter entitled "The Pet and Child Development," but the interested reader should take note of the other topics included in the book: animals in mythology, history, and art, pets and adults, pets in old age, grieving over pet loss, the use of animals in psychotherapy, the role of the veterinarian, and pets in caretaking and correctional institutions. I should comment that, to Levinson's credit, each of these topics is now the object of concerted research efforts.

Levinson began his chapter on pets and child development by noting a number of challenges facing families in the era he was writing and it is remarkable that these challenges still remain. He listed the economic stresses that often require both parents to be employed outside the home, children who may be left without adult supervision, high rates of mental health problems in young people, and the alarming number of children who were victims of abuse. Levinson was not so naïve as to suggest that pets in a home would alleviate these problems. In fact, in his prologue, he stated, "It will take more than providing children and adults with pets for them to function as productive, happy members of the human family" (1972, p. 3). However, he would make clear that pets' contributions to family harmony and health had not been sufficiently appreciated, especially by the mental health professions.

Levinson first addressed the role of pets in the life of the infant. And it is not surprising that most of his comments focused on attachment processes. We now know that the development of a close and intimate relationship with a nurturing caregiver in the first two years of a child's life is critical for healthy human development. If attachment is absent or proceeds in dysfunctional ways, serious psychological disturbance may result. I will elaborate on this in a later section on attachment disorders in chapter 6. Levinson saw the availability of pets as an opportunity for infants to experience pleasurable touch (see Tiffany Field's marvelous book on the role of touch in human development, *Touch*) and a sense of stability in what might otherwise be a changing and shifting social environment, for example, in cases where an infant has multiple caretakers outside of the home. He also stressed the importance of pets as "transitional objects," like a security blanket or favorite toy, that help infants soothe themselves, experience safety, and bridge the gap between themselves and the outside world. In the absence of adult presence, a pet could provide comfort and security.

The tasks of the toddler period can also be facilitated by the presence of pets. Animals in a home may provide a child with a model of exploring the environment and the parallel between a young animal's need to be "house-broken" and the toddler's toilet training is obvious. Parents play a critical role as well. If a young child sees his or her parents respond to a kitten's or puppy's "accidents" in a tolerant, gently corrective manner, it may reassure the child about how his or her occasional failures will be treated. During this period, pets may also become part of a child's fantasy life, facilitating a child's role-taking, perspective-taking, and empathy, and some children may actually create imaginary animal companions (Taylor 1999). Both real and fantasy play may therefore be enhanced by the presence of pets.

As children approach school age, learning responsibility for others is another developmental task in which pets can play an important role. Parents can help make this a successful experience by modeling appropriate pet care, giving children responsibilities for pets that match children's current level of competence, and by being present to gently correct errors children may make in fulfilling their responsibilities. Levinson believed that children's successes in these care taking activities could only improve their sense of self-esteem. Since peer relations become more important at this stage of development, children's ability to care for pets can be a sign of competence noted by peers. And when inevitable strains occur in peer relations, children can turn to pets for unconditional love.

During late childhood and early adolescence, children are learning and constructing their early identity, beginning to focus more on gender issues and sexuality, learning to be accepted and productive members of groups, and developing more complex forms of prosocial behavior and kindness toward others. Levinson suggested that pets can facilitate each of these developmental tasks. How children behave with their pets can be a mirror revealing to children their own personality characteristics, both their assets and their flaws. Children may learn that their occasional cruelty to animals is distressing to their pet and the development of such empathy can serve to make further cruelty less likely. Children need to learn that they may need to control their pets but that this must be done through "benign authority" and not abusive manipulation.

When pets die. The shorter life span of most pets also means that children will see the unfolding life cycle of animals, including their death. Again, I reflect on the words of Willie Morris, "The dog of your boyhood teaches you a great deal about friendship, and love, and death: Old Skip was my brother" (1996, p. 118). The loss of a pet, especially when a child and pet have formed a significant attachment, is not only an emotionally wrenching event for a child but also an opportunity to learn the appropriate expression of grief and mourning. Again, sensitive parents can facilitate this process by validating their children's sense of loss. More recently, in a book for parents and caretakers of infants through 3-year-olds, the well known and beloved pediatrician, T. Berry Brazelton (1992) offered parents the following advice:

> The death of a pet. This should be taken as seriously as the loss of a person. Never lie about it to a child. You will lose her trust. Tell her what you can about the animal's life and the animal's death. Encourage the child to unload her grief and her anger at losing a beloved friend. Allow her a period of mourning before you introduce another pet into the family. It is important for the child to realize the loss and to experience the sense of caring that goes with losing a beloved pet. Again, expect her to feel personally responsible for having caused the loss, and explain whether it was an accident or a natural death. (pp. 331–332)

Brazelton's advice should also be heeded by parents of older children. Joann Jarolmen independently surveyed 433 children 6 years old and older as well as adults in the same family about their reactions to the recent (past year) death of a pet, usually due to illness (1998). Most of the pets who had died were dogs (56.4%) and cats (27.5%). Jarolmen found that, although adults reported stronger attachment to the pets than either children or adolescents, children 6 to 10 years old expressed more grief over the loss of their pet than did the adults (children's grief was not significantly different from that of adolescents). It would be of interest to conduct a similar study of cases where pets have met a violent death.

The significance of the death of pets and the distress this can create for their human caretakers, young or old, makes this a topic of obvious interest to the veterinary professional. A recent book that addresses this issue and includes a chapter on helping children cope with the death of a pet is Mary F. Stewart's (1999) *Companion Animal Death.* Advice is provided for both the veterinarian and the parent and Stewart considers the varying impact of pet loss depending on a child's level of development.

As children enter adolescence, pets highlight a number of new developments. Animals' uninhibited sexual activity may help illustrate sexuality and the reproductive process and adolescents' expanding cognitive abilities help them appreciate the financial and economic aspects of caring for a pet (e.g., food, veterinary care). Pets may also reduce the stress or loneliness some young people experience during this period of development (Rew 2000). For example, Erika Friedmann and her colleagues found that the presence of a dog in a room where 9- to 16-year-olds were given a reading task was related to lower blood pressure in these young people (Friedmann, Katcher, Thomas, Lynch, and Messent 1983). This likely calming effect has recently been enlisted to "assist" readers who experience difficulties with this skill; dogs present a nonjudgmental and accepting environment for even the most challenged of readers!

At this stage, young people also confront the contradictions and ambivalence present in humans' relations with animals more generally. We may keep certain animals as pets, but other species we treat as food, some animals are destroyed when they interfere with or endanger humans, and adolescents may have to deal with peers whose behavior toward animals is cruel or abusive. Pets may help adolescents' introduction into this complex and ambivalent adult world of human-animal relationships.

B. Levinson provided a rich picture of all the reasons why developmental psychologists and others interested in the human development should make pets a focus of developmental analysis. He also mentioned the issue of cruelty to animals a number of places in his book. For example, he suggested a case where an emotionally disturbed child who associated a pet with the parent who gave them the pet might, upon the parent's death, abuse or even kill the animal (1972, p. 121). One case he described alluded to inappropriate sexual activity between a young girl and her dog (p. 77). And in another section, he notes that veterinarians may see pets harmed or injured by the pet's young caretaker (p. 169) stating later in his book, "eventually veterinarians will become members of mental hygiene teams" (p. 162). It seems that

Levinson did not overlook or fail to anticipate any of the contemporary issues related to children and animals, kindness and cruelty.

Although Levinson's work remained in the shadows of mainstream developmental psychology, a handful of developmentalists have illuminated and expanded on his ideas. The three who stand out in my mind are the late Aline Kidd, her husband, Robert Kidd, and Gail Melson. The Kidd's research represents a methodical dedication to understanding children's attitudes towards pets and other animals across developmental stages and examining children's artwork and their attachment to pets. Samples of their research include "Children's attitudes toward their pets" (1985) and "Social and environmental influences on children's attitudes toward pets" (1990) and a review of the topic of children and pets can be found in chapter 7—"Are pets good for children" of Barrie Gunter's *Pets and People* (1999, pp. 89–105). A summary of their work on pet ownership is available in Phil Arkow's *The Loving Bond: Companion Animals in the Helping Professions* (1987, pp. 68–82).

The noted Purdue University developmental psychologist Gail Melson is a pioneer in our understanding of the role of pets in the development of children's capacity for nurturance. Her book *Why the Wild Things Are: Animals in the Lives of Children* (2001) is an excellent overview that integrates mainstream developmental psychology topics with the often overlooked contributions of pets and other animals to children's social and cognitive development. Also of note and worthy of your attention is Gene Myers's *Children and Animals: Social Development and Our Connections to Other Species* (1998), a fascinating excursion into the lives of preschoolers and their classroom pets.

The efforts of these social scientists and others suggest that we may be seeing a renaissance of scholarly interest in animals' role in the unfolding of children's social, cognitive, and emotional development. What are some of the challenges facing those who study children's relationships with animals, especially in cases where animals are abused? In the next chapter, I introduce an overview of these challenges and will elaborate on them in later chapters.

CHAPTER 3

Old wine in a new bottle

Over 100 years ago, Marshall Saunders wrote *Beautiful Joe* (1893/1922), the fictionalized account of a real dog who had been abused by his master, Mr. Jenkins. The book has a happy ending since, after being cruelly mutilated and disfigured, Joe is adopted by a family known for its humaneness and love of all animals. This general theme—animals maltreated by humans are rescued from further harm—is a common one in children's literature. What sets *Beautiful Joe* apart from other books of this type is the author's attention to the link between animal abuse and the maltreatment of people, a link that received renewed attention during the 1990s.

Beautiful Joe was written during a period of U.S. American history when the animal cruelty issue was a prominent social concern. In fact, Saunders dedicated the book to George Angell, President of the Massachusetts Society for the Prevention of Cruelty to Animals. Nine years before the publication of this book, Angell made a presentation entitled "The new order of mercy; or, crime and its prevention," to the National Association of Superintendents of Public Instruction (1884). The essence of Angell's presentation was that although animal abuse should be a concern in its own right, society should heed animal abuse as an omen of violence between people. In Angell's words, "I say, then, that our remedy against the lawlessness and crime now so rapidly growing in this country lies in the humane—which will be found also to include the moral—education of the children, and that this is also the shortest road to reach the parents" (p. 28). Remember, this was 1884! When asked why he spent so much of his time and money talking about kindness to animals when there was so much cruelty to people, Angell's reply was "I am working at the roots" (p. 32).

As I write this chapter, I am still reeling from the spectacles of school violence in Pearl, Mississippi and Springfield, Oregon. In these two high-profile cases, the children responsible for killings at their schools had histories of abusing animals, histories that were apparently ignored by the adults and classmates who knew these children. What were Marshall Saunders and George Angell calling our attention to over a century ago? Why did their message remain dormant for so long?

I believe some hints to the answers to these questions can actually be found in *Beautiful Joe*. Recall that Joe's abuser was a Mr. Jenkins. Jenkins is portrayed as a man with antisocial tendencies, many of which he displayed within his own family context. Jenkins' capacity for emotionally abusing his own children is clear when he kills Joe's littermates while his children watch. When Jenkins is tried for his abuse of Joe, there is the intimation that Jenkins' wife and children are also victims of his physical abuse and neglect. Suspicions of domestic violence and child abuse and neglect prompt the court to contemplate removal of his wife and children from his home.

"Rediscovering" violence to children, women, and animals

In the era during which *Beautiful Joe* was written, society was aware that animals could be abused, that women could be battered by their husbands or boyfriends, and that children could be victims of physical and sexual abuse and neglect (Gordon 1988). And yet, social scientists paid little systematic attention to these separate forms of violence and virtually no attention to the possible relations among animal abuse, domestic violence, and child maltreatment. Society's inattention to these phenomena was sharply interrupted in the 1960s and 1970s with the "rediscovery" of battered children, battered women, and battered animals. And today, rather than being viewed as unrelated forms of violence, social science is finally grappling with the potential interrelations among these types of maltreatment. The messages offered by Marshall Saunders and George Angell are finally being heard and it is beginning to make a difference in the lives of children, women, and animals.

If animal abuse is such a potentially significant sign of a person's tendency toward interpersonal violence, why has it taken so long for laypersons and professionals to take it seriously? I think there are three main reasons for slow progress in this area. One has to do with how we define animal abuse. A second involves measuring and keeping records of animal abuse. And a third deals with researchers' interest in focusing their scientific lenses on how animals are treated or mistreated in our society. I turn to these issues in the next section.

Animal abuse: A childhood "phase" or a significant omen?

> The dance of bloodless categories that broad theories present to us cannot show us the particular textures of the horrors—Philip P. Hallie (1982, p. xv)

Defining animal abuse

How do we know when animal abuse has occurred? For many of us, our response might be "I know it when I see it!" and, to a certain degree, we would be correct. There are many publicized incidents of cruelty to animals that virtually every person would consider serious maltreatment of a living creature. Pasado, a donkey in a

Bellevue, Washington petting zoo, had a noose placed around his neck and then was bludgeoned for 45 minutes by three young men until he died (Fox 1999). If we consider that animal maltreatment can range from teasing to torture, the reader will surely agree that the Pasado case falls at the "torture" end of the continuum. And the Pasado case is not an isolated incident. In the course of my own work, it seems that not a week goes by without a report of some type of animal—pet, wild, farm, or stray—horribly abused by a child or an adult. This also seems to be the case with child abuse. Shaken babies, children burned with lit cigarettes, toddlers raped by a family member—when we read about such cases, we know our horror is shared by nearly everyone in the human community.

But what about the incidents that are less dramatic, less likely to appear in newspaper headlines? In the United States, most cases of child maltreatment are cases of neglect and animal neglect dominates humane societies' caseloads. Improper care of both children and animals can have devastating effects on their welfare. Yet we often seem unaware of these cases unless, again, the neglect is so severe or involves so many victims that it makes the evening news.

Definitions of child abuse and neglect are not exactly the same in every State in the U.S. but the definitions do share common characteristics. Usually, four types of abuse and neglect are differentiated: physical abuse, sexual abuse, psychological or emotional abuse, and neglect (which can include educational and medical neglect). Each type of abuse and neglect can also be rated on a continuum ranging from minor to severe/lethal. The age of the victim may also be a factor in applying these definitions and ratings. For example, the same hard slap on the buttocks of a 6-year-old (not a recommended practice) would have a more serious impact on a 6-month-old infant.

Defining animal abuse is even more challenging. First of all, there are no national standards for defining different types and severity of animal abuse. In fact, definitions of what an animal is vary from state to state! Animals can be physically and sexually abused, some suggest animals are capable of being psychologically abused (e.g., keeping a prey animal next to but not accessible to its natural predator, isolating a social animal from other members of its species), and there is no doubt that animals can be neglected. As with child abuse and neglect, animal abuse and neglect can range in severity from mild cases to those that are severe or lethal. But there is a further complication.

Definitions of animal abuse will be dependent on the age and type of animal involved. Shaking a puppy's head might cause permanent injury but the same shaking of a large adult domestic dog could be inconsequential. Societies also classify some species of animals as pests or vermin and are not likely to view their destruction, no matter how torturous and deliberate, as abusive. Which species are classified in this way can vary from one culture to another. The species issue clearly makes animal abuse more difficult to define and is very likely one reason why progress in this area has been slower than efforts to define child abuse.

In an earlier review of this topic (Ascione 1993), I defined animal abuse as "socially unacceptable behavior that intentionally causes unnecessary pain, suffering, or distress to and/or the death of an animal" (p. 228). Although this definition excludes veterinary procedures, medical research, and agricultural practices that may injure or cause the death of animals, I believe it still captures the clinically and psychologically relevant behavior that may bring a child or adolescent to the attention of mental health professionals.

Sociocultural standards of animal care and treatment. First let me focus on the part of the definition that refers to "socially unacceptable behavior." Societies vary dramatically in animal welfare standards and in their internal debates about such standards. For example, as the Salt Lake City 2002 Olympics were approaching, there was debate about the appropriateness of a rodeo as an adjunct to these winter games. Utah and the rest of the U.S. would be unanimously appalled if a proposal to include bullfights had been offered. But a similar proposal in Spain would likely be less controversial. Sensitivity to varying cultural standards of animal treatment is laudable. But, as so convincingly argued by Robert B. Edgerton in his book, *Sick Societies: Challenging the Myth of Primitive Harmony* (1992), there is a limit to cultural relativism.

Edgerton describes cases where adults encourage children to torture small animals and birds to death (p. 79) or treated hunting dogs with "callous cruelty," forcing the dogs to eat hot chili peppers (p. 80). He labels these practices and others, like female genital mutilation, as "culturally maladaptive," observing that "As much as humans in various societies, whether urban or folk, are capable of empathy, kindness, even love and as much as they can sometimes achieve astounding mastery of the challenges posed by their environments, they are also capable of maintaining beliefs, values, and social institutions that result in senseless cruelty, needless suffering, and monumental folly in their relations among themselves and with other societies and the physical environment in which they live" (p. 15). Yet in other cultures, perhaps equally "primitive" by our Western standards, parents take seriously teaching respect for and benevolent treatment of animals (Edwards 1986).

There are many other morally relevant issues concerning standards of animal care in our society. Cosmetic surgery to alter the appearance of domestic pets, conditions of maintenance and training at zoos and circuses, sport hunting practices, the slaughter and consumption of animals for food, the use of assistance animals and the manner in which they are trained, the use of animals in cosmetics testing, and the role of animals in medical research are considered by some to be examples of institutional cruelty and all are worthy of study in their own right. But since our focus is on individual psychological dysfunction that may be signaled by animal abuse, these important topics are beyond the scope of this book.

Being cruel on purpose. Second, the definition includes the criterion of "intentional" harm. This element is included because we want to exclude cases where animals are injured or killed due to accidental acts. All of us cringe with distress when an animal crosses the path of a car on the highway or a raptor is electrocuted on a power line but I doubt anyone would consider the human agents in such circumstances to be abusing animals or displaying cruelty toward them. Likewise, a rambunctious toddler, still mastering her coordination skills, might fall on and break the leg of the family kitten but we would not label this abuse. Intention requires understanding that one's actions can have effects on others and some level of self control such that an individual is free to choose to act or not act. Our world has been witness to horrific tragedies in which children have been exposed chronically to violence and have been coerced into committing atrocities against other human beings. In these cases, the question of whether the children had any freedom to choose their behavior is moot.

In Kari René Hall's photographic essay, *Beyond the Killing Fields* (1992), we confront the plight of Cambodian refugees who had fled the Khmer Rouge to camps on the Thailand-Cambodian border. The author notes that "Children in the camp laugh and play naturally, but they take their cues from the war and violence that permeate their environment. Like their parents, the children are eyewitnesses to theft, murder, assault, and rape" (p. 102). Having missed many of the normal opportunities to learn about their native land and its animal inhabitants, children may not even recognize common work animals. "A father tells how his seven-year-old son pointed to a picture in a magazine and exclaimed 'Chke' (dog)! 'It nearly broke my heart,' The father said. 'He did not know the water buffalo.'" (p. 102). But it's not only their knowledge of animals that has been affected: "Children treat animals and each other with indifferent cruelty" (p. 113).

Another recent report describes how children and adolescents were "drugged, abused, and tortured" as part of their induction into the vicious maiming and killing for which Sierre Leone's Revolutionary United Front became notorious (Whitelaw 2001, p. 28). James Garbarino, Kathleen Kostelny, and Nancy Dubrow (1991) tell of similar coercive tactics used by the rebel army in Mozambique to enlist child soldiers. These children may commit unspeakable acts but, given the threats and abuse under which they were performed, it is unlikely we would consider them intentional. "In judging the significance of animal abuse by young people, we must always determine whether the youth's behavior violates community and cultural standards and whether sufficient cognitive maturity is present to indicate that the behavior was intentionally harmful. Both of these factors are relevant for clinical assessment and may also be related to legal statutes pertaining to the treatment of animals" (Ascione, Kaufmann, and Brooks 2000, p. 326).

Adults are not immune from circumstances that may reduce their inhibitions against violating community and cultural standards. One of the most difficult national memories of the Vietnam war for U.S. citizens was the March 16, 1968 My Lai incident, where hundreds of Vietnamese civilians—unarmed men, women, children, the elderly—were slaughtered by American servicemen. The actions of these servicemen was such a clear violation of civilized standards of conduct, even in war time, that another U.S. service man, Hugh C. Thompson, Jr. who later received a citation and the Soldier's Medal for his intervention, who came upon the scene of the massacre actually ordered his men to shoot their own compatriots if they failed to stop killing the civilians (Vistica 1997, p. 41). And the brutality of this incident was not confined to human victims: "nearly every living thing in the village had been shot: cows, chickens, dogs, babies, and unarmed women" (Wilson 1990, p. 49).

Defining what hurts. Finally, the definition refers to pain, distress, and suffering but does not limit these to physical manifestations. In a later chapter, I will give examples of ways that animals may be neglected and physically or sexually abused (which may also cause physical injuries). The subject of the emotional abuse of animals has received much less attention. Perhaps we can think of examples where isolating a social animal like a dog or always verbally berating a pet would be considered emotional abuse. A more extreme example was provided by Donna Ferrato in her book *Living with the Enemy* (1991), a photographic essay on domestic violence. One of the batterers who abused his wife in front of their 3-year-old son also kept a boa constrictor and a ferret in adjacent aquaria. "The ferret was forced to live in a state of constant anxiety next to the eye of the ever-hungry snake" (p. 145).

Measuring animal abuse

The second reason that attention to animal abuse has been dormant so long is the absence of standardized reporting and recording of such cases. In the child abuse and neglect field, methods have been devised to collect national data on reports of child abuse and neglect. Health professionals are mandated to report suspected cases of child abuse and neglect and, in some states, all citizens are mandated reporters. These methods are not perfect and they continue to evolve but they do allow us to compare, from year to year, reported and substantiated cases of child abuse and neglect. Attaching numbers to a phenomenon (e.g., one million children abused in some way in 1997) allows the public to grasp the scope of the problem. In addition, changes in these numbers from year to year can tell us whether our prevention programs are working.

We have no comparable national system for tracking reports of animal abuse and neglect, in part, because so few states mandate reporting of suspected animal abuse. As a result, we do not know the annual rate of animal abuse and cannot determine if the rate of animal abuse is increasing, staying the same, or decreasing in American society. Furthermore, even though cruelty to animals is a crime in each of the states in the U.S., there are no national records that allow us to determine, for example, the number of juveniles or adults arrested for crimes involving animals.

We could obtain information on rates of animal abuse and neglect by contacting humane societies and animal control/services agencies. But we would find that their record keeping and reporting practices vary dramatically. Another source of information is mental health professionals who work with children, adolescents, and adults. One of the most prominent advances in our understanding and assessing animal abuse occurred in 1987. This was the year when "cruelty to animals" was first included in the major diagnostic manual used for assessing psychological and psychiatric disorders (DSM-III-R 1987).

What type of mental disorder would include animal abuse as a symptom? Let me answer this by first describing a case noted in the news a few years ago (*Courier Chronicle* 1993). Three Humboldt, Tennessee brothers, ages 6, 7, and 9 years, were apprehended after a series of incidents including stealing, beating and throwing a knife at another child, and killing cats. All three of these behaviors are listed among the 15 separate symptoms of what is called "Conduct Disorder" (CD). The 15 symptoms are now (DSM-IV 1994) grouped under the following categories: aggression to people and animals (including bullying, fighting, cruelty, stealing with confrontation of a victim, and forcing someone to have sex), destruction of property (including setting fires and vandalism), deceitfulness or theft (including breaking and entering, lying to "con" others, and behaviors like shoplifting and forgery) and serious violation of rules (including running away from home and truancy). Children must have displayed at least three of the symptoms in the past 12 months to receive a diagnosis of CD. CD reflects serious antisocial behavior and can, in some cases, persist from childhood into adolescence and adulthood. (It is ironic that an earlier classification system for symptoms juvenile delinquency also included cruelty to animals—it was published in 1925 by Cyril Burt, a well known British psychologist.)

I will have more to say about CD later, but the point here is that only within the last decade and a half has animal abuse been formally listed among CD symptoms. This means that professionals evaluating children and adults are now more likely to ask about a child's violent behavior toward animals and we can now get a better idea about how common this behavior is in childhood and adolescence.

> It would, therefore, seem wise to include a more carefully planned handling of behavior toward living creatures in our school curriculum on the one hand, and to alert all child therapists to watch for any record of killing or torturing a living thing. It may well be that this could prove a diagnostic sign, and that such children, diagnosed early, could be helped instead of being allowed to embark on a long career of episodic violence and murder. (Mead 1964, p. 22)

Estimating the percentage of children and adolescents who abuse animals. One of the most significant advances in our understanding of psychological problems in childhood and adolescence is the development of checklists that ask caretakers to identify problems displayed by their children. One widely used version of these checklists is Thomas Achenbach's *Child Behavior Checklist,* which is available in separate versions for 2- to 3-year-old children and for 4- to 18-year olds (Achenbach 1991; Achenbach 1992).

Usually a parent, most often the mother, or a child's primary caregiver (e.g., foster parent, grandparent) completes the checklist by noting whether each problem mentioned is a) not a problem for the child, as far as the parent knows, b) is sometimes a problem or somewhat characteristic of the child, or c) is very true or often true of the child. The 2–3-year-olds' version lists 99 behaviors that could be considered problems (Achenbach 1992) and the person filling out the checklist is asked to use "the past 2 months" as the time frame for making judgments about the child. The version for 4–18-year-olds lists 112 specific problem behaviors (Achenbach 1991) and asks the respondent to use "the past 6 months" as the time frame.

One of the items that appears on both of these versions relates to whether the child has been "cruel to animals." In the graph below, I present the results for this cruelty to animals item that have been found with hundreds of children who were assessed using the Child Behavior Checklist but I also include results for another item, "vandalism," for comparison purposes and to prepare the reader for a point I will try to make later in this chapter.

In Figure 3.1 below, the percentages on the left or vertical axis represent the percentage of caregivers who said the problem behavior was somewhat or sometimes true for their child plus the percentage who said it was very true or often true. The children's age groups are shown on the horizontal axis. "Referred" indicates groups of young people who were being seen at mental health clinics for a variety of childhood and adolescent psychological problems. "Nonreferred" indicates comparable groups of young people who formed the normative sample; it is assumed that there are no significant clinical problems for children in these groups.

Let's begin by examining the data for "cruel to animals" on the left side of this graph. First, for the Nonreferred children in the 2–3 year age range, we find that 9% of the girls and 15% of the boys were reported to have displayed cruelty to animals. The corresponding percentages for Referred children were 31% for girls and 40% for boys. Therefore, for this age group, Referred children are two to three times more likely to be reported as cruel to animals than the Nonreferred children.

Cruelty to animals is also reported by the parents of children who are very young. A study of children *under* 2 years of age being examined at well-care pediatric clinics, by Larzelere, Martin, and Amberson (1989), used the Toddler Behavior Checklist, which was modeled after Achenbach's (Larzelere, Martin, and Amberson 1989). They found that 4 to 5% of parents reported the presence of cruelty to animals in their infants and toddlers within the past month. Unfortunately, the authors do not provide information on the types of behavior these parents considered cruel.

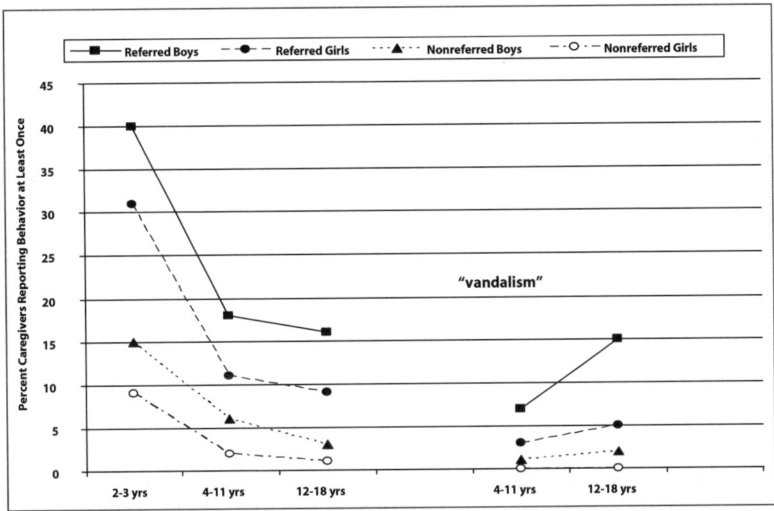

FIGURE 3.1. Responses to the "Cruel to Animals" items from the CBC/2-3 and CBC/4-18 (Achenbach,1991;1992), compared with "vandalism." Reporting in past 2 months (for 2–3-year-olds) or 6 months [responses of somewhat/sometimes true; very/often true].

Between the ages of 3 and 4, there is a dramatic overall drop in the percentage of children reported to be cruel to animals but the difference between the Referred and Nonreferred groups persists. For example, for 4–11-year-olds, 2% of girls and 6% of boys in the Nonreferred group were reported to be cruel. For the Referred children in this age group, 11% of girls and 18% of boys were reported to be cruel. A similar pattern is present when we look at the data for the 12–18-year-olds. In fact, the rate of cruelty to animals for referred children seems remarkably stable across the 4–11 and 12–18 year age groupings—this is a behavior that may not just "go away" as children get older.

Depending on the age group we focus on and the sex of the child, from 1 in 10 to 4 in 10 *Referred* children are reported to have been cruel to animals. In contrast, for *Nonreferred* children, the rate of cruelty to animals never exceeds 1.5 in 10 children and by the time these children reach school age, fewer than 1 in 10 are reported as cruel to animals. Keep in mind that these may be underestimates since not all children who are assessed have access to animals. Cruelty is less likely if victims are unavailable.

As you can also see by examining the graph, girls, regardless of referral status or age, are less likely, on average, to be reported as cruel than are boys. This latter finding may be related to the greater empathy displayed by girls found in a number of studies reported in the research literature or the correspondingly greater levels of physical aggression in which boys engage.

Let me share with you the reason I superimposed data for vandalism on the same graph. As you examine the right side of the figure, you will first notice that vandalism is not recorded on the 2–3-year-old version of the Child Behavior

Checklist. This makes sense, since there are few toddlers out there who graffiti walls or throw rocks through the windows of abandoned buildings. However, for 4- to 18-year-olds, vandalism appears to be reported at a rate that is, overall, *less* than the rate for cruelty to animals. (Although I have not plotted the data in the graph, "setting fires" is reported at roughly the same rate as vandalism. More information about arson and fire setting will be provided in a later section.) You should also note that vandalism seems to become more of a problem as children get older, especially for referred boys.

Vandalism is also a symptom of Conduct Disorder and the property destruction involved may not only be financially costly but also a danger to human welfare (think of cases where objects are thrown from an overpass at the windshields of oncoming vehicles). Because vandalism is included as a specifically defined offense that is common to criminal codes nationwide, we can access yearly reports on the incidence of vandalism provided by the Office of Juvenile Justice and Delinquency Prevention. These reports are quite detailed, including a breakdown by age and sex of the perpetrator. Similar national reports on cruelty to animals by juveniles do not exist.

Let me be clear—I believe that juvenile vandalism can be a serious offense and should be tracked in juvenile crime statistics. Arnold P. Goldstein (1999) makes a compelling case for the potential for vandalism to escalate into more dangerous forms of violence. But isn't cruelty to animals at least as serious? In fact, I would suggest that because cruelty to animals involves a living victim (as distinct from an inanimate object or structure), it should be given more weight as a crime. The primary reason I believe this is as follows: In order to hurt or kill an animal, children or adolescents have to suppress their sense of empathy—this is unnecessary if the target of an attack is inanimate. Smashed windshields and graffitied walls do not weep or cry out in pain when they are damaged. Animals do express their distress when they have been abused and the forms of their distress are sometimes quite human-like (there will be more on this topic in chapter 6).

Since records of cruelty to animals are so rare, let me provide one more example of the data we can access. These data come from the use of an assessment instrument that is very similar to the Child Behavior Checklist. Using the Achenbach-Conners-Quay (ACQ) Behavior Checklist, Achenbach, Howell, Quay, and Conners (Achenbach, Howell, Quay, and Conners 1991) collected parent or guardian reports of problem behaviors for 2,600 nonreferred and 2,600 referred boys and girls 4 to 16 years of age. The nonreferred children comprised a representative sample of the U.S. population, based on ethnicity, socioeconomic status, and place of residence (urban/suburban/rural and national region [e.g., Northeast, West]). These children had been screened for the absence of mental health referrals in the past year. The referred children were drawn from 18 mental health clinical settings across the U.S. Most of the referred children were being evaluated for outpatient mental health services. Potential candidates for inclusion in the nonreferred and referred groups were excluded if they were mentally retarded, had a serious physical illness, or had a handicap.

Item #39 on the ACQ asks the respondent, again, usually a parent or caregiver, whether being "cruel to animals" has been true, of a child or adolescent, in the past two months. Respondents can answer using the following 4-point scale: 0= Never or not at all true (as far as you know), 1= Once in a while or just a little, 2= Quite often or quite a lot, or 3= Very often or very much.

In Figure 3.2 below, I have represented the percentage of caregivers, for each age group, child gender, and referral status, reporting the presence of cruelty to animals, that is, scores of 1 or 2 or 3 (Dr. David Jacobowitz, personal communication, July 17, 1992). Each data point in this graph represents a percentage based on 100 children (for example, 100 nonreferred 6–7-year-old girls). In their statistical analyses for individual ACQ items, Achenbach, et al. note that cruelty to animals was significantly (p<.01) higher for referred youth, for boys, and for younger children.

The data in this graph again illustrate the relatively low frequency of cruelty to animals in the nonreferred sample (0–15%) in comparison with the referred sample (5–35%). Between the ages of 6 and 16 years, 15%–25% of referred boys are reported to be cruel to animals and the data suggest this symptom's incidence has greater stability through childhood and adolescence for boys than for girls.

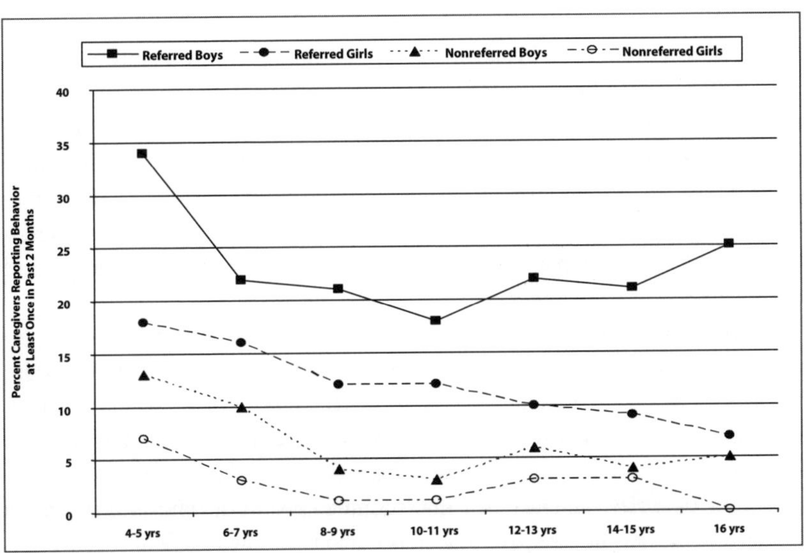

FIGURE 3.2. Responses to Item 39, "Cruel to Animals" from the ACQ Achenbach, Howell, Quay, & Conners (1991).

But I must add a few words of warning about the results of studies like these. First, when parents are asked about "cruelty to animals," this behavior is never defined. One parent might consider teasing an animal as cruel, another parent might not consider animal abuse as cruel unless their child maimed or killed a family pet (a similar observation has been made in Pickles and Angold 2003). In my own interviews of parents, I have found they may have dramatically different standards for judging children's cruelty. Rather than only relying on single questions like "Has your child been cruel to animals?" I have recommended that we also ask respondents to answer the following question, "What would your child have to have done to an animal for you to have considered it cruel?" Illustrations of more detailed assessments of types of animal abuse will be presented in chapter 7.

Second, some animal abuse may occur in the presence of parents but in other cases the abuse may occur secretively or, at least, out of the parent's view. This is also likely to be true for vandalism and fire setting. If you look back over the list of other CD behaviors I mentioned earlier, it's easy to see how parents *may not know about* their children engaging in some of these antisocial behaviors (e.g., fire setting, shoplifting). One study of non-clinic 12- to 16-year-olds that included both direct interviewing of these adolescents as well as parental interviews (Offord, Boyle, and Racine 1991) found that boys' and girls' *self-reported* cruelty to animals was five times higher than parental reports! Either the adolescents and their parents had very different definitions of cruelty to animals or parents were not aware of some of their children's activities. I suspect the latter explanation is more likely since Offord and his colleagues found similar discrepancies when they asked about vandalism and fire setting, activities whose definition is less ambiguous.

A colleague of mine (J. Richters, personal communication, September 10, 1996) shared with me the following quote attributed to David Berkowitz, New York City's "Son of Sam" killer: "I have often noticed just how unobservant people are. It's been said that parents are the last to know. This may be true in my case, for I wonder how I, at ages nine, eleven, thirteen, etc., managed to do so very many negative things and go unnoticed. It is puzzling indeed. And I think you will agree it is sad." Berkowitz pled guilty to more than a dozen murder and attempted murder charges. He'd also shot a neighbor's dog (Lockwood and Hodge 1986).

Berkowitz's observation and the findings of Offord, Boyle, and Racine suggest that parents and other adults may not be aware of some incidents of animal abuse because they may take place in settings where children are alone or out of direct adult observation and supervision. In fact, even if some children do not themselves perpetrate animal abuse, they may be exposed to it in their community.

In my own view, animal abuse may be another form of community violence children may witness but we have little information on how prevalent it is. We also have little information on how witnessing community violence to and abuse of animals affects children's psychological health. For example, during the 1980s and 1990s, the high rates of violent crime in many U.S. urban areas prompted psychologists to begin paying more attention to the effects of witnessing community violence on children, for example, heightened aggression, anxiety, and posttraumatic stress symptoms. These studies ranged from cases where children were present during a sniper attack at a schoolyard to seeing the body of a victim of violent crime on the street of a local neighborhood (Pynoos, Nader, Arroyo, Steinberg, Eth, Nunez, and Fairbanks 1987; Nader, Pynoos, Fairbanks, and Fredrick 1990; Osofsky 1999). Even college-aged students who report high levels of exposure to community violence are more likely to show compromised mental health including greater depression and aggression (Scarpa 2001).

As noted by an expert who recently reviewed research on the potentially devastating effects on young people of witnessing violence, sometimes "children see too much" (McAlister Groves 2002). Although many of these reports are case studies of thankfully rare but lethally violent events that children witnessed, other researchers have tried to obtain more representative data on children's exposure to a range of community violence. To facilitate gathering such information, John Richters and his colleagues developed the *Survey of Exposure to Community Violence: Self-report Version* (SECV) (Richters and Salzman 1990; Martinez and Richters 1993). The items on the SECV ask young people to report on whether and how often they have seen or heard various forms of crime and violence. In the Martinez and Richters' study both mothers and children separately completed the measure of violence exposure and, in keeping with my discussion so far and the findings of Offord, Boyle, and Racine, mothers were found to significantly underestimate what their children had seen or heard and the level of their children's distress.

Unfortunately, the SECV does not contain any animal-related items. It is clear from this work that we must ask children directly about their experiences; parents may simply not know the types and frequency of violent events, including violent attacks on animals, to which their children are exposed. And when children are asked, they may readily provide examples of animal abuse in their communities (Spitzer 1999).

The inventory of animal-related experiences developed by Barbara Boat (1999) and my "Children and Animals Assessment Instrument" (Ascione, Thompson, and Black 1997) both include items on witnessing violence to animals and it would be of value to add similar items to more general community violence exposure self-reports for use with children.

The stability of cruelty to animals across development. The lines used to connect the data points in the graphs I've discussed so far can be deceptive. They suggest that the same groups of children are followed from one developmental period to another (for example, first we study 2–3-year-olds, then re-examine them when they are between 4 and 11 years of age). Actually, in these graphs, different groups of children are represented in the data for the differing ages—this is referred to as a "cross-sectional" study in child psychology parlance. Different aged children are studied at the same point in time. Although this type of study is efficient, economical, and informative, cross-sectional research cannot tell us about the "stability" of a characteristic in a particular child. If a 5-year-old is cruel to animals, does the child continue to display this behavior four years later, when 9? If a child has not been cruel by age 10, could cruelty emerge when this child is 14? These and similar questions about past history and patterns of future development are unanswerable with cross-sectional approaches which assess individual children at only one point in time. Is there an alternative?

"Longitudinal" research refers to an approach that studies the same children at different points in time, at different developmental stages. As you can anticipate, such an approach can be time consuming and expensive. But the important advantage is that it allows us to track patterns of behavior over time. The questions I posed at the end of the previous paragraph can only be answered with longitudinal research.

I wish I could share with you graphs derived from longitudinal studies that were as comprehensive, detailed, and represented as large groups of children as the graphs derived from cross-sectional research using behavior checklists. I could do this if we were discussing aggression in general. However, I am not aware of any research with large numbers of children that specifically focuses on cruelty to animals using a longitudinal, or "prospective," design. But a pair of classic, pioneering studies completed more than thirty years comes close.

Fernando Tapia, a psychiatrist at the University of Missouri and later, the University of Oklahoma School of Medicine completed two studies (the second, with his colleague, John Rigdon) that represent the only published research designed to follow up, over a significant period of time, children displaying cruelty to animals. In the first paper, entitled "Children who are cruel to animals" and published in 1971, Tapia searched through the clinic files at the University of Missouri Child Psychiatry Section and selected the records of 18 children using the following criteria:

- Cruelty to animals was the *main* reason for the child being referred to the clinic.
- Cruelty to animals was included as one of the reasons, among others, that led to the child's referral.
- Only cases where the animal abuse was chronic or persistent, as distinct from insolated events, were included.

Using these criteria, Tapia identified 18 patient case files that spanned an 11–year period: all involved boys between the ages of 5 to 14 years. As I have mentioned before, cruelty can range from teasing to torture. In the case of these children, their behavior was clearly at the "torture" end of the continuum. Let me share some of the examples Tapia found in his review of these cases:

- a 9-year-old who tried to choke and smother his pet dog; when he was 4 years old he had successfully killed two other animals
- a 10-year-old who stabbed a cat and nearly killed it by trying to dismember it

- a 7-year-old prone to continuously beating the family dog
- a 5-year-old who "generally destroyed pets and other available animals . . ."
- an 8-year-old who was "constantly killing the chickens in the barnyard"
- a 14-year-old who "slowly choked a cat to death" and drove an ice pick through the head of a dog

Tapia also noted that in 16 of the 18 cases, the boys also displayed aggression and violence, either physical or sexual, toward human beings. A number of children were abusive toward their siblings, one tried to anally penetrate a 3-year-old girl with a stick, and another tried to smother his baby brother. Tapia found that 5 of the 18 boys were known to have set fires and 3 displayed bed wetting, or enuresis. I mention these two other behaviors because there was a time when the combined presence of cruelty to animals, fire setting, and enuresis (the "triad") was considered to be highly predictive of extreme interpersonal violence. The literature to date has not, however, confirmed the predictive value of this triad of symptoms (Barnett and Spitzer 1994).

One other factor makes this 1971 paper by Tapia so significant. In his discussion of these cases, he noted that physical and sexual abuse of the boys was common to many of the cases as was the presence of domestic violence. Tapia was clearly a pioneer in calling our attention to how an accumulation of risk factors in a child's life (see, for example, Dong, Anda, Dube, Giles, and Felitti 2003) might be manifested in their abusive behavior toward animals.

Six years later, Rigdon and Tapia (1977) published a study that involved locating as many as possible of the 18 boys studied in Tapia's 1971 paper. They were successful in finding 13 of the original 18 boys who had been evaluated between 2 and 9 years earlier; one of these 13 boys refused to participate but his parents did provide an update on his status. Rigdon and Tapia solicited information about their current functioning from the boys themselves, their parents or guardians, teachers, employers, and, if applicable, their current therapists. The researchers found that 8 of the 13 boys, 62%, were still behaving in inappropriate ways with animals and 4 of these 8 boys, 31% of the 13, displayed animal abuse that was severe in nature.

Tapia's two studies definitely shed some light on the issue of the stability of cruelty to animals in childhood and adolescence. Nearly 1 out of 3 of the young people still displayed animal abuse 2 to 9 years after their original assessment. This suggests that cruelty can be a persistent behavior that may not simply disappear with increasing maturity. Of course, one limitation of this longitudinal research project is the relatively small number of children who were studied. But I believe these were the first two published studies to focus specifically on the childhood animal abuse issue. It is unfortunate that Tapia's pioneering work did not yield more immediate research attention by others. When I wrote to Dr. Tapia over 10 years ago to request copies of his publications, he ended his note back to me with the following comment: "I still feel that the psychopathology of these interesting children needs further unraveling" (F. Tapia, personal communication, June 22, 1990).

Professional attention to animal abuse. I have covered two of the factors related to the relative neglect of animal abuse as a potentially significant clinical sign of disordered development—the challenges of defining animal abuse and measuring its prevalence. The last factor is related to these and involves the lack of training some clinicians have on this topic. When psychologists and psychiatrists think about violence, their attention is likely focused on *interpersonal aggression*—bullying, fights between peers, aggression during the commission of crime, and so forth. Violence toward animals has only recently been highlighted in the professional literature and mental health professionals still do not always ask their clients, child or adult, about this behavior. Recall that it was not until 1987 that cruelty to animals was even listed in the manuals of psychiatric disorders. As we learn more about how animal abuse is often embedded in the lives of children who are victims of abuse, young people who grow up in violent community environments, and children whose home life is distorted by domestic violence, I believe professionals will be more likely to incorporate information about animal abuse in their strategies for assessment and intervention. Signs of this change will be addressed in the next chapter.

CHAPTER 4

Animal abuse: Revisiting the past and looking to the future

Renewed research interest in animal abuse. The potentially common roots of child maltreatment, domestic violence, and animal abuse have been acknowledged for centuries. In the thirteenth century, Saint Thomas Aquinas recommended sanctions against animal abuse, "lest through being cruel to other animals, one becomes cruel to human beings." In the late 1600s, the philosopher John Locke wrote, "For the custom of tormenting and killing of beasts, will, by degrees, harden their minds even towards men; and they who delight in the suffering and destruction of inferiour creatures, will not be apt to be very compassionate, or benign to those of their own kind" (1693, Sec. 116).

In 1751, the British artist William Hogarth (1697–1764) created a series of engravings he entitled "The Stages of Cruelty" (Shesgreen 1973). The central figure in this series is a boy named Tom Nero who, as a child, is depicted joining other children in tormenting and abusing stray animals on a London Street. Tom is depicted as an abandoned child, since he wears clothing marked with the insignia of an almshouse, places where homeless and destitute adults and children resided.

In the first engraving of the series, animals are seriously abused in ways that insult our sensibilities and overwhelm our capacity for sympathy. In one corner of the engraving, a dog fight is ending with a serious abdominal injury to one of the "contestants." In another, children have tied makeshift wings to a cat and thrown it from the third floor of a building. A pointed stick is thrown at a rooster, a dog is having a bone tied to the root of its tail—other dogs will try to get the bone, injuring the dog's tail in the process, the tails of two cats are joined with a rope and they are then suspended from a lamppost, a boy smiles as his companion pokes the eyes of a live bird with a burning stick. And Tom Nero is joined by another boy shoving an arrow into the anus of a dog. A sole young man attempts to intervene and save the dog by offering the tormenters a small pie. The words accompanying the first engraving were penned by Rev. James Townley:

> While various scenes of sportive woe the infant race employ
> and tortured victims bleeding show the tyrant in the boy
> Behold a youth of gentler heart to spare the creature's pain
> O, take, he cries—take all my tart but tears and tart are vain
> Learn from this fair example you who savage sports delight
> How cruelty disgusts the view when pity charms the sight
>
> (Shesgreen, Plate 77)

In the second engraving, we encounter Tom again, now as an adolescent who is mistreating a work horse, beating it with the butt end of a whip to make it get up—the horse has a visibly broken leg and Tom has now gouged one of the animal's eyes with his assault. Tom, again, is not alone in his cruelty—adults are shown overworking a donkey, baiting a bull to attack a dog, clubbing a lamb to death, and running over a playing child because the driver of the cart is asleep or drunk.

When we encounter Tom again in the third engraving, he is an adult. Hogarth depicts him in a churchyard at nighttime with a gun in the pocket of his coat and watches that have fallen to the ground; Tom has apparently graduated from his earlier cruelty to animals to the life of a thief and highwayman. With keen insight for what we know more clearly today, Hogarth makes one further critical connection between Tom's childhood and adolescent animal abuse and his current character. Tom is apprehended and physically restrained by authorities. On the ground lies a young, obviously pregnant woman with her throat and wrist slashed. A note that fell at her side indicates that she has been stealing from her mistress, as Tom commanded her. Tom Nero has murdered his girlfriend.

In the fourth engraving of the series, Tom's body, a hangman's noose still around its neck, is being dissected by surgeons as part of a medical school anatomy lesson.

It is disturbing to visualize the depictions of cruelty and violence Hogarth illustrated and we may be tempted to click our tongues and shake our heads at such deplorable acts, thinking that such cruelties were confined to the dangerous streets of eighteenth-century London. Unfortunately, what Hogarth called his audience's attention to more than 250 years ago is still a problem in the twenty-first century. Contemporary newspaper and magazine articles as well as many conversations I have had with humane society agents, cruelty investigators, and animal control officers indicate that the cruelties Hogarth depicted still occur today and are complemented by forms of animal abuse even more horrid that those in *The Stages of Cruelty.*

My purpose was not to offend you in describing Hogarth's *Stages.* I call your attention to Hogarth's work because it represents one of the earliest attempts, in this case, through art, to increase public awareness not only of the tragedy of animals being tortured, maimed, and killed, but of the connection between animal abuse in early development and later violence toward humans. Hogarth purposely reproduced his engravings in a format by which they could be sold inexpensively and, therefore, would be accessible to all economic classes in his society. In a sense, Hogarth was producing public service announcements (PSAs), in the form of affordable art, similar to the PSAs about gun safety, substance abuse, and other human welfare issues produced today for radio, television, and print media. Since I will discuss animal abuse in the context of family violence in a later section, keep in mind that Hogarth used a violent, lethal assault against an intimate partner as the culmination of Tom Nero's cruel and antisocial life. *Research* on the association between animal abuse and domestic violence has only emerged in the past 10 years.

Novelists and other writers have drawn our attention to the relation between violence toward animals and violence toward people. In Edgar Allen Poe's story "The Black Cat," a man's descent into madness is charted as he first kills the family's pet cat and then murders his wife (1843). Pat Conroy describes the casual cruelty toward animals displayed by an abusive and controlling father in *The Great Santini* (1976) and the callous abuse of local animal life by young boys living on an island off the coast of South Carolina in *The Water Is Wide* (1972). Peter Shaffer's *Equus* (1973), a play about an adolescent who blinds six horses, was based on an actual incident in England. And recall the book that, I think, all of us had to read in high school—William Golding's *Lord of the Flies* (1959). Among the many moral messages Golding conveyed in this book is one illustrated by the sequence of scenes in which the boys on the island are violent and sadistic toward the island's resident pigs, acts that are a prelude to the violence and sadism the boys eventually practice on each other. One can read this book as a philosophical argument for children's inherent cruelty, especially when adult socialization agents are unavailable to monitor and deter aggression. But let's also recall that the boys find themselves on the island because they have been evacuated from a society where the adults are at war! We don't condone the boys' behavior but, with our current knowledge about the effects of exposure to community violence, traumatic separation from and, perhaps, loss of parents, and experiences of abandonment and displacement to an unfamiliar and dangerous land, the behavior of the boys is, at least, understandable. Children's positive and negative relations with animals in real-life evacuation from war zones in England during World War II were mentioned in Amy Strachey's *Borrowed Children: A Popular Account of Some Evacuation Problems and Their Remedies* (1940). Even across the Atlantic, concerns about the effects of the war on U.S. and Canadian children, including aggression, lowered empathy, and acting out by abusing animals, were noted by educator Dorothy W. Baruch (1943).

Best known to parents and children for his *Chronicles of Narnia*, C. S. Lewis also wrote a fascinating fantasy trilogy on human morality that included the novel *Perelandra* (1944). The story's protagonist, Dr. Ransom, representing the good in humankind, travels to the once unspoiled planet Perelandra and encounters the evil

Weston. Lewis uses an animal abuse incident to portray the cruelty of which Weston is capable. Walking along the edge of a beautiful sea, Ransom comes upon

> a damaged animal. It was, or had been, one of the brightly coloured frogs. . . . Weston . . . was standing about thirty feet away: and as Ransom watched he was tearing a frog—quietly and almost surgically . . . ripping it open . . . (Lewis 1962, pp. 108–110)

> The thing was an intolerable obscenity which afflicted him with shame. It would have been better, or so he thought at the moment, for the whole universe to never have existed than for this one thing to have happened. (p. 109)

And in a more contemporary vein, Andrew Vachss, in his 1991 novel, *Sacrifice*, describes a child victim of sexual abuse who is forced to observe animal mutilation as a way of coercing him into silence and later turns his own rage on a human infant victim.

Although philosophical, artistic, and literary treatments of an issue can sometime move us to focusing on the realities of our human condition, there are enough real and actual events that can serve the same purpose. For example, the Pasado case I mentioned earlier was, in part, responsible for galvanizing communities in Washington State to enact stricter penalties for animal abuse. A similar scenario developed in Utah a few years ago when a family's dog was severely beaten by its owner in front of the owner's children—the community's outrage and subsequent legislative action now makes intentional animal cruelty a more serious offense in Utah.

The interest of social scientists in animal abuse and its relation to interpersonal violence has intensified in the past two decades, adding scientific validity to the philosophical, artistic, and literary messages placed before us (see ten Bensel 1984). But there are still limitations on how widespread this interest is. Let me provide an illustration. In 2000, the cover of an issue of *Science*, the premier journal of the scientific community in the United States, displayed a stylized primate, looking rather human, pointing a revolver at the viewer of the cover. This cover highlighted a number of articles in the issue focusing on the problem of violence in my country and others. I was excited that a publication of such stature was grappling with and bestowing scholarly attention on this topic. But as soon as I found the editorial essay introducing the articles, I was disappointed as I read the following passage: "First, a disclaimer. This issue does not attempt to penetrate all the ugly visages of violence, purposefully ignoring, for instance, violence inflicted by predators upon their prey, *human cruelty to animals*, and that uniquely human capacity for waging war" (my emphasis) (Stone and Kelner 2000, p. 569). Although this journal issue contained excellent articles on topics ranging from school shootings and hooliganism at soccer matches in England and Europe to violence among non-human primates and the physiological and neurobiological correlates of aggressive and violent behavior, I was discouraged that human cruelty to animals had been excluded by fiat. Nevertheless, given my interest in this general topic, I read on.

Then, to my surprise I read an article, in this issue, by Constance Holden that was entitled "The Violence of the Lambs." Holden provided an overview of the developmental origins of aggression and violence in infancy and early childhood. Reading her paper rewarded my persistence since the article contained the following case study information: "By the time Joshua had reached the age of 2, says his mother . . . he would bolt out of the house and into traffic. He kicked and head-butted relatives and friends. He poked the family hamster with a pencil and tried to strangle it" (Holden 2000, p. 581). So here, in the same journal issue that was not going to address cruelty to animals was an example of a disturbed child displaying this very behavior! This is clearly the case of a phenomenon being "right under our noses" but not receiving the attention it is due. Scientific change is often slow but I do believe that we will see increasing attention to the issue of animal abuse, especially its relation to interpersonal violence.

There is now an accumulation of studies, relatively small in number, focused on the relations among child maltreatment, domestic violence, and animal abuse. Although I will expand on these relations in chapters 8, 9, and 10, let me illustrate them with the following samples of research.

Child physical abuse and neglect

> "Even a pet dog knows it is unloved when it is beaten." (Gilligan 1996, p. 47)

In 1983, DeViney, Dickert, and Lockwood examined the home life of 53 New Jersey families who had met legal criteria for child abuse and neglect. Each of these families also had at least one pet in their home. The observers who visited these homes discovered that in 60% of the families, pets were also abused and/or neglected. When the researchers focused on the 21 families specifically referred to social service agencies for the *physical* abuse of their children, animal abuse or neglect was found in 88% of these homes! It is clear from this study that children and animals can both be victimized in the same family. Unfortunately, some children who are victimized may become victimizers—children in 26% of the 53 families were abusive toward their pets.

In Mary Wertsch's book on growing up in military families (1991), she recounts the background of a woman physically and emotionally abused by her father. In reminiscing about her childhood experiences, it is remarkable that the following memory stood out in this woman's mind:

> I'm ashamed to tell this. . . . I remember bringing this dog in (the hallway) once, a small dog, and I remember shutting all of the doors to the hall so it had no escape, and getting a belt, and *whipping* this dog. Just

whipping. And delighting in hearing this dog cry. I could cry now to think of it. What a terrible thing. But I remember doing it. *Then* I remember trying to hug the dog, to make the dog realize I really loved it.

And I've never forgiven myself for that. But I also know that I had to do it for survival. I had to act it out....

My brother used to be very cruel also . . . he used to throw bread out the window to attract the birds, and then kill them. Just like our father used to set us up and trap us. (Wertsch 1991, p. 236)

Child sexual abuse

Many of us respond even more strongly when we learn that children can become victims of sexual abuse, often in the presumed safety of their own homes, schools, or church groups, by individuals who are supposed to be their caregivers. William Friedrich examined data for 271 cases of substantiated sexual abuse in 2- to 12-year-old children and 879 non-abused children. "Substantiated" cases are ones where an agency, for example, child protective services, has determined that there is evidence verifying the child's victimization. The rates of parental reports of their children being cruel to animals were 7 times higher for sexually abused boys than for non-abused boys and 8 times higher for sexually abused girls than for non-abused girls. One of every three sexually abused boys and one of every four sexually abused girls were reported to be cruel to animals (see Figure 4.1).

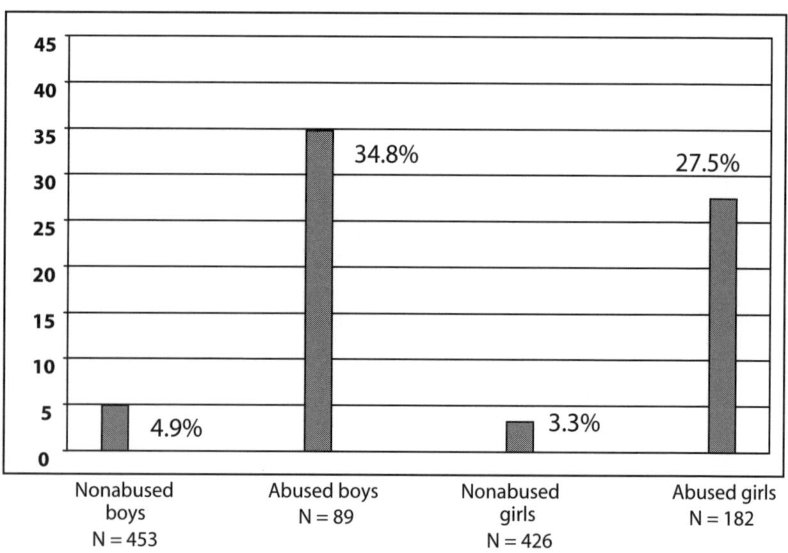

FIGURE 4.1. Parental Reports of Children's Cruelty to Animals on the Child Behavior Checklist (2–12-year-olds), Percent reporting "Sometimes/Often True." (Friedrich, personal communication, April 1992)

Domestic violence

I need not mention all the high-profile cases of domestic violence reported in the media or the countless non-celebrity families touched by wife battering. In reading many of the books published on this topic, I frequently encountered anecdotes about women enduring threatened or actual abuse of their pets by their adult partners, including a number in one of the first published books on this topic (Pizzey 1974). One example is the book written by Neil Jacobson and John Gottman (1998), *When Men Batter Women,* where the authors note that "the most violent batterers in our sample also tended to behave sadistically toward pets" (p. 149). What I did not find, however, was systematic research that examined such animal abuse.

Over the past few years, I have studied over 100 women who were battered by their partners, husbands or boyfriends, and who had sought safety at domestic violence shelters. Some women were accompanied by their children to these shelters. We discovered that over two-thirds of these women reported that their pets had been threatened or actually harmed by their partners. Over half of the women reported incidents where their pets had been hurt or killed and, in my most recent research, 62 percent of the women with children reported that their children had witnessed these incidents of pet abuse. We also know from other research studies that children in families where there is wife battering are at heightened risk for being abused themselves. Chapter 10 will be devoted to animal abuse in the context of domestic violence and I will expand on this research and that of others who have replicated these findings in other states in the United States as well as two Canadian provinces.

Animal abuse: Worthy of attention in its own right

It might seem obvious and it should come as no surprise that the veterinary profession is most likely to encounter cases where animals have been abused and it is the profession with a great responsibility to call society's attention to the plight of animals injured or killed by humans. This is parallel to the role that the profession of pediatric medicine played in our heightened awareness of child maltreatment. In a landmark study published in 1962, a group of physicians in Denver, Colorado and Cincinnati, Ohio, headed by the pediatrician C. Henry Kempe published a paper entitled "The battered-child syndrome" that galvanized U.S. society's concern for abused children. What was disconcerting about this report was not the fact that infants and children were victims of injury and, at times, fatal abuse. It was the fact that the maltreatment experienced was most often at the hands of the children's caregivers, caregivers who themselves often brought the children to be examined by doctors and emergency room staff. Pediatrics is concerned with the welfare and health of the young and this profession was sounding an alarm that our country had a problem of potentially epidemic proportions.

It is of historical interest that a similar attempt to raise society's awareness about child maltreatment including fatal abuse was made over 100 years earlier by Dr. Ambroise Tardieu, a Professor of Legal Medicine at the University of Paris and President of the French Academy of Medicine. In reviewing a number of cases, Tardieu noted "that the executioners of these children should more often than not be the very people who gave them life—this is one of the most terrifying problems that can trouble the heart of man" (quoted in Masson 1984, p. 19). Tardieu's words seemed to fall on deaf ears, perhaps reflecting society's willingness to believe that caregivers harming their own offspring was nothing but a rare anomaly.

Twelve years following the publication of the historic "battered child" paper, the United States Congress passed the Child Abuse Prevention and Treatment Act (PL 93-247) providing federal impetus to address child maltreatment. Mandatory reporting of suspected child maltreatment would eventually be required in every state and the law included a mandate for periodic national tallies of the number of abused infants, children, and adolescents as well as research into the causes and prevention of maltreatment. The most recent federal report on national child maltreatment rates was released in 1996 (Sedlak and Broadhurst). Based on a 1993 reporting period (p. 3-3), the study estimated that 1,555,800 children were victims of maltreatment that resulted in demonstrable harm. This reflected a 67% increase from the 1986 study and a 149% increase from the rates reported in 1980 (pp. 3-4). And it should be emphasized that these cases are ones that were reported to agencies or had come to the attention of professionals. We know that many other cases of child abuse and neglect never leave the privacy of the family, childcare center, school, or church.

As we open a new century, I believe we are witnessing parallel developments related to animal abuse within the veterinary community. Although he is not a veterinarian by training, Phil Arkow is a long-standing and well known member of the animal welfare community. In the 1990s, he published two articles in veterinary medical journals encouraging the veterinary profession to address societal concern with what appeared to be increasingly prevalent animal abuse, especially abuse perpetrated by young people. In an article directed at the Canadian veterinary community (1992), he reviewed existing research on animal abuse and human violence and urged veterinarians to consider the reporting of suspected animal abuse an ethical obligation to their animal "client" I should clarify for the reader that, according to a 1999 report, only two states in the U.S., Minnesota and West Virginia, mandate veterinarians to report suspected cases of animal abuse (Frasch, Otto, Olsen, and Ernest 1999). This is ironic since many states mandate veterinarians to report suspected child maltreatment! In a similar article directed to the U.S. veterinary profession (1994), Arkow again recommended that veterinarians play an active role in both child and animal abuse prevention and intervention and consider the benefits of reporting suspected cases to the appropriate agencies or authorities. This same argument was made by Robert Reisman and Cindy A. Adams in an essay entitled "Should Veterinarians Tell?" (1999).

In what I believe will become a landmark paper in the field of animal abuse and animal welfare, Dr. Helen Munro, a veterinarian at the University of Edinburgh, Scotland, published "Battered Pets" in 1996, making a purposeful parallel to the 1962 Kempe et al. paper on physicians' responses to non-accidental injuries in children. Given current veterinary training and practice, Dr. Munro observed, "although animal abuse is acknowledged to occur, there has been no attempt to describe the clinical signs and pathology of the 'battered pet.' In other words, the situation is remarkably similar to the one in which physicians found themselves, pre-Kempe" (p. 712). Her report did not present statistics but cited anecdotal evidence (e.g., cases of unexplained or repeated injuries or cases where injuries did not match the account provided by the pet's owner; such inconsistencies also raise a red flag in suspected child maltreatment cases) and urged veterinarians to establish criteria to facilitate the diagnosis of animal abuse.

Since the anecdotes she provided were derived primarily from veterinarians' experiences, they demonstrated that pet owners who abuse their animals may still seek medical care for them, just as child maltreating caregivers may take their children to doctors' offices and emergency rooms. As observed by psychiatrist James VanLeeuwen more than 20 years ago, "It would be sad, therefore, if in analogy to child abuse there persisted a reluctance to recognize the existence of animal abuse among the so-called accidental injuries brought to the veterinarian's attention. Greater awareness of animal abuse may lead veterinarians to initiate mental health intervention for the abusing family in addition to treating the animal" (VanLeeuwen 1981, p. 182).

In an effort to obtain more systematically collected and representative information about suspected animal abuse that comes to the attention of veterinarians, Dr. Munro and her colleague, Dr. M. V. Thrusfield conducted a survey of 1,000 small animal practitioners in the United Kingdom. In a series of four articles published in 2001 in the *Journal of Small Animal Practice*, they reported on the percentage of veterinarians who had encountered suspected or confirmed animal abuse, described the types of non-accidental injuries found in pet dogs and cats, demonstrated that animals could be victims of sexual abuse, abuse that in some cases led to the death of an animal, and noted a small number of cases in which the pet owners apparently induced or fabricated illnesses or injuries to their own pets. Because studies such as these are virtually nonexistent in the veterinary medical literature, allow me to expand on Munro and Thrusfield's findings.

In the first paper of their "Battered Pets" series of studies, subtitled "Features That Raise Suspicion of Non-accidental Injury" (2001a), the authors describe their methodology of sending surveys to 1,000 small animal practice veterinarians in the U.K., approximately 25% of the total number of practitioners. Of the 404 respondents who completed the survey (40.4% of the total), 195 or 48.3% reported that they had encountered from one to six cases of suspected or actual animal abuse during the course of their practice. The 448 animals affected included dogs, cats, horses, hamsters, and rabbits. Due to the extent of the injuries suffered by abused animals, 15% of the dogs and 13% of the cats died and an additional 8% of dogs and 10% of cats required euthanasia. Although the authors urge caution in generalizing the results to all veterinarians in the U.K., it is clear that nearly half of the sample of veterinarians they surveyed had come into contact with suspected or actual animal abuse.

The second paper in the series, "'Battered Pets': Non-accidental Physical Injuries Found in Dogs and Cats" (2001b), elaborates on the types and severity of injuries suffered by these animals, noting the similarities of these injuries to those displayed by children who are victims of physical abuse.

In their third article, "'Battered Pets': Sexual Abuse" (2001c), Munro and Thrusfield focus on the 6% of the 448 cases that involved abuse of a sexual nature, specifically injuries to the genitals and anorectal areas of 21 dogs and 5 cats. It should be noted that, in contrast with cases of child sexual abuse that may include acts such as fondling that may not physically harm a child, cases of sexual abuse of animals brought to the attention of veterinarians almost always involve physical injury. The seriousness of these attacks is illustrated by some of the examples Munro and Thrusfield provide:

- A border collie with vaginal injuries probably caused by the male owner penetrating the dog (as reported by his wife).
- A crossbreed dog found with a 12-inch knitting needle in her vagina.
- A collie with an elastic band tied around the base of its scrotum.
- A cat with a bloody and infected foreign object (probably a tampon) inserted in her vagina.

"'Battered Pets': Munchausen Syndrome by Proxy (Factitious illness by Proxy)" (2001d) is the topic of the fourth paper in the series. Before elaborating on the animal-involved cases described in Munro and Thrusfield's article, let me provide a brief overview of this phenomenon. In 1977, the British pediatrician Roy Meadow published an article entitled "Munchausen Syndrome by Proxy: The Hinterland of Child Abuse," in which he described two cases of mothers simulating or producing illness in their children; a six-year-old girl's mother was contaminating her daughter's urine samples with her own urine and menstrual blood and another mother's toddler died of excessive sodium the mother had her child ingest. A scene in the haunting film *The Sixth Sense* (1999) depicted a lethal case of this disorder. Often, the child's symptoms are directly correlated with the presence of the mother. For example, in the urine contamination case, Meadow found that when the child was separated from her mother, her urine tested clear; it was only when the mother had access to her child or collected the child's urine herself that tests showed contamination. Although this is a complex and relatively rare psychological disorder, Meadow suggested that the phenomenon has three common characteristics: the mother usually lies about the child's care and condition (it is estimated that over 90% of cases involve the mother as the perpetrator), it can produce serious health consequences for the child not only in cases where the mother produces actual illness but also in cases where only simulation occurs since the child may have to undergo painful and invasive diagnostic procedures, and the mother seemed to enjoy being in the hospital environment and receiving the attention of hospital staff. Donna Rosenberg, another expert in this field, described Munchausen syndrome by proxy as a "profound disorder of empathy" (p. 31) since the caregiver seems inured to the suffering experienced by her own child (1995).

Equally rare in cases involving animals, Munchausen syndrome by proxy was noted in only one earlier case report I could locate (Feldman 1997) and suspected in 2% of the 448 animal abuse cases reported to Munro and Thrusfield. In one of these cases, a dog owner called a veterinarian to his home three times in one day to determine if the animal had been poisoned. This person was later convicted of poisoning his own child. Other cases involved repeated visits (up to four times a day) to the veterinary practice with injured animals suggesting that the owner may have been thriving on the attention of the clinic staff. (In the Feldman case report, a 45-year-old woman contacted a veterinarian daily about her dog's presumed gastrointestinal problems; two other dogs had died under this woman's care. The dog eventually lost half its body weight but the woman refused overnight evaluation at the clinic. A breeder who cared for the dog while the woman was on vacation, noted absolutely no digestive problems in the dog and observed that the dog ate "ravenously." The breeder refused to give the dog back to the woman when she returned from vacation, at which point the woman admitted starving the dog to get attention from others.) Although these cases are small in number, 3 of the 9 animals died and 2 others had to be euthanized due to the extent of their injuries.

Animal and human victims of abuse may differ on many dimensions but their victimization may share certain characteristics, as so effectively illustrated in the research conducted by Munro and Thrusfield.

RECAPPING THIS INFORMATION, please keep in mind that the concerted scientific study of animal abuse is a relatively new field.

We have seen that one obstacle to progress in this area is reaching consensus on how we define animal abuse and neglect, how we determine when it is trivial and when it is worrisome, and maintaining sensitivity to cultural variations in how different animals are treated. We have also seen that the absence of state-wide or national statistics on existing cases and new cases of animal abuse prevent us from determining the extent of this problem in American society. Recall how child abuse and domestic violence seemed invisible until we were confronted with yearly statistics on the prevalence of these problems.

Finally, we noted that the overlap of child maltreatment, domestic violence, and animal abuse is now being directly studied by a number of researchers. We have discovered that, at times, children may be exposed to adults who may cruelly treat the animals in their care. And we have seen that children who abuse animals may be displaying a warning sign of their own psychological distress. Research is also emerging that illustrates animals may be subjected to the same categories of abuse that children may experience. We know that each form of violence—child maltreatment, domestic violence, and animal abuse—can occur independently but we are also starting to acknowledge that understanding one form of violence may provide insights about the other forms. Each form of violence and its relation to animal abuse will be covered in more detail in chapters 8, 9, and 10.

Defining, describing, and documenting the prevalence of a problem are usually the first steps in a scientific analysis. But once the description and documentation are completed, we are left with a critical question: why does animal abuse occur? The next chapter addresses this issue.

British artist William Hogarth's prescient depiction of the relation between animal abuse and interpersonal violence. The link to domestic violence is especially remarkable since it predates research on this topic by nearly 250 years.

SECOND STAGE OF CRUELTY.
THAVIES INN
The generous Steed in hoary Age
Subdu'd by Labour lies;
And mourns a cruel Master's rage,
While Nature Strength denies.
The tender Lamb o'er drove and faint,
Amidst expiring Throws;
Bleats forth it's innocent complaint
And dies beneath the Blows.
Inhuman Wretch! say whence proceeds
This coward Cruelty?
What Int'rest springs from barb'rous deeds?
What Joy from Misery?

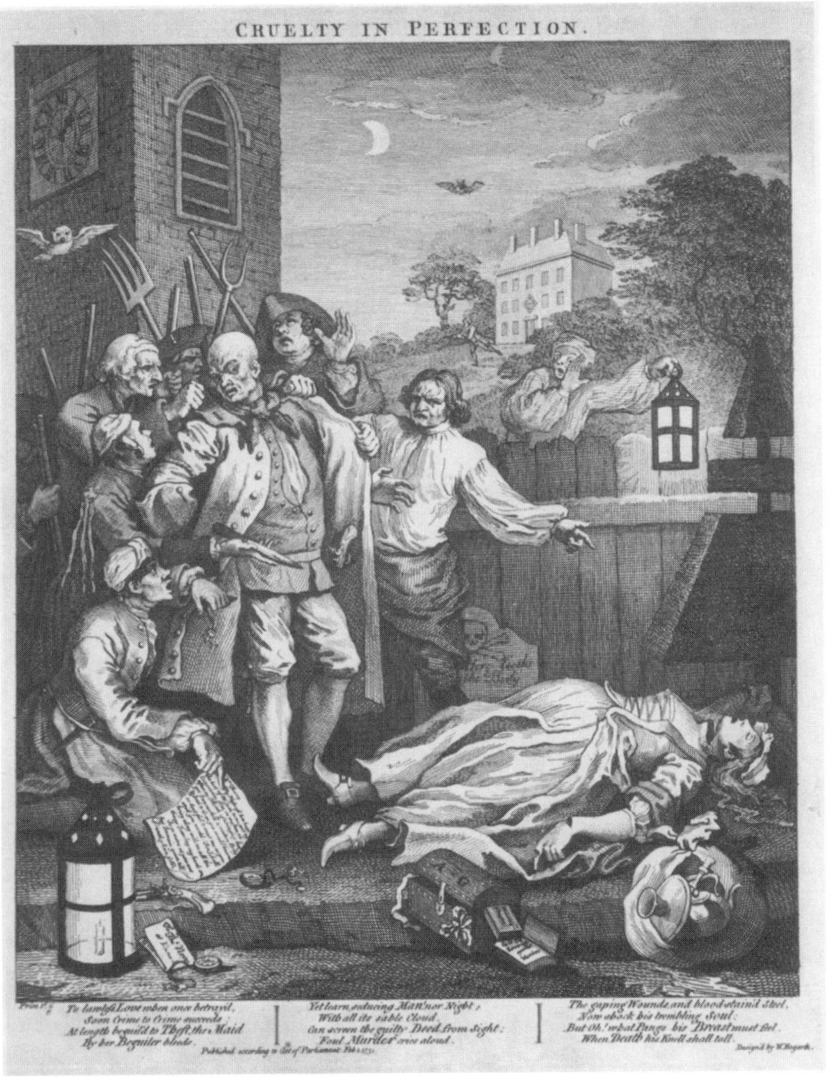

To lawless Love when once betray'd,
Soon Crime to Crime succeeds;
At length beguil'd to Theft, the Maid
By her Beguiler bleeds.

Yet learn, seducing Man! nor Night,
With all its sable Cloud,
Can screen the guilty Deed from Sight;
Foul Murder cries aloud.

The gaping Wounds and blood-stain'd Steel,
Now shock his trembling Soul:
But Oh! what Pangs his Breast must feel,
When Death his Knell shall toll.

Published according to Act of Parliament Feb 1 1751

Design'd by W. Hogarth.

THE REWARD OF CRUELTY.
Behold the Villain's dire disgrace!
Not Death itself can end.
He finds no peaceful Burial Place;
His breathless Corse, no friend.
Torn from the Root, that wicked Tongue,
Which daily swore and curst!
Those Eyeballs, from their Sockets wrung,
That glow'd with lawless Lust!
His Heart, expos'd to prying Eyes,
To Pity has no Claim:
But, dreadful! from his Bones shall rise,
His Monument of Shame.

CHAPTER 5

The critical question: Why are animals abused?

> The expression of hostile feelings may take the form of recurrent cruelty, as when a child hatches schemes to hurt another innocent person, or sets fire to ant hills, or goes out of his way to kill frogs, toads, and other creatures. The subject of cruelty in children is in need of study from a developmental point of view, for 'cruel' behavior may represent varying combinations of hostility, thoughtlessness, and exploratory interest at different developmental levels. (Jersild 1954, p. 888)

> Coco the Spaniel is sent plunging three stories. D.C. Police are searching for boys who dropped dog from roof, injuring her two front legs. (*Washington Post,* Sept. 18, 1996)

Whenever we confront human behavior that puzzles or disturbs us or is in some way out of the ordinary, one of our first reactions is to ask, "Why?" Specifically with regard to animal abuse, we want to know what factors might motivate someone to hurt animals, animals that we usually hold in high regard. One reason why understanding motivations is so critical to dealing with animal abuse and violence, generally, is that this understanding can inform the way we try to prevent and treat such behavior. In this next section, I will explore some answers to the question: Why do people abuse animals? I begin with an overview of the reasons why adults might abuse animals. Although this book is not focused on adult animal abuse, children can be exposed to it and it therefore deserves attention. Then I will explore some of the factors that might lead children and adolescents to abuse animals. This exploration will be more detailed since I will revisit these developmentally related motivations in a later chapter examining ways to prevent animal abuse and intervene in cases where it has already occurred.

> I am convinced that violent behavior, even at its most apparently senseless, incomprehensible, and psychotic, is an understandable response to an identifiable, specifiable set of conditions; and that even when it is motivated by 'rational' self-interest, it is the end product of a series of irrational, self-destructive, and unconscious motives that can be studied, identified, and understood. (Gilligan 1996, p. 102)

Adult motivations for animal abuse. In 1985, Kellert and Felthous published an article summarizing much of their work with adults who had a history of abusing animals (Kellert and Felthous 1985). One important contribution included in this paper was a listing of the motivations that may underlie animal abuse perpetrated by adults. As I describe these motivations, think about how, in some cases, motivations for animal abuse may be similar to the motivations that may be present in cases of child abuse and domestic violence.

Attempts to *control or discipline* a pet animal can be abusive. Controlling an animal's behavior or limiting its range of exploration is an important element of making our lives with pets a satisfying experience. Efforts to control can, however, be violent and abusive. Beating a dog for a toileting accident or taping shut a cat's mouth because it chewed the end of a couch are examples of an owner using abusive discipline in an effort to limit or change an animal's behavior.

Animal abuse may be a form of *retaliation* against a particular animal. In the "discipline" example I just provided above, if the dog responded to its beating by attacking its owner, the owner might "get back" at the dog by punishing it even more severely.

In some cases, animal abuse may represent *retaliation against a person* for whom the animal is significant. A person who judges they were mistreated by a neighbor, co-worker, or partner may not confront these individuals directly but, instead, abuse their beloved pets. In addition, some victims of stalking report that stalkers may threaten to harm or kill their pets (Tjaden 1997).

Just as people hold prejudices toward certain human beings, adults may abuse animals to *satisfy a prejudice toward certain species or breeds of animals.* I once encountered a young man with a deep affection for horses who was horribly cruel to cats. He could not explain his prejudice toward cats but used this prejudice to justify his abusive behavior.

Animals are abused when they are directed to become *instruments of aggression.* Training dogs to engage in dog fights or using a dog to purposely attack another person essentially converts an animal into a weapon. The animal becomes an extension of the antisocial behavior of its owner. In the 1500s, The Spanish priest Bartolomé de Las Casas, who deplored the treatment of the indigenous peoples of the New World, described how his countrymen used their dogs to track down, attack, and devour fleeing natives (1552/1992).

Enhancing personal aggressiveness may also motivate the abuse of animals. A person who tortures an animal while you watch may be sending you an obvious message about his or her capacity to be violent and destructive. Our wariness and avoidance of such an individual may be the very outcome he or she hopes to achieve. Another example of this motivation would be a person who practices shooting animals in preparation for using the weapon against a human being.

As difficult as it is to imagine, animal abuse can be used as a form of *entertainment.* A recent disturbing phenomenon is the production of what are labeled "crush" videos. Small mammals and other animals are filmed being tortured and killed under the spiked heel of an abuser. It has also been reported that adolescents may give drugs to pets as a form of amusement (Buchta 1988). Sometimes the abuse of animals is sexual and I must caution the reader that depictions of human sexual behavior with animals, or bestiality, are not uncommon in printed, video, and computerized forms of pornography.

Sadism, in which the motivation for behavior is the satisfaction derived from seeing another suffer, may also underlie animal abuse. Seeing an animal writhing in pain or hearing its cries while being abused may be the actual reinforcer for the abuse. A Utah murderer who abducted, tortured, and killed young boys (this case will be examined in chapter 6) described abusing puppies in a similar way because he enjoyed the sounds they made when he abused them!

Clearly, this list is not exhaustive, but the reader should now have some understanding of the varied motivations that might prompt someone to hurt or kill animals. Veterinarians may hurt animals and workers in slaughterhouses may kill animals, but the list of motivations provided by Kellert and Felthous describes socially unacceptable reasons for causing animals' distress, pain, or death. The reader will also note that intervening with an individual who abuses animals to control or discipline them will require a different approach than that used with a sadistic abuser. Knowing about motivations can inform the choice of an appropriate intervention.

Child and adolescent motivations for animal abuse. In this section, I will rely on research and analysis my colleagues and I have conducted on why young people may abuse animals (Ascione, Thompson, and Black 1997—see chapter 3) and material from case reports provided by colleagues in the field. Although adult and child/adolescent motivations for animal abuse may sometimes be similar (e.g., both an adult and a child may be retaliating against a particular animal, both may hold similar prejudices toward particular animals), developmentally-related motivations are worthy of attention in their own right.

Let me first describe the approach that Teresa Thompson, Tracy Black, and I took to learn more about young people's motivations for abusing animals. With a grant of funds from the Geraldine R. Dodge Foundation, I developed a set of interview questions that I named the *Children and Animals Assessment Instrument* (CAAI). It was designed in two forms: one that could be used to interview children between the ages of 5 and 18 years and another that could be used to interview a parent or guardian. Although I was familiar with the interview protocol that Alan Felthous had developed for use with adults (see below), it was immediately clear that it would *not* be acceptable for children. One of the main reasons for this is that Felthous specifically named a variety of physical and sexual abuses of animals and asked the adults he was interviewing whether they had engaged in these behaviors. I judged that it would be ethically inappropriate and potentially psychologically disturbing to use the same approach with children and adolescents. Therefore, I designed my questions to be open ended, asking children to describe incidents when they or others had been "mean" to animals or hurt them in some way. I also balanced these questions with others about the kind and humane treatment of animals. These questions about the positive treatment of animals were placed at the end of the interview so children would complete the session on a more uplifting note.

The CAAI asks young people to self-report on a variety of animal-related issues including whether they have abused animals or seen others abuse them. Since children grow up in many different contexts, they were asked these questions in reference to pet animals, stray animals that might be in their neighborhoods, wild animals that might be found in parks or wooded areas, and farm animals. A parallel set of questions asks children about incidents where animals have been treated in a kind or nurturing way. When children could describe examples of cruelty or kindness to animals, follow-up questions prompted children to indicate *why* they thought that they or the person they had described had acted in this way. This was the method we used to obtain information about motivations. The parent form of the CAAI asks similar questions but the parents or caregivers provide answers about their children's behavior, similar to the process used in the behavior checklists I discussed in chapter 3. However, unlike the checklists that ask only a single question about animal cruelty, the CAAI includes multiple opportunities for animal abuse to be reported.

After my university's human research ethics board approved the project, we were able to enlist the cooperation and informed consent of 20 parents or guardians and their children, who, on average, were ten and a half years of age. Some children were drawn from the local community but most were in day treatment or residential facilities for emotionally disturbed youth, were incarcerated adolescents, or had accompanied their mothers to shelters for women who were battered. We focused on distressed children since we knew that in the non-clinical population, cruelty to animals is a fairly uncommon behavior problem (5% or less) and expected it would be more prevalent among children who were stressed or already disturbed in some way (e.g., undergoing therapy for juvenile sex offending).

As I mentioned earlier, one of the reasons psychologists are interested in the motivations for behavior and the factors that maintain behavior is to inform prevention and intervention efforts. Let's take fire setting as an example. A great deal of research has been conducted on juvenile fire setting and will be discussed in more detail in chapter 11. Two general categories or types of juvenile fire setters have been identified: curiosity and pathological fire setters. Curiosity fire setters are usually younger, typically between 3 and 7 years of age, and their fire setting is associated with poor parental supervision, lack of education about fire danger and safety, and no fear of fire. By understanding these factors, intervention takes the form of teaching parents to more closely supervise their children and to store potentially incendiary materials out of children's reach. In addition, children can be taught about fire danger and safety rules about fire.

Pathological fire setters are a more problematic group since they are older, usually between 7 and 13 years of age, and usually have had adequate fire safety education. For these children, fire setting may be motivated by anger, a need for power and attention, or a desire to retaliate against someone. Designing effective interventions for these children demands an understanding of what motivates their fire setting and requires assistance and intervention by a trained mental health professionals.

As we explore some of the possible motivations for children and adolescents abusing animals, I think you will see parallels to the fire setter distinctions I just described. Understanding these motivations will also be important when we discuss preventing and treating animal abuse. For example, if a child were interviewed with the CAAI, we might find a number of instances where the child had abused kittens, imitating something the child may have seen neighborhood adolescents do. But we might also discover that this child adores dogs. This information about the child's affection for dogs could be used to strengthen the child's empathy toward other animals.

Let's turn now to a number of motivations that might underlie children's mistreatment of animals. This list is not meant to be exhaustive and as research on this topic continues, we may discover other significant motivations.

Children may abuse animals in the course of their *curiosity* about and *exploration* of their natural world. Infants and toddlers, especially, may occasionally behave in ways that are harmful to animals and yet their behavior is unlikely to reflect intentional cruelty. The 11-month-old who rolls onto the hind leg of a puppy or the 3-year-old who grabs a kitten's tail, dragging it to the milk saucer are, technically, abusing these pets. But their behavior is more a reflection of youthful exuberance and lack of education than a sign of malevolence. As the French developmental psychologist Gabriel Compayré wrote in 1902, "The child's conduct, then, when he maltreats animals comes from the same needs that make him tear open his cardboard horses or demolish his drums: from an eagerness to know" (p. 196).

If we reach back into our own childhood memories or have had occasion to observe very young children around pets and other animals, we recall the thoughtless harm that animals may suffer. Burning ants with a magnifying glass, crushing the luminous end of a firefly, poking a dog with a stick, scattering a group of birds with a thrown rock can almost be expected in young children. These incidents can be opportunities for adults (and even older children or siblings!) to teach children about the appropriate treatment of pet animals and animals in the wild. Although animal abuse that reflects curiosity and exploration is most likely in older infants, toddlers, and young children (similar to the case for curiosity fire setters), we need to be alert to older children's animal abuse that may also be motivated by "scientific" curiosity. For example, a middle school child may propose an animal experiment for a science fair that could harm the animals involved.

We must also remember that chronological age may not be an accurate guide to a child's or even an adult's mental maturity. In John Steinbeck's classic *Of Mice and Men* (1937), an almost parental alliance has formed between George and his developmentally delayed yet adult companion, Lenny Small. In his exuberance and excitement about touching and fondling small living creatures, Lenny, in part due to his size and strength, has sometimes "loved them to death." There is no maliciousness here, no delight in the suffering and death of the victim, only hands too powerful and undisciplined for handling vulnerable creatures. The animal abuse Lenny inflicts is not intentional and his remorse when animals die makes his plight even more pathetic.

Animal abuse may be motivated by the *peer reinforcement* young people receive for such behavior. A group of children may behave in ways very different from the way each member of the group might behave if they were alone. Children may be challenged or "dared" to act in ways that hurt animals and in some cases this may actually be part of a group ritual. A recent report described animal abuse in fraternities on some of our college campuses (Hoover 2003). There also have been cases where the torture and killing of animals is part of a gang initiation rite and the pressure to belong to the gang may overwhelm a young person's empathy for the animal being harmed.

Boredom, sadness, depression, insecurity are, by definition, unpleasant states to experience and we work hard to escape them, usually in socially acceptable ways. We have encountered young people who abuse animals to *modify their mood*. In interviews with juvenile sex offenders who were asked about why they also abused animals, some said that they had been bored and abusing an animal was exciting and "fun." These young offenders revealed that they not only physically abused animals but, on occasion, sexually abused them as well. The excitement experienced while abusing animals may be experienced as pleasurable, producing feelings akin to the effects of substance abuse.

Related to the motivation just mentioned is the abuse of animals for *sexual gratification.* As I will elaborate on in chapter 9, some children may engage in sexual activity with animals. If this involves gentle touching, the animal may not be harmed. But in some instances, violent penetration of the animals may occur and, in some instances, cause the animal to be injured or to die. The association of a child's or adolescent's sexual arousal, the violent control of the animal victim, and the animal's distress, pain, or death is a terrible recipe for a disordered sexual arousal pattern.

Children may be *enticed, coerced, or forced* to abuse animals. One case I encountered involved three young sisters befriended by a 40-year-old male neighbor (B. Fennessy, MSPCA investigator, personal communication, November 18, 1992). These children were described as lonely and needing attention. The man provided them with companionship (there was no evidence that the young girls were maltreated either physically or sexually by this man) and offered them spending money. However, to earn this money, the girls were required to torture a variety of small mammals while the man filmed their acts ($15 for mice, goldfish, and lizards). Eventually, when the man requested that the children progress from abusing insects and small mammals to larger mammals (he offered them $50 plus cosmetics to torture a rabbit), they refused to participate. We only know about this case because the man was so bold (and, perhaps, stupid) that he took his 8mm film to a processing lab to be transferred to videotape! Thankfully, the film processor alerted authorities and the perpetrator was arrested; the girls were counseled. Here is another example where parents may be unaware of the animal abuse in which their children are engaged.

I recall describing this case when I testified, a few years ago, before a legislative committee of the Washington state legislature when they were considering strengthening their animal cruelty laws. One of the legislators was so disturbed by this story that he successfully added forcing a child to abuse animals as an offense in the revised law.

Abusing animals may be a way of *emotionally abusing others.* Vernon R. Wiehe (1990) has described how siblings may psychologically abuse their brother or sister by torturing or killing the pets these children hold dear. We will also encounter this motivation when we explore issues related to domestic violence.

Abuse may also be related to *animal phobias* experienced by some children. If a child cannot escape from an animal he or she is frightened of, the child may make a preemptive attack on the animal. I will have more to say on fear of animals in the next chapter.

In contrast, *attachment to an animal* can also be the underlying reason for a child's animal abuse. If a child has been threatened with the torture of a beloved pet, that child may kill the animal rather than allowing it to suffer at the hands of someone else. I recall a documentary about U.S. prisoners of war in Vietnam that vividly illustrated this. An American soldier, imprisoned in a cage, began to care for a bird he had attracted to his "dwelling." After a few days, he realized that his captors had noticed his fondness for the bird. Rather than giving his captors the pleasure of torturing the animal, a fate he was sure would soon occur, he quickly killed the bird himself.

One well-documented phenomenon in human psychology is *identification with the aggressor.* When children are exposed to others being harmed and abused or when the children themselves are the victims, children may imitate the behavior of the person in power. We see this in cases of domestic violence when children may begin to display behavior that is similar to a batterer's behavior. "Pecking order" aggression may also appear—the child who is physically abused "takes out" his or her anger and pain on a more vulnerable victim. That victim may be a peer, a younger sibling, or an animal. Becoming a victimizer may alleviate the feelings of powerlessness and shame a child experiences when he or she is victimized.

Related to identification with the aggressor is the more general case of *imitating adult treatment of pets and other animals.* If children witness respected adults, like their parents, using severe and abusive methods of controlling, disciplining, or punishing animals, the children may assume that these are proper methods of treating animals (see chapter 6). Children may learn abusive ways of treating animals from their experiences at home but we cannot discount the role of media (e.g., films, videogames) in promoting animal abuse. Recall the furor when some young children, after seeing *Beavis and Butthead*™ episodes that portrayed animal abuse and fire setting tried to imitate that behavior (Patsuris 1993).

Another opportunity for imitating adult animal abuse is related to certain practices of the Afro-Caribbean religion known as Santeria, a religion most often practiced in the United States in Florida. Animal sacrifices are sometimes included among the rituals performed by practitioners of this faith and children are often required to be witnesses to the killing of the animals. During the hearing of the initial case in Florida, two psychologists gave opposing views on whether children would be negatively affected by seeing such sacrificial killings (Greene 1993, p. 6). Animal welfare professionals attempted to outlaw such practices but the U.S. Supreme Court eventually ruled in favor the practitioners of this religion (*Church of the Lukumi Babalu Aye, Inc., et al. v. City of Hialeah* 1993) and animal sacrifices continue to be permitted. Readers with certain religious backgrounds might recall pretending to play the role of priest, minister, or nun during their childhood. I fear what children reared within the Santeria faith might reenact in *their* play.

In certain forms of psychological disturbance, children and adolescents may harm their own bodies. Severe rubbing or cutting of skin, hair pulling, and eating disorders are just a few examples. We have encountered one case where an *animal was used as an implement of self-injury.* The young child involved had a long history of physical and sexual abuse inflicted by a number of different adult perpetrators. This child's mother described occasions when the child would restrain and agitate the family's cat until the animal would severely scratch the child's arms and hands. Rather than being distressed, the child displayed facial expressions of pleasure during these encounters. Self-injury is not uncommon in abused children (Murray 1993), but this animal-involved self-injury may be a rare phenomenon.

Since I have just described a case of severe child abuse, let me focus on another developmental phenomenon found in certain cases—*posttraumatic play.* There is research with children who have been traumatized suggesting that one way some of these children attempt to master and control their trauma is to re-enact elements of their experiences. A young child who has been severely beaten may repeatedly take a stuffed animal and re-enact the abuse. Lenore Terr, in *Too Scared to Cry* (1990, p. 242), illustrated this phenomenon by referring to a film entitled *Forbidden Games* (Clément 1952) based on the novel *The Secret Game* (Boyer 1950). During the Second World War, a preschool-aged girl witnessed her parents killed as the family tried to escape their village during an airplane attack. The surviving adults bury her parents and the group continues their escape. She is adopted by villagers from nearby and at this point her posttraumatic play begins. Finding small dead animals, she buries them, continuing this ritual until she cannot find animals that are already dead. At this point, she begins to kill animals and place them in her "cemetery." As Terr describes it, "she has turned her game to reenacting the killing of her parents as well as their burial" (p. 242).

Recently, in my own community, I encountered a case where an animal was threatened *for monetary gain.* A 15-year-old was apprehended after making a threatening call to a cat owner, stating, "We have your cat. . . . If you don't give us money, we'll kill her." Fortunately, the cat was found, apparently tortured but alive (Oliver 1998).

Finally, for some children (we hope, a small minority) animal abuse may be a form of *rehearsal for interpersonal violence.* We all recall Jeffrey Dahmer, whose fascination and experimentation with dead animals was a macabre omen of acts he would later perform on his human victims. Recall also the case of Luke Woodham, the Pearl, Mississippi adolescent accused of killing his mother and two of his high school classmates in 1997. Luke had tortured and fatally abused his own dog, Sparkle, describing the incident in his diary as "my first kill." Just weeks after the Woodham rampage, a Japanese 15-year-old was convicted and sentenced for the beheading of a younger child (see *Salt Lake Tribune,* October 18, 1997; *Newsweek,* September 22, 1997). Prior to this, he had dismembered live frogs and cats.

AS YOU CAN NOW SEE, the answer to the question, "why do people abuse animals?" is complex and may vary from individual to individual. As we explore the overlap among child abuse and neglect, domestic violence, and animal maltreatment, we may discover that these forms of violence may sometime share common motivations. When we know the answer to the question "why?" we will be in a better position to design effective prevention and intervention programs. Many of the child and adult motivations involve terrible insensitivity to the suffering of animals. As you have read parts of this book, you no doubt have been distressed by descriptions of the pain and suffering endured by animal victims of abuse and have empathized with their plight. The potential role of empathy and disturbances in empathic development in cases of animal abuse is the next topic to which I turn.

CHAPTER 6

Children, animals, and empathy: Sharing emotions—antidote for aggression and violence?

> **A**s a boy, I naturally assumed animals experienced the same sorts of thoughts and feelings I did. When a kid down the street chucked a box turtle into the air just to watch the turtle's shell split open, I imagined that the turtle probably had a friend turtle somewhere nearby, mourning the death and hating the kid. I was projecting I know, but that is the essence of empathy in children, and it is not all that different for adults. (Myers 1995, p. 558)

". . . in the moment that the horse turned from the stream and nudged Jonas's shoulder affectionately with its head, he perceived the bonds between animal and human." In this scene from Lois Lowry's Newbery Medal–winning novel, *The Giver* (1993, p. 122), Jonas lives in a fictional utopian world where benign control and regimentation are the rule. It's a safe world where all the significant fears and joys that humans might experience have been eliminated. Even an adolescent's search for identity and a future role in the society has been made unnecessary since the community chooses for the adolescent.

Real animals are not permitted in this world, only stuffed ones, called "comfort objects." These, children must relinquish on their eighth birthday so the playthings can be recycled for use by younger children. Jonas has had his twelfth birthday and, in his society, is about to become an adult. Comfort objects have been absent from Jonas' life for a number of years. As he turns twelve, Jonas' future identity and role are conferred on him, selected for him. And as the story unfolds, we discover that his future place in this society is a critical and awesome one because he alone will be the keeper of his world's memories, both the painful and the glorious. He alone will preserve these memories, sparing his fellow humans the "complications" that memories of the past can present. He will be "the receiver" of these memories and one day, he will become "the giver," passing the remembrances to the next child selected for this all-important role.

Among these memories is the abuse and misuse of real animals by adults. Jonas is wounded and pained by these memories because of his human capacity for empathy—the ability to imagine and feel a part of the emotions being experienced by another, human or animal. Lowry's story suggests that real animals have no place in this controlled and antiseptic world. Animals connote spontaneity, change, deep affection, fear, and the potential for the anguish that accompanies loss and death. There is no place for these characteristics in Jonas' world and Lowry effectively uses this depiction to show us how emotionally impoverished we would be in a world devoid of animal life.

It is not hard to imagine that Jonas contemplated the commonalities he shared with the animals of his newly discovered memories. As so beautifully described by my Italian colleague, Dr. Camilla Pagani, greater concern for animal welfare "is fundamentally related to the perception of a common fate that humans and animals share. . . . The perception of a common fate is considered an integral part of identification with others, either humans or animals, of empathy with them, and of an attitude of respect toward nature in general" (2000, p. 66).

Identification, empathy, respect—Dr. Pagani considers these characteristics to be essential in the prevention and amelioration of violence. And she is in good company since, over the past 30 years, developmental psychology and related disciplines have focused on the importance of our sense of belonging to family and community, our increasingly refined ability to connect with the emotional life of others, and respect for, or at least toleration of, others even others who are very different from us.

> The human animal is never truly self-sufficient. Babies are the personification of need. Children are needy. And the need to give, to love is the transfusion that mutates the feral savagery into which we are all born. Empathy. To feel the pain of another as our own. Hardest to learn, the most valuable of all we are allowed to feel. (A. H. Vachss 1993, p. 13)

In this chapter, I will focus on empathy, what we know about its developmental origins and course, and the complex ways that empathy toward people and empathy toward animals may be related. Empathy is believed to be a critical component of prosocial behavior, a term that connotes kindness, helping, cooperation, nurturance, and unselfishness in our relations with others. In essence, it means *car-*

ing about and *caring for* others. And it is very likely that these qualities develop in human children when these children themselves experience being cared about and cared for by family, community, and society. Empathy is a component of "emotional intelligence," a capability that some believe may be as important if not more so than our cognitive intellectual prowess (Goleman 1995). And, although beyond the scope of this book, research has demonstrated the roles our brains and physiology play in our capacity to display both types of "intelligence" (Eisenberg and Fabes 1998; Goleman 1995, pp. 13–29, 102–104).

> . . . compassion and the language to express it is the regulator of impulsive anger and the opposite of human violence. (ten Bensel 1987, 138–139)

> I don't think it's possible to be a detective and always remain kind. But if you ever find that cruelty is becoming pleasurable in itself, then it's probably time to stop being a detective. —Chief Inspector Adam Dalgliesh (James 1982, p. 252)

Dr. Nancy Eisenberg, a developmental psychologist at Arizona State University, is a world-renowned scholar in the areas of prosocial development and the development of empathy. A summary of developmental research on these topics appeared in her very readable book, *The Caring Child*, published in 1992. In the following overview, I rely on this book by Eisenberg and a more recent review she completed with Richard Fabes (1998) to discuss empathy, prosocial behavior, and moral development in the context of children's relations with animals.

But before I begin, a word of caution—empathy and related topics are complex phenomena even at the level of basic definitions. For example, my dictionary defines empathy as "the intellectual identification with or vicarious experiencing of the feelings, thoughts, or attitudes of another" (Flexner 1987, p. 638). The definition highlights a number of distinctions developmental psychologists have tried to make about this concept. Let me use a hypothetical example to illustrate these distinctions.

If a child sees and hears a puppy yelping, with its hind leg caught at the bottom of a chain link fence, what thoughts and emotions and plans for action go through this child's mind? On one level, we need to ask, is this child capable of *perceiving* this puppy's predicament? Visually, the child needs to identify that the animal is trapped by the fence and, through hearing, identify the yelping as a sign of distress, discomfort, and, very likely, fear. Does the child compare the puppy's dilemma to situations the child might have experienced in the past—a toe caught in a door jam, a finger in a car door, a foot in a hole on a soccer field? Here we're referring to the cognitive ability to compare the puppy's circumstances to one with which the child is familiar. This role taking ability assumes the child can place herself in the puppy's experience and differentiate this living creature's situation as different from that of an inanimate object "caught" in some way (e.g., the branch of a shrub tangled in a car bumper). The child must use and integrate her perceptual abilities and intellectual capabilities to come to this understanding. These skills are important, yet, as Robert Coles observes in *The Moral Intelligence of Children,* "The intellect can grow and grow . . . in a person who is smug, ungenerous, even cruel" (1997, p. 179). But does the child also "feel" what the puppy is presumed to be feeling? Does the child experience pain? Fear? Anger? Worry? Embarrassment? Desperation? This is another level to the concept of empathy that assumes we can not only understand but, in some cases, "feel with" the emotional experiences of another, human or animal.

Human and nonhuman animal emotions

> Like the owl and the pussycat in their pea-green boat, birds, cats, people, and animals all play out the contradictions we feel in their human-like animality and our animal-like humanity. (Shepard 1996, p. 72)

Before I return to examining the example of this child and puppy, allow me a brief aside to consider emotions in nonhuman animals. I do not wish nor am I competent to enter into a philosophical, comparative psychological, and scientific analysis of emotions in animals and their degree of comparability to human emotions. Attributing human emotions to non-human animals (a form of anthropomorphism) is an age old phenomenon, one, perhaps first given the greatest scientific credibility by Charles Darwin in *The Expression of Emotions in Man and Animals* (1872). Since Darwin's focus was on nonhuman animals, he relied on nonverbal cues as signs of animals' emotional experiences, a reliance we display when considering how an infant, who has not yet acquired speech, feels. Humans are aficionados of nonverbal and symbolic emotional expression through the visual arts, music, drama, and religion. Being able to talk about, describe, depict, evoke, and write about emotions may be uniquely human capabilities but the *experience* of emotions most likely exists in many species other than our own and empathy may cross species lines. As Eisenberg notes, "there is no reason as yet . . . to believe that humans' sympathy with animals differs greatly in quality or functional outcomes from their sympathy for humans" (1998, p. 15).

The direction of such sympathy may also be from nonhuman animals towards humans. You may recall the August 16, 1996, case of a 3-year-old boy who fell into a gorilla enclosure at Chicago's Brookfield Zoo (Graft 1996; Sawyer 1996). After hitting his head on the concrete and losing consciousness, the toddler was approached by Binti Jua, a female gorilla with an 18-month-old baby of her own. Binti picked up the toddler, cradled him in her arms, and then laid him near a gate where Binti was accustomed to finding humans. Binti followed a zoo keeper's instruction to move to another gate and the toddler was retrieved by paramedics. The toddler recovered from his serious injuries and Binti made the national and international news. As noted by Frans de Waal, what was remarkable was not Binti's attempt to assist another primate who was injured and in distress—according to de Waal, those who study gorillas know this is a common phenomenon (2001, pp. 79–80). It was Binti's willingness to come to the aid of a *human* primate that captured the attention of people around the world.

For those of you who would like to explore the issue of emotions in nonhuman animals, I recommend the following sources which I have found entertainingly written and grounded in scientific research. The first is Jeffrey Moussaieff Masson and Susan McCarthy's *When Elephants Weep: The Emotional Lives of Animals* (1995). The second is Carl Sagan and Ann Druyan's *Shadows of Forgotten Ancestors* (1992), especially chapter 6, "Us and Them"; chapter 9, "What Thin Partitions . . . "; chapter 15, "Mortifying Reflections"; chapter 19, "What Is Human?"; and chapter 20, "The Animal Within." The last two recommendations are books that focus primarily on nonhuman primates and both were authored by Frans de Waal (*Good Natured: The Origins of Right and Wrong in Humans and Other Animals* [1996] and *The Ape and the Sushi Master* [2001]). To close this (too long!) aside, I quote Sagan and Druyan (1992):

> The limbic system in the human brain, known to be responsible for much of the richness of our emotional life, is prominent throughout the mammals. The same drugs that alleviate suffering in human mitigate the cries and other signs of pain in many other animals. It is unseemly of us, who often behave so unfeelingly toward other animals, to contend that only humans suffer. (pp. 371–372)

Let's return to the child and puppy. We are going to assume that the child is competent to perceive the puppy's entrapment and that the puppy's distress signals are disturbing to the child, perhaps reminding her of times when she has been in pain. The child also needs to recognize the puppy's helplessness (it's unlikely that the puppy can free himself, even with continued struggling) and make a decision about whether to help and, if so, how. Even though, in this case, the child was not responsible for the puppy's dilemma, Eisenberg would suggest that the child's cognitive perspective taking and her emotional empathy will combine to make sympathy for the puppy more likely. Eisenberg defines sympathy as "other-oriented concern or compassion," qualities we often display toward members of our own species but qualities that can occur *between* different species. This sequence of changes in the experience of this child may make it more likely that she will try to assist the puppy to alleviate the puppy's suffering.

The child's physical competencies may also come into play now. If the child is a preschooler, she may judge the fencing too difficult to manipulate herself and might seek out an older sibling or adult to help the animal. An older child might be capable of and willing to intervene on her own but might also be wary of the puppy's behavior being unpredictable, and potentially dangerous, since the puppy is in such distress. The child's familiarity and history with this particular puppy would affect her decision (for example, if it's the child's own puppy as distinct from a puppy belonging to a neighbor who trains dogs for fights).

Eisenberg also notes that sometimes children may be overwhelmed by the intense, painful emotions they imagine another is experiencing. Children's own *personal distress* may result in their focusing on their own emotional turmoil and turning away from the object of their empathy to reduce their own distress. Prosocial behavior will be less likely to occur under such circumstances. Experiences in children's own history of development may influence whether sympathy or personal distress predominates when they are confronted with the suffering of another, human or animal.

Let me complete the example of this hypothetical child and puppy. She runs to the fence, beginning to cry herself because the puppy is one of her own. The girl is able to lift the fencing enough to free the puppy's leg. The puppy is still whimpering but it becomes clear that the injuries are only minor scratches. The girl cradles the puppy in her arms, caresses him, and the puppy begins to lick her face. The girl's father who witnessed the end of this rescue when he happened by the kitchen window, runs out to see if all is well. He's relieved that the injuries are minor and then, smiling and gently holding his daughter's arm, compliments her on her watchfulness, responsiveness, caring, and helpfulness, and tells her how secure the puppy must feel having such a devoted caretaker. The girl smiles meekly, with tears still wetting her cheeks. Perhaps we can see pride in her face too.

The complexities of human empathy. Before we begin to explore the development of empathy and its relation to child-animal interactions, I would like to describe an example of human empathy in adults that illustrates its richness and complexity and its relation to animal abuse. In 1917, Susan Glaspell published a short story entitled "A Jury of Her Peers" (1996). As the story opens in rural Nebraska, a woman, Martha Hale, joins her husband, the local sheriff and his wife, Mrs. Peters, and the county attorney on a car ride to the scene of a crime at a neighboring farm—Mr. Wright had been strangled with a rope as he lay in bed. His wife had been arrested and held in the local jail; the women had been asked to come to retrieve some of Mrs. Wright's clothing and personal items. The sheriff also asked the two women to be alert to anything they saw in the downstairs kitchen that might indicate why Mrs. Wright apparently killed her husband. But just after he asks them this, the sheriff remarks, " But would the women know a clue if they did come upon it?" The men go upstairs to see if they can discern a motive for the crime, a reason why Mrs. Wright apparently murdered her husband, leaving the women to their task and allowing them to explore Mrs. Wright's kitchen.

The women discover a quilt Mrs. Wright had been sewing, beautiful save for the last block whose stitching was erratic and disorganized. And then, the sheriff's wife discovers an empty bird cage, the hinge of its door roughly broken. The women wonder whether Mrs. Wright had bought a canary from the itinerant salesman who had visited their town and, if so, what happened to the bird. They had recalled how Mrs. Wright enjoyed singing in her youth and how a songbird might have brought joy to a childless woman living on an isolated farm. The women knew the Wrights kept no other pets, not even a farm cat that might account for the bird's absence.

Deciding Mrs. Wright might like to continue quilting in jail, the women search for additional blocks of cloth in her sewing basket. When they open a box in the basket, a smell takes them both aback. Wrapped in a silk cloth in the box is the body of the pet bird, its neck wrung and twisted to one side; ". . . the eyes of the two women met—this time clung together in a look of dawning comprehension, of growing horror" (p. 89). When the men return from their upstairs investigation, the sheriff inquires about the birdcage and missing bird. The women suggest that a cat, who must have departed a house shrouded in death, probably killed it. Satisfied with this explanation, the men resume their investigation.

It becomes clear that the women presume Mr. Wright was responsible for the violent killing of the bird and that Mrs. Wright is, no doubt, responsible for her husband's death. That the women understand and connect emotionally with Mrs. Wright's actions is revealed in the following passage:

> "She liked the bird," said Martha Hale, low and slowly. "She was going to bury it in that pretty box."
>
> "When I was a girl," said Mrs. Peters, under her breath, "my kitten—there was a boy took a hatchet, and before my eyes—before I could get there—" She covered her face an instant. "If they hadn't held me back I would have"—she caught herself, looked upstairs to where footsteps were heard, and finished weakly—"hurt him." (p. 90)

The women continue their dialogue reflecting on Mrs. Wright's loneliness in living out a difficult marriage with no children, the joy the bird must have brought her, her anguish when the bird was so cruelly silenced. Yes, the women could understand. But they decide, perhaps rightly so, that the men would not. The women hide the box and its contents from the men as the story ends and the reader realizes that Mrs. Wright's motivation, unless she herself reveals it, will remain a secret the two women will preserve.

As you read this synopsis (which does not do justice to the richness of the story or the sensitivity and skill of the story's author), with whom did you identify? Whose perspective did you take—the sheriff and his men investigating the upstairs crime scene? The human victim? Mrs. Wright? The two women reflecting on Mrs. Wright's life? The dead songbird? The story, perhaps, causes us to reflect intellectually on each of these perspectives, to some degree. But what stirred your strongest emotional response? With whom did you empathize most strongly? I believe that

Susan Glaspell has effectively captured the richness of the concepts of role taking, empathy, and sympathy in this heartrending tale.

Mrs. Hale and Mrs. Peters understand, on a cognitive level, what life might have been like for Mrs. Wright. After all, they, too, live on farmland and have experienced their own share of difficulties and challenges and disappointments. They know they are not too different, as human beings, from Mrs. Wright. They understand the inevitable loneliness of a farm wife, especially one without children and unconnected to her neighbors. They understand the impact of the loss of a loved one, Mrs. Peters even comparing the death of the bird to one of her own children's death. And they understand how such a loss when deliberately and cruelly caused could lead one to violence. But we also see in these women a vicarious experiencing of Mrs. Wright's emotional life, their ability to empathize with her and understand her act even though neither woman probably condoned it.

The origins of empathy and prosocial behavior. What makes a caring child? How do we account for the behavior of the girl in the fictional puppy rescue I described earlier? What if the scenario I described had been different? What if the girl had either ignored the cries of the puppy or, worse, had gone over to the fence and purposely pushed the sharp ends of the fencing into the puppy's leg, seeming to delight in the increased intensity of the puppy's cries? What factors might contribute to such childhood cruelty? Our attempts at understanding and explanation must account for the behavior of both of these hypothetical children. We have already examined some of the factors that may underlie animal abuse perpetrated by children and adolescence. How might we account for youthful benevolence toward animals?

Sigmund Freud noted that children identify strongly with animals and this may be valuable if animals are treated kindly in a child's world but terrorizing if animals are abused. "The child does not yet show any trace of the pride which afterwards moves the adult civilized man to set a sharp dividing line between his own nature and that of all other animals. The child unhesitatingly attributes full equality to animals; he probably feels himself more closely related to the animal than to the undoubtedly mysterious adult, in the freedom with which he acknowledges his needs" (1938, p. 905).

Eisenberg (1992) and Eisenberg and Fabes (1998) provide excellent frameworks for addressing and suggesting some answers to this question. First, they suggest that it's likely that our biology, genetics, neurophysiology, and culture must make some contribution to shaping our responses to the distress of other human beings and, very likely, to animals as well (Eisenberg 1988). After all, babies seem to find the cries of other infants distressing and significant cognitive disabilities (e.g., profound mental retardation) and mental illnesses with a strong biological substrate, like depression, may interfere with our responsiveness to the emotional needs of others. But Eisenberg believes that we should focus on the contexts of children's lives for clues to the development of a caring child (Azar 1997). In the following elaboration, I will take the liberty of applying Eisenberg's analysis to examples that involve children's relations with animals as distinct from their relations with other human beings.

Eisenberg describes three broad contexts within which we can examine the development of empathy and prosocial behavior. One of these is the child's own intellectual competencies. Cognitive abilities will be related to children's ability to perceive the needs of differing species and types of animals. A family puppy and a wild squirrel cannot be treated identically. The signs of wariness in a dog are quite different from those of a cat. Thus, children's knowledge about animals, their needs, and appropriate ways of interacting with and caring for them is likely to increase with age, experience, instruction, and exploration.

A second context has been referred to as socioemotional or sociocognitive development. Perhaps this context comes closest to the idea of "emotional intelligence" so effectively elaborated and popularized by Daniel Goleman (1995). This context relates to the development of emotions and their expression, understanding the perspective and emotional experiences of others, learning how to interact socially in constructive, collaborative ways with others, understanding a variety of strategies for solving conflicts with others in nonviolent ways, making moral choices that are respectful of the needs and rights of others as well as respectful and ennobling of the self, and learning to care for the welfare of others.

A third context is comprised of the myriad influences on the socialization of young people. These influences include the family (parents, siblings, extended family members), peers, schools, faith communities, and broader societal and cultural influences. It is in interaction with others that children learn appropriate ways of behavior, when and how to express their emotions, and to construct an evaluation of themselves as valued and esteemed members of society. The mechanisms by which these influences exert their effects include direct teaching, teaching by example, and factors that help young people identify with and seek belonging to social groups. One of the goals of socialization is the child's internalization of patterns of desirable behavior and adoption of positive and productive social values like responsibility, honesty, and unselfishness. When internalization is successful, children may behave in keeping with socially appropriate norms even when socialization agents are not present to prompt and reinforce such compliance or punish infractions.

These three contexts of development correspond to the ecological model proposed by U. Bronfenbrenner and P. A. Morris (1998). In an earlier paper (Ascione 1999), I described how this model "examines individual human development within nested contexts that extend from face-to-face family relationships (with parents, siblings, pets) and relations with peers and adults in school settings, neighborhoods, and churches to institutions such as social welfare, mass media, law enforcement, animal welfare, and human and veterinary health care. The model also includes the societal and cultural elements of beliefs and practices in which human development is embedded" (p. 51). And, of course, we must include at the most basic level the physical and behavioral characteristics of the individual child. Let's begin our exploration of the origins of empathy at this very basic level.

Infant empathy—learning to care by being cared for

Infants learn a great deal about the world through their senses especially vision, hearing, smell, and touch. These senses are present at birth (and, to some degree, prenatally) but their proper development depends on a stimulating environment. And that stimulation comes from the social world as well as the physical environment. We now know how important the infant's early caregiving environment is in promoting physical and psychological health. This has become most evident when we examine cases of infants reared in exceptionally impoverished physical and social environments. Recall the experiments of Harry Harlow with rhesus monkeys reared in isolation as well as cases of human infants in poorly staffed orphanages or reared by neglectful and/or abusive caregivers. The first year of a baby's life is the crucial time for the development of a healthy attachment to the baby's caregiver(s). There are, of course, the baby's essential needs for food, safety, and shelter that must be met. But we also know how important it is for caregivers to be sensitive to their baby's shifting psychological needs for touch and soothing, smiles and playful stimulation, relief from fear and distress, and a sense that the caregiver can be depended on, counted on to be there when needed. When a caregiver successfully provides for an infant's needs, expresses emotions appropriately, and is attuned to the infant's emotional states, the caregiver is also providing the infant with a model of what human relationships are like. And it may well be that the origins of empathy are present in the infant's earliest experiences of being cared for by others. When infants feel safe and secure in their relationships with their caregivers, this will positively affect their ability and willingness to explore their wider physical and social environments. Eisenberg notes that signs of empathy and attempts to console or help someone in distress emerge by 18 months, a time when infants begin to give clear indications of recognizing themselves as psychologically separate from other humans around them. When caregiving is chaotic, inconsistent, absent, or abusive, the infant's exploration may be inhibited by fear, anger, uncertainty, emotional distress, and apathy.

The importance of the attachment process becomes most evident when we examine cases where the process has been disrupted or distorted. The *DSM-IV* (1994) defines Reactive Attachment Disorder as "markedly disturbed and developmentally inappropriate social relatedness in most contexts that begins before age 5 years and is associated with grossly pathological care . . . that may take the form of persistent disregard of the child's basic emotional need for comfort, stimulation, and affection" (p. 116). Although disagreement exists on the critical symptoms of this particular disorder and how it may be distinguished from other childhood dysfunctions, such as Conduct Disorder (Hanson and Spratt 2000), cruelty to animals is often listed among the signs. There are some who suggest that cruelty to animals may be one of the core symptoms of this disorder (Magid and McKelvey 1987; Parker 1997; Randolf 1999). In the words of Magid and McKelvey:

> In most families with unattached children family pets are the target of cruelty. There is a common saying among therapists working with such children: The family pet is an endangered species in the home of an unattached child. Pets will die with no explanation. One mother said her son would run after neighborhood dogs and cats, teasing, kicking and hurting them. (1987, p. 83)

Children with severe disorders of attachment that include violent behavior may have been removed from the care of abusive parents and placed in foster care. This raises the important issue of informing foster parents of the potential for aggression in some of their young charges, including aggression toward the foster family's children and pets.

In a disturbing 1990 HBO documentary (*Child of Rage*), viewers were introduced to a 6-year-old girl named Beth who had been the victim of severe neglect and both physical and sexual abuse dating from her infancy. Placed in foster care with her younger brother, Beth admitted to abusing the foster parents' dog, describing how she would stick pins into the animal to make it cry, abused her brother's genitals, and made an attempt on her brother's life. Beth talked about how she wanted to kill her brother and her foster parents while they slept. Thankfully, this child was placed in a residential treatment program. Her case, however, illustrates how critical it is to warn foster parents of the need for careful supervision of such children, especially if animals and other children reside in the same home. Children like Beth should not have unsupervised access to family pets or vulnerable younger children.

In my own state, a lawsuit was brought on behalf of children in foster care (S. Davis, personal communication, April 15, 1993). The lawsuit raised concerns about the treatment of some children while in foster care but also addressed cases where foster parents were not given critical information about the level of psychological disturbance present in children they care for. One example involving animal abuse can be found in the class-action suit that was filed: "Now seven years old, he . . . has killed several farm animals at his foster home." In other cases, foster children or the biological children of the foster parents were abused or molested. Clearly, these are not rare problems.

In anticipation of my later discussion of animal abuse and domestic violence, I should also note that Hanson and Spratt refer to a study by Charles Zeanah and his colleagues in which attachment was examined for low-income mothers and their 15-month-old infants. All the mothers had a history of partner violence. Disorganized attachment was more common for the infants of women with severe violence experiences (Zeanah et al. 1999). The authors speculate that since families experiencing domestic violence also have a higher risk for child maltreatment, some of the children rated as disorganized in their attachment may have been child abuse victims. Furthermore, growing up in such families exposes the child to both frightening "caregiving" and a frightened caregiver. We know that young children, even younger than the 15-month-olds in this study, will look to others for cues about how to respond in ambiguous situations, a process called social referencing that is implicated in the development of some fears (i.e., "catching" the fear from an adult or peer). Children this young may not be able to cope adaptively to the violence between their adult caregivers.

A vivid example of such a terrorizing environment was reported in a recent report of a fatal child abuse case (Boglioli, Taff, Turkel, Taylor, and Peterson 2000). A 19-year-old father is awakened by his girlfriend's and his one-week-old infant. During a diaper change, the infant urinated on the father who, in a rage, shook the infant and smashed his head on the floor, killing him. The father then attempted to completely dismember the infant and fed parts of the body to the family's German Shepard. This couple also had an 11-month-old child and we can only imagine whether or how much of this grisly scene she witnessed and her reactions to and interpretation of the dog's behavior and the behavior of her "caregiver."

Preschool prosocial behavior

The period from infancy through the preschool years is a time of remarkable change in physical and cognitive abilities including the development of language. The growing independence of the child in moving from place to place is both a joy and challenge for the caregiver. Two-year-olds may try to help in caregiving for a younger sibling and their prosocial efforts to assist another person in distress become less self-centered and more attuned to the victim's needs. An 18-month-old may egocentrically try to give his own security blanket or favorite stuffed animal to console a distressed peer; a wiser 2½-year-old may try to get the peer's mother to come or find the distressed peer's favorite toy.

Dangerous places in the home that were inaccessible to an infant who cannot crawl, for example, electrical outlets and stairwells, become points of fascination for the toddler and prompt the caregiver to take new measures to ensure the child's safety. Although disciplinary encounters between infant and caregiver may occur in infancy—teaching a 4-month-old that hair pulling and scratching cause the victim distress and cannot be tolerated—these encounters increase in frequency as the caregiver sets appropriate limits on the child's behavior toward and exploration of the physical and social world. How this limit setting is implemented may affect the development of prosocial behavior. Eisenberg and others suggest that discipline that is based on pointing out the negative effects of the child's behavior on others is likely to instill a healthy sense of guilt that may reduce the likelihood of future misbehavior. The displeasure of a valued caregiver coupled with the caregiver's explanation of why the child's actions are unacceptable are believed to help the child eventually internalize control of his or her own behavior. Discipline that is physically abusive may, instead, create fear and anger, generating more personal distress instead of guilt about harming another.

When children observe how pets are treated in a home, they are vicariously learning about the treatment of other vulnerable members of the family and the strategies their caregivers use to redirect, shape, and modify behavior that may have a negative effect on other members of the family. These strategies may be adopted by the children themselves. Robert Coles provides an excellent example: "to protect a puppy being teased by a child by paddling that child hard and long so that he or she is scared badly may secure a temporary reprieve for the animal, but at a high cost" (1997, p. 81). He then describes a case, related to him, of a boy who'd hurt the family dog during rough play and was severely beaten for this by his father. The boy no longer hurt the dog but he also avoided the animal and became frightened of the dog. Coles continues:

> I am asked what I'd have done, how I'd handle a child who is making life unpleasant for a family pet—that is, a child who needs to learn self-control and compassion and empathy. . . . [I] told them of the ways my wife and I handled such times with our own children; told how we'd taken notice of the situation . . . and intervened to protect the animal, our dog Grady, and how we'd taken the child aside, in order to say a firm no but also to give a brief, explanatory speech: this dog is part of our family, is quite friendly to us, and deserves a similar attitude from us. . . . When such episodes were over I also recalled realizing that our dog in his own way was a teacher, one who had helped all of us come to terms with the meaning of *understanding*, to put oneself in another's shoes, to see and feel things as he, she, or it does. We need to keep doing so, again and again over this life. (1997, pp. 83–84)

Young children need guidance in interpreting the body language and sounds by which family pets and other animals signal their emotional states. Parents must teach toddlers about not interfering with or disturbing a dog who is eating, that a drowsy cat probably doesn't want to chase a toy, and that growls can indicate an angry or frightened animal. This kind of instruction can heighten children's awareness of and attentiveness to the emotional experience of animals and facilitate more positive and benevolent interactions between children and their pets. They will learn when their behavior creates delight and playfulness in their pets and when their behavior may cause animals distress or pain.

This kind of sensitivity to animals' emotional characteristics and needs presupposes that children understand that animals are living creatures. Dr. Susan Carey reviews research indicating that such understanding changes dramatically during the age period from 4 years to 7 years (1987, pp. 72–110). Although even infants younger than 6 months of age are able to categories animals into groups (e.g., dogs vs. cats) and distinguish them from inanimate objects, this ability is probably based on the observable perceptual features of the animals and objects (Cole and Cole 2001, pp. 198–203). What about children's understanding of the "aliveness" of animals, that they eat, sleep, grow, die, and experience pain? By showing children pictures of various animals, Carey found that "4- and 5-year-olds do not know that all animals eat and breathe" (p. 78). For some of the animals tested, only 67% or fewer of the 4- and 5-year-old children assessed thought these animals could "get hurt." The performance of the 7-year-olds, however, approached the accuracy of adults who were tested. Thus, basic lessons about the "aliveness" of animals may be a prerequisite before we can expect children to empathize with other living creatures.

Carolyn Zahn-Waxler, Barbara Hollenbeck, and Marion Radke-Yarrow, pioneers in research on the development of empathy and prosocial behavior, also provide examples of "teachable moments" some handled well, some poorly, by parents with their young children (1984). I will discuss their work in some detail since it one of the first and most detailed observational analysis of young children's empathy toward animals in the context of their own homes.

In one project, they trained mothers of 1- to 2½-year-olds to observe and keep records of their children's reactions to naturally occurring distress in the home, distress experienced by either humans or animals. Over the course of months, the researchers noted that "Several hundreds of these incidents involved reports of children's feelings and behaviors toward animals" (p. 29). Here are some examples from their records:

> "Child pulls the dog's foot hard and the dog yelps. Mother says, 'Oh, don't pull Suzy's foot like that.' Child looks serious, touches foot and says 'hurt.' Mother becomes very excited because this is the first time child has used a word that expresses a feeling. She says, 'Yes, it did hurt, but it doesn't anymore.' Child then pats dog's paw very lovingly and gently, and hugs the dog."

> "The dog comes in making little crying sounds. The child turns around and says very sympathetically, 'What's the matter, Lady? What's the matter?'"

> "Child pulls dog's ears and dog gives a high little squeak. Mother notes that the child doesn't seem to realize that those are squeaks of pain. So she has to tell him, 'No, don't hurt the doggie, be gentle.' Then he puts his arms around the dog's neck, puts his cheek on the dog's head and is sweet and gentle. (On another occasion like this, the mother explains but also slaps the child thus giving a mixed message.)" (p. 30)

Zahn-Waxler, Hollenbeck, and Radke-Yarrow also provide examples where parents do not handle these disciplinary encounters and opportunities to teach empathy and caring in a positive or benevolent manner:

> "Father is 'real harsh' with the dog and the child, in turn, starts to berate the dog—yelling at him in the same kind of tone of voice."
>
> "Child is squeezing a kitten's neck. Mother is worried that he might be able to hurt it. So she wraps her hands around the child's neck, to give him the idea of how unpleasant it is to have one's neck squeezed. He drops the kitten and she stopped squeezing." (p. 31)

These researchers found that the mothers with children most likely to show empathy and prosocial behavior shared the following characteristics:

- in cases where the child had caused distress in another, the mother explained to the child the negative effects of the child's behavior on the victim;
- the mother often stated moral rules and made judgmental comments like "It's not nice to bite the cat's tail" or "I don't want to be around you when you behave that way";
- the mother stated verbal rules about not hurting people or animals; and
- the mother prohibited the child from aggressing against the victim and provided the child with alternative, positive ways of interacting.

The researchers conclude that "Young children can be made to understand that animals as well as people, have feelings, are receptive to affection, and sometimes require consolation" (p. 32). And the parents' role in fostering the development of empathy, sympathy, and prosocial behavior is clear from the examples described above and may be related to a decreased propensity to be violent toward others (Hastings, Zahn-Waxler, Robinson, Usher, and Bridges 2000).

We must not forget that, at times, young children become the teachers for their adult caretakers. The late Philip Hallie (1997) described a visit to his 3-year-old grandson Daniel's home where, on an early morning, Hallie found one of the family's six cats with its hind paw in Mr. Hallie's cereal bowl (p. 44). Hallie "seized the cat, picked him up off the table, and let him drop to the kitchen floor with a little downward push of anger and disgust." Daniel's reaction was that "he was anguished by what he had just witnessed. He loved me and he loved the cat, and he was baffled by the disapproval he felt for me and the pity he felt for the abused cat. . . . After a few moments he sought out the cat and took it in his arms—it was almost as big as he was—and he sat on the floor in the kitchen petting it, weeping a little, and not looking at me."

Variations on the theme of empathy—deficits and perversions of perspective taking. Recently, Vernon R. Wiehe, a pioneer in studying sibling abuse, published a paper encouraging a greater emphasis on the role of empathy in facilitating interventions with and treatment of caregivers who have abused their children (1997a).

First of all, he reviews a number of studies demonstrating that mothers who have abused their children tend to score lower on measures of empathy. Some of these mothers may not be very skilled in perceiving, interpreting, and attending to the emotion cues of their children and some abused children show similar deficits. He also notes that children growing up in families where there is child maltreatment or domestic violence are missing out on opportunities to see models of caring and compassion between members of their own family. Wiehe cites research showing that empathy often reduces the likelihood that aggression and violence will occur. This relation between empathy and violence has also been described by Roy F. Baumeister in referring to the common cruelty toward animals found in some young children. He notes that "what generally brings these activities to a halt is the intervention of adults, who tell the child to imagine how that would feel if someone did that to you: Put yourself in the other's place. As the child develops some empathy with the victim, the cruelty subsides. Empathy is an important inhibiter . . . but it takes years for empathy to be developed and refined into a common response—and to be strong enough to keep people from inflicting harm" (1997, pp. 220–221).

Secondly, because of this empathy deficit in some caregivers who abuse their children, Wiehe recommends that these caregivers be given specific training in perspective taking and identifying and relating to the emotions experienced by their offspring. He observes that some programs for treating juvenile sex offenders do focus on increasing the offenders' capacity to empathize with their victims. Empathy training is also a component of the Nurturing Program, a child maltreatment prevention program developed by Stephen Bavolek of Family Development Resources (Bavolek 2000).

Extensive evaluation of these types of programs is ongoing and there is a caveat. Greater perspective taking and understanding of another's emotions may help a perpetrator become a more competent victimizer!

For example, in the notorious 1994 case of the abduction, rape, and murder of 7-year-old Megan Kanka by Jesse K. Timmendequas (Jenkins 1998), it is likely that Timmendequas had sufficient perspective taking skills to understand a young girl's desire to see a puppy, the ploy by which he enticed Megan to his home (Burney 1997). Timmendequas had previously sexually assaulted a 5-year-old in 1981 and attempted to sexually assault a 7-year-old in 1982. According to another report ("Killers" 1997), one of the psychiatrists who testified at the trial indicated that Timmendequas' confessions indicated "he was in control of his actions, was not 'panicked', and knew fully what he was doing and what the consequences were."

I should also emphasize that individuals considered sadistic or cruel, by definition, take pleasure in the suffering of another. It seems obvious that, at least on a cognitive level, these individuals "understand" the emotions accompanying the terror experienced by their victims. Although I don't mean to imply that children who abuse animals are necessarily on a path to becoming psychopaths, reflect on Jonathan Kellerman's observation that " Skillful, intelligent psychopaths can learn kindness, sensitivity, and morality as abstractions and weaknesses to be exploited, but they don't integrate these qualities into their personalities" (1999, p. 54). Again, some chilling words from Roy Baumeister: "Yet the most extreme cruelty makes use of empathy. To be seriously, thoroughly cruel, it is necessary to know what the victim is feeling, in order to maximize the suffering" (p. 245). The notorious Utah case of Arthur Gary Bishop illustrates this point. Between 1979 and 1983, Bishop abducted, tortured, and killed five young boys, ranging in age from 4 to 13 years ("Slayer" 1988). Bishop was tried, convicted, and later executed for these crimes, an execution he did not protest or legally contest. At one point, Bishop told an Associated Press reporter that after his first human murder he had tried to "cure himself" of his sexually violent urges by buying dozens of puppies and torturing and killing them. However, his plan backfired—he discovered that he enjoyed the cries of the animals suffering too much and so he continued his serial killing of children (M. Carter, personal communication, March 23, 1998; Hickey 1991, p. 11).

Now contrast Bishop's sadism with a recollection of childhood by André Theuriet (qtd. in Compayré 1902, pp. 195–196): ". . . at the age of four years he took a fancy to seize four new-born puppies and carry them to the fountain, 'just to see.' 'When I saw them,' he says 'miserably swimming and struggling in the water, I had a consciousness of my infamy; my sensibility was aroused, and I wanted to rescue the poor things. When I failed in doing this, I fled, full of terror, thinking in my soul of four years that hell, of which my mother had often spoken to me, would certainly punish such misdeeds.'" Theuriet provides a vivid example of animal abuse motivated by curiosity, the ensuing empathy with the puppies' distress, sympathy that motivated an unsuccessful prosocial rescue attempt, and the deep guilt felt by this child as he considered his mother's admonishments. Clearly, Theuriet had already internalized standards for how to treat other living creatures. It would be fascinating to compare the socialization histories of Arthur Gary Bishop and André Theuriet!

School-aged children and adolescents

The beginning of school does not mark the end of young people's education and socialization about empathy and caring but rather the opportunity for the scope and quality of these characteristics to be refined and extended to peers, other adults in roles of authority, and the wider community. Many school-based intervention programs will often include components aimed at enhancing children's empathy with and prosocial behavior toward others (see, for example, Lantieri and Patti's (1996) *Waging Peace in Our Schools* and Slaby, Roedell, Arezzo, and Hendrix's (1995) *Early Violence Prevention: Tools for Teachers of Young Children*). For example, Eisenberg (1992, pp. 119–122) describes the Child Development Project in the San

Francisco area (Battistich, Watson, Solomon, Schaps, and Solomon 1991). This program fosters prosocial development by embedding in the regular curriculum opportunities for children to cooperate on tasks, teaching children to take the perspective of others and be aware of emotions in themselves, their peers, and adults, specifically stating that prosocial values are important and desirable. Children are provided actual opportunities to engage in helping behavior and experience classroom discipline that is not physically or emotionally coercive but instead that is based on empathy, self-regulation, and a healthy sense of responsibility and guilt. This type of classroom atmosphere mirrors many of the qualities of the effective mothers described by Zahn-Waxler, Hollenbeck, and Radke-Yarrow in the section above.

Concern for animal welfare has also been included in attitudinal assessments of children's more general prosocial behavior (Ma and Leung 1991). In this study of Chinese second to sixth graders, the authors found that the higher a child's prosocial orientation, the lower their self-reported delinquency.

In the first chapter, I described a variety of efforts to teach school-aged children kindness and compassion toward animals, what has been called "humane education." One example of this type of program was described in a newspaper article by Cortland Milloy (1994). Reminiscent of the "Bands of Mercy," Debbie Duel and her associates at the Washington (DC) Humane Society conduct such education programs in the local schools. Children are also given an opportunity to take an oath to take appropriate, and safe, measures to prevent cruelty to animals. The article describes a number of young people who had "graduated" from this program and who had been commended for their actions on behalf of animals. In some cases, it was calling animal control to report an abandoned litter of puppies or a starving cat trapped in an apartment building crawl space. Some children were even more proactive in displaying their empathy, sympathy, and prosocial behavior toward animals. According to a 15-year-old, "You know how teenage boys can be, they just feel like being bad and hurting something," Daiquon said. "They might see a turtle and say, 'Let's smash it,' and I'll say, 'No, I want that one.' And I'll take it home and let it go free the next day." Daiquon and some of the other children like him live in housing complexes that prohibit pets so their empathy and compassion is all the more remarkable.

The ability of psychologically challenged youth to reach out to help animals was one of the themes of Glendon Swarthout's *Bless the Beasts and the Children* (1995), a wonderful counterpoint to Golding's *Lord of the Flies.* A group of troubled and probably neglected young boys, attending a summer camp for youth with "problems," band together to save a herd of buffalo destined for slaughter. "Beasts and boys considered each other. They smelled each other. And suddenly boys of fifteen, fourteen, and twelve were children once more. The breath of innocent animals blessed them" (1995, p. 142).

Helping children identify danger. School-aged children may be growing in their capacity for empathy and their competency to engage in prosocial behavior but this does not mean that their socialization and education in these domains is complete. Take, for example, the issue of dog-bites. One report ("Dogs bite" 1998) noted that 334,000 yearly dog-bite incidents are serious enough to require emergency room care, most involve dogs a child knows (including the families' pets), and that the children at greatest risk are 5- to 9-years-olds. Although the vast majority of dog bites are not fatal, injuries can be devastating and disfiguring (Gomes, Ribeiro-Filho, Giron, Mitre, Figueira, and Arap 2000; Rohrich 1999). Boglioli and her colleagues (see the study above on the infant who was killed and dismembered) note that dog attacks may be related to the following circumstances (p. 392): children may not identify a dog's growling or body language that precedes fear biting, a child may interfere with a dog's feeding, or a child's behavior or vocalizations may elicit aggressive behavior in a dog. These problems implicate the ability to read the emotional state of the animal and interpret correctly what the animal's sounds and body cues indicate about its emotions. Given the number of children bitten, it is clear that many children are missing or misinterpreting these emotion cues and need to be taught by adults to pay attention to them.

A recent and excellent contribution to the topic of dog bites is Molly Love and Karen L. Overall's "How Anticipating Relationships between Dogs and Children Can Help Prevent Disasters" (2001). This is the first article I have seen that integrates information about the behavioral and psychological characteristics of children from infancy to early adolescence with canine signaling and social and behavioral development from "puppyhood" to maturity. The authors anticipate problems that may arise in child-dog relations and provide detailed charts at the end of their paper (p. 453) that provide advice and guidance for human caregivers with children about managing child-dog interactions, factors to consider even before a pet dog is acquired, signals that dogs may give indicating that interactions with a child are distressing to the animal, and child behaviors at various developmental stages that may affect the family dog or place a child at risk. This is an excellent resource that will, no doubt, become a standard information packet provided to prospective dog adopters/purchasers by animal welfare agencies, veterinarians, and, I would hope, pediatricians. The paper also makes clear that both children *and their caregivers* must be educated about the potential for danger and the need for parental supervision of the contexts in which children interact with dogs. Dr. James VanLeeuwen, the child psychiatrist I referred to earlier, went so far as to suggest that in some cases, "the mutilation of children by their family dog may result from parental neglect and should be reported to the Children's Aid Society" (1981, p. 183).

One example of a formal attempt to provide such instruction comes from a study conducted with Australian school children by S. Chapman, J. Cornwall, J. Righetti, and L. Sung (2000). Children who were 7 to 8 years old from eight schools participated and 346 children were involved. Four of the schools were provided with a half-hour lesson by an accredited dog handler who instructed children about ways to identify friendliness, anger, and fear in dogs, how to make safe approaches to a dog, circumstances under which dogs should be left alone and not disturbed, and how to respond if knocked down by a dog. The other four classrooms served as a control group and did not receive this instruction. The truly innovative part of this study took place about a week later. The researchers set up a scenario on the schools' playgrounds where a "docile Labrador" was tied up near its owner, who was dressed as a worker. During playtime, children from all the schools were videotaped to record their reactions to and behaviors toward the dog. The videotapes were later scored by three different people, one of whom had no idea which children were in the trained group and which were in the control group.

The researchers found that children trained in dog safety were much more cautious about approaching the dog and spent more time just watching the dog from afar. In fact, only 9% of the trained children petted the dog in contrast to 79% of the control group children! These results demonstrate that children can be taught skills that will make them respond to an unfamiliar animal in ways that could increase the children's safety. Of course, as the authors themselves note, we still need studies to determine how long these training effects last and whether the effects will generalize to animals who are unleashed. Nevertheless, this pioneering study is an excellent start on addressing a significant child safety issue.

If you would like more information about dog-bite prevention education, see the following resources:

> Health Tips: Preventing Dog Bites. (2001) *Mayo Clinic Health Letter, 19,* 3.
>
> Preventing Dog Bites. (2001). *American Family Physician, 63,* 1573–1574.
>
> The Centers for Disease Control published a brief report about dog bites that includes a one-page (p. 467) list of measures for preventing dog bites (Centers for Disease Control 1997). In addition, your local humane society or animal welfare and control organization can very likely provide you with educational materials. The national animal welfare organizations listed in the Appendix are also excellent resources.

More detailed treatments of the topic of dog bites and dog-bite fatalities can be found in Overall and Love (2001) and Sacks et al. (2000).

Children frightened by animals. As I noted in chapter 5 dealing with children's motivations underlying animal abuse, fear of an animal may cause a child to harm or even attempt to kill the animal in a kind of preemptive strike. Here, the child may be attempting to take the perspective of the animal but may misinterpret the animal's behavior, assuming there is danger where there may be none. In such situations, rather than experiencing empathy, the child may be focusing on their own personal distress and anxiety. For example, fear of snakes, insects, and animals in general is not uncommon in young children (Lapouse and Monk 1959) with fear of snakes among the ten most common fears expressed by young people between 7 and 16 years of age (Ollendick, King, and Frary 1989). These fears may not be inherent in children but may develop as part of the socialization process. Remember Little Albert's interest in the rat before Watson "conditioned" him. Earlier, I discussed the process of social referencing where children look to others for cues about how to react to certain novel events. Paul Shepard describes the process with his typically rich language: "Acutely scrutinizing and attending raptly, children seeing their first snakes do not loathe or love but simply wonder. The mood and words of grown-ups direct and exploit the child's aroused awe, shaping and suffusing passion with terror or reverence, approach or avoidance" (1996, pp. 271–272).

The circle of compassion: How wide? Referring to an Indian tribe in Central Brazil, Paul Shepard observes:

> Red macaws are the only pets kept by the Bororos. There are other domestic animals—chickens, dogs, and pigs—but the people show no affection for them. The macaws are the property of women. They are admired, well fed, groomed, given proper names from the owner's matrilineage, taken on trips, and become part of an estate. Allowed to wander freely in the village, they are regarded with indulgent pleasure and protective care. They are never punished or eaten, seldom sold, and mourned when they die. (1996, p. 108)

Understanding the development of empathy toward animals is complicated by the diversity of animal species and the particular status that each species holds in each society. In the United States, cats, dogs, gerbils, birds, aquarium fish are common pets but these same animals may be considered food in other cultures. In the U.S., insects rarely seem to be considered pets—perhaps one of the few exceptions is the popularity of ants and ant farms. We consider some wild insects beautiful and worthy of our protection (e.g., praying mantises, butterflies, certain species of spider) but it is uncommon in the U.S. for insects to be brought into our homes and become the objects of our affection and nurturance. Think about how much time and money we spend on ridding ourselves of many insect species like cockroaches, flies, mosquitoes, and lice! But in Japan, insects—*mushi*—may commonly achieve the status of "pet" for many children in that society. Erick L. Laurent (2000) describes the major commercial enterprise that exists in Japan's marketing of crickets, singing grasshoppers, and rhinoceros and stag beetles. Earlier examples that are no longer common included dragonfly catching and spider fighting. Department stores that sell mushi and related insect breeding and raising equipment often locate these items next to insecticides! Laurent also notes that catching fireflies used to be popular but fireflies are now an officially protected species—one who catches them may be reported to the police and fined! This is an excellent example of how empathy and concern for the welfare of a particular animal species may supercede the public's desire to collect them and keep them for display or as pets.

We might ask: Are insects really considered pets in Japan or is this phenomenon more like the collecting of interesting inanimate objects? Laurent provides some evidence that children do consider these insects as pets ("petto," in Japanese) or playmates. Mushi are referred to as pets, are anthropomorphized as characters in the songs that children sing, and are "participants" in children's play. And yet, Laurent observes, mushi kept as pets are rarely given names and their eventual death does not seem to distress the children who reared them. Perhaps the significant physical and behavioral differences between insects and humans and the insects' relatively short life span make empathy with these creatures more difficult.

Misplaced empathy? Keeping insects as pets seems a rather benign activity. However, there are cases where keeping certain pets may jeopardize the welfare of the individual animals involved or, in some cases, entire populations. Empathy may be the sincere motivation behind such pet keeping but the empathy may be misinformed and misdirected. In a study conducted in Costa Rica, Carlos Drews surveyed members of over a thousand households in that country, 71% of which kept pets—a figure higher but comparable to pet keeping in the U.S. (2001a). Drews found that, in addition to keeping pet dogs and cats, 33% of the households with pets kept wild species, most often (76%) illegally caught wild birds. A number of these wild species are considered endangered or vulnerable under international or national criteria or laws. Drews lamented, in a recent address at an international conference, that despite benevolent attitudes toward wild species kept as pets, some Costa Ricans do not realize that the conditions under which such animals are maintained in homes rarely match the animals' behavioral and species-specific "psychological" needs (2001b). He stressed that educating the public was needed to help people redirect their empathy toward some of these species in more humane directions.

Loving animals to death. Another, more extreme, example that may involve people believing they are acting in the best interests of animals when in fact the animals' welfare is being endangered is the case of "animal hoarding." We can all recall a newspaper or TV news story on investigations of homes where, in some cases, literally hundreds of animals are being housed and "cared for" by the home owner. In cases of animal hoarding, the issue is not necessarily the shear number of animals present but the fact that the number exceeds that for which the human could possibly provide humane and healthy care. As noted by Dooley Worth and Alan M. Beck in one of the first published papers on this topic (1981), many animal hoarders believe they are "rescuing" strays from harsh environments and may distrust or disagree with the values of official animal control and welfare agencies. Unfortunately, the animals kept in such numbers and unhygienic conditions often suffer from disease, illness, and may die prematurely. Although virtually every case Worth and Beck studied involved adults (one 14-year-old boy was included), the authors observed that "all these people had developed strong feelings about animals very early in childhood" (p. 295).

In a more recent study, Gary J. Patronek examined 54 cases of animal hoarding throughout the U.S. (1999); in four of these 54 cases, more than 100 animals had been discovered in a single residence. Patronek notes that animals were found dead or in poor physical condition in 80% of these investigations. Although mental health problems probably underlie a number of these cases (for example, investigation in 26% of the cases resulted in the hoarder being institutionalized, placed under supervised living, or placed under guardianship), hoarding may be the epitome of misdirected empathy. In a current and ongoing study of hoarders (Frost 2000), interviews with nine women who hoarded animals revealed the following characteristics: ". . . the beliefs that they had special abilities to communicate or empathize with animals, that animal control officers failed to recognize the care the interviewees give to their animals and that saving animals was their life's mission. Typically, animals played significant roles in their childhoods, which were often characterized by chaotic, inconsistent and unstable parenting." Obviously, the developmental origins of this phenomenon, especially its potential relation to disorders of attachment, are worthy of additional study.

I will share one last example of misplaced or misguided empathy (Delk 1977). It involves an adult but we can imagine cases where children might develop similar problems. The client was a 25-year-old woman who sought therapy for depression. She told her therapist that she thought her depression was related to her obsessions about the welfare of animals, primarily pets. She experienced a great deal of distress when she encountered stray animals and avoided TV and films since she was afraid of seeing an injured or dead animal. Car trips created a similar concern. It is clear that this woman's life was miserable as a function of her intense empathy with helpless animals. Her concern was also interfering with her own enjoyment of food, sleep, and normal sexual relations with her husband. Here is a clear example of how extreme personal distress can override a sympathetic response and reasonable efforts to aid a victim in need.

The woman also described spending time looking for stray animals and finding homes for them. But animals she could not place she cared for in her own home. Given our earlier discussion, it would be of interest to know *how many* animals she kept in her dwelling and whether her behavior might be an example of hoarding. The maladaptive empathy displayed by this woman is captured in the therapist's comment that "the more she helped animals, the more depressed she became—because she could not help them more!" (p. 938).

The happy ending to this case was that, over the course of ten weeks of weekly sessions, the therapist used relaxation training with feedback on muscle tension and systematic desensitization that allowed the woman to imagine more and more distressing examples of injured or dead animals yet remain relatively calm. The therapist was not attempting to make the woman callous toward animal suffering but to bring her reactions within normal limits. Six months after the conclusion of therapy, the woman reported that she was no longer depressed and that her improvement had also been noted by her husband and friends.

Empathy: General or specific? One of the age-old assumptions in philosophy and in the animal welfare movement is that empathy toward animals may promote the development of empathy toward humans. The parallel argument for animal abuse is that those who learn to be cruel to animals may be prone to cruelty toward fellow human beings. It is not surprising, then, that a great deal of research, much of it with young people, has been directed at exploring the nature of the relation between empathy toward animals and empathy toward humans. Setting aside the complex issue of which species of animals each culture considers a proper focus of empathic concern (I still struggle with my own lack of empathy for mosquitoes and their high-pitched whine when they settle into my ear on warm summer nights!), we can ask, "In what ways might these two kinds of empathy be related?"

Empathy could be a highly generalized characteristic in that people who are empathic toward animals would be more likely to be empathic toward people. This makes sense if we assume that many of the processes underlying empathy (a living creature is involved, distress cues can be perceived and correctly identified, relieving the distress of another is a valued trait) are applicable to both people and animals. Unfortunately, a *lack* of empathy may also be a general characteristic of some people; little concern or care is shown toward victims of distress, human or animal. There is also the possibility that empathy is more specific. Some people may be highly empathic toward the plight of other human beings but oblivious to or unconcerned with animal distress. The opposite may also occur in cases where a person has great affection and empathy for animals but cares little for the concerns and welfare of other people.

There are also serious developmental questions that surround this issue. Some might suggest that, in young children, empathy toward animals occurs first and then is extended to humans. But there are many children who do not have contact with pets or other animals until after they have already achieved a number of milestones in the development of empathy toward people. Clearly, the presence of a pet in a home is no guarantee that empathy will emerge—in my estimation, pets are neither necessary nor sufficient for the development of caring toward others. But pets, if present, may provide one more opportunity for children to develop a healthy sense of compassion for vulnerable others.

A recently published chapter by Elizabeth S. Paul provides an excellent overview of research that has been conducted on this topic (2000). Although she addresses both child- and adult-focused research on the generality of empathy, I will concentrate on the studies involving children and adolescents (one study I conducted with Claudia Weber found that empathy toward people and animals were positively related for both children and adult [Weber and Ascione 1992]). I also caution the reader that one of the limitations of most of our understanding of empathy toward people and animals is that the information has been derived from participants' responses to questionnaires and surveys rather than observation of their behavior. Also, since virtually all of the research has been correlational, we cannot determine if empathy toward animals affects empathy toward people or if the direction of the effect is in the other direction (empathy toward people affects animal-directed empathy). There is, in addition, the possibility that some other factor (sociability? assertiveness? heightened sensitivity to distress cues?) affects both forms of empathy.

Citing research conducted by Robert Poresky with young children (Poresky 1990; Poresky 1996; Poresky and Hendrix 1990), Paul notes that "empathy with other children was positively associated with empathy with pets . . . and that while pet ownership per se was not related to child-oriented empathy, the reported strength of the child's bond with the pet was" (pp. 173–174). These findings reinforce the observation that knowing there are pets in a home tells us little about how well the animals are treated; unfortunately, as attested to by the high rates of child maltreatment, the presence of children in a home is no guarantee that their caregivers are empathic or nurturing. Gail Melson, another researcher who has focused on pets and children's development, also cites research she has conducted showing that the child's *attachment* to pets is what is related to empathy not the mere presence of pets in a home (1998).

So, as Boris Levinson noted years ago, the mere presence of pets is not a panacea for insuring healthy psychological development, no more than the presence of children or a spouse guarantee a healthy family. It is the *quality* of relationships that is important for both humans and the animals for whom they provide care.

I turn next to cases where the quality of human relationships has been compromised by violence and abuse and describe how these experiences may be related to the maltreatment of animals.

CHAPTER 7

Animal abuse, violent offending, and Conduct Disorder

> Cruelty to animals and other children is a characteristic, though not common, feature of the affectionless delinquent, and occasional outbursts of senseless cruelty are well known in some forms of mental illness. (Bowlby 1953, p. 94)

> Specific childhood indicators of aggression include temper tantrums in infancy, physical aggression toward peers and siblings, cruelty to animals, disobedience, quarreling, and disruptiveness in class. . . . (Reiss and Roth 1993, p. 354)

Although there is good news that the past few years have witnessed *decreases* in violence committed by juveniles, it is also true that the past few decades in the United States were filled with too many violent crimes perpetrated by young people and too many children and adolescents who were victims of those assaults. As the age of the perpetrators becomes younger and younger, our gasps of disbelief intensify.

- "Student, 15, accused of killing 3 and wounding 26 in Oregon" (*New York Times*, May 22, 1998)
- "Japanese teen goes to youth prison for beheading boy" (*Salt Lake Tribune*, October 18, 1997)

- "Boys, 11 and 13, silent after killing spree." (*Salt Lake Tribune*, March 25, 1998)
- "11-year-old convicted in baby's death." (*The Logan Herald Journal*, November 20, 1997)
- "Britain murder trial for 11-year-olds winding down." (*The Logan Herald Journal*, November 22, 1993)
- "When killer boys grow up. Two infamous 10-year-old murderers in Britain have become men. Do they merit new, anonymous lives?" (*Time*, January 22, 2001)
- "If 6-year-old did beat a baby, should he be helped or jailed?" (*Salt Lake Tribune*, April 29, 1996)
- "Boy, 6, fatally shoots classmate." (*USA Today*, March 1, 2000)

In the summer of 2000, Stephanie Verlinden completed a doctoral dissertation at Pacific University in which she reviewed 9 school shootings involving fatalities that took place in the United States between 1996 to 1999. The perpetrators included 11 young people about whom Verlinden gathered information about their history and background from a number of sources including official reports and media coverage. Later published as a journal article (Verlinden, Hersen, and Thomas 2000), her dissertation examined the individual, family, peer, situational, and psychological characteristics associated with these young perpetrators. In her analysis of background variables, she reported that 5 of the 11 young people or 45% had alleged histories of animal abuse.

Obviously, this was not the only risk factor she identified in this sample of lethally violent youth but the high rate of animal abuse suggests that in a substantial number of cases, the violence of these young people targeted both people and animals. And as we know, the animal abuse these young people display may not be considered significant by parents, peers, or other adults until the violence directly affects human victims. For example, I already made a brief reference to the case of Luke Woodham who, on October 1, 1997, killed his mother and two high school students in Pearl, Mississippi. This case was one of the 9 incidents reviewed by Verlinden in her dissertation. Let me share some other aspects of this case that I wrote about in a chapter for the book I co-edited with my colleague and friend Phil Arkow (Ascione 1999.

> "Sometime prior to this mayhem, Luke had allegedly written in his diary about the torture and killing of his own dog, Sparkle (Morello 1997). After being beaten with clubs, Sparkle was doused with lighter fluid, set on fire, and thrown into a pond. The diary entries include: "I'll never forget the sound of her breaking under my might." "I will never forget the howl she made . . . it sounded almost human. We laughed and hit her more" (Hewitt, Harms, and Stewart 1997).

> "Sparkle's killing was witnessed by an adult neighbor. The incident was never reported to the police or animal control (Barr 1997). Was this an omen ignored, a portent that could have prompted intervention and prevented the human tragedy on October 1?"

In another chapter of the same book, Lynn Loar, a clinical social worker well known in the fields of both child and animal welfare, began by describing the case of Eric Smith, a 13-year-old Savonna, New York boy who killed a 4-year-old child named Derrick Robie on August 2, 1993. A newspaper article reported that four years earlier, at the age of 9, Eric had strangled a neighbor's cat to death by putting a laundry hose clamp around the cat's neck and then tightening it until the cat died (Nordheimer 1993). Eric had been made to apologize to and perform yard work for the neighbor in "reparation" for this fatal animal abuse but there is no indication that the incident was ever brought to the attention on law enforcement authorities or mental health professionals. Lynn Loar laments that the significance of this animal abuse was overlooked and a potential opportunity to intervene in the life of an obviously troubled child was missed.

Animal abuse was clearly not the only sign of problems in the histories of Luke Woodham and Eric Smith, any more so than in the other 10 young people studied by Verlinden, but why didn't this sign raise more significant concerns *before* the incidents of human victimization occurred?

Both animal abuse and interpersonal violence toward humans share common characteristics: both types of victims are living creatures, have a capacity for experiencing pain and distress, can display audible or visible physical signs of their pain and distress (with which humans could empathize), and may die as a result of inflicted injuries. Given these commonalities, it is not surprising that early research in this area, much of it using retrospective assessment in which the person is asked to reminisce about past periods of development, examined the relation between childhood histories of animal abuse and later violent offending.

Violent offenders. Alan Felthous, a forensic psychiatrist whose work I referred to in chapter 5, and a number of his colleagues produced some of the most compelling research on this issue in the 1970s and 1980s. One of the limitations of these research studies is that they were based on the self-reports of adults reminiscing about earlier periods of their lives. It is possible, therefore, that some of the recollections were inaccurate or even, in some cases, confabulated to deceive the interviewer. Since there was generally no independent verification of the adults' reports, we must keep these potential biases in mind.

Felthous developed an interview model that was very extensive and included hundreds of questions about the adults' history of contact with and abuse of animals. The interview results were presented in a number of published papers written by Felthous and his colleagues.

In one study, Kellert and Felthous (1985) interviewed 152 men. Some were inmates in federal penitentiaries. This group was divided into three subcategories. Using the ratings of prison counselors based, in part, on the inmates' behavior while incarcerated, the prisoners were categorized as highly aggressive and violent, moderately aggressive, or nonaggressive. A group of noncriminals from the community was also interviewed.

In anticipation of my later discussion of family factors associated with animal abuse, I should mention that these researchers also collected data on the men's reports of being physically abused. Recall that both Tapia (1971) and Rigdon and Tapia (1977) had found severe abuse, as well as domestic violence, to be common to a number of the cases they studied. "Excessive and repeated child abuse" was reported by 75% of the two aggressive criminal groups (highly and moderately aggressive), 31% of the criminals who were not aggressive, and 10% of the community, nonincarcerated men.

One of the measures that was derived from the interview information was whether the respondent had abused animals 5 or more times. This was labeled "substantial cruelty" to separate it from less frequent and possibly less severe animal abuse. The researchers found that the violent, incarcerated men reported the highest rates of "substantial cruelty to animals" in childhood—one in four (25%) were so classified. Similar results have been reported in a more recent study of incarcerated child molesters (Beyer and Beasley 2003). "Substantial cruelty" was found for only 5.6% of the moderately aggressive and 5.8% of the nonaggressive criminals and for none (0%) of the comparison group of men who were not criminals.

These kinds of results were not limited to samples of incarcerated men. Felthous and Yudowitz (1977) interviewed 31 incarcerated women and categorized them into "assaultive" and "nonassaultive" subgroups based on the presence or absence of their inflicting personal injuries, as noted in their official records. For women incarcerated for violent offences, 36% reported cruelty to animals. None of the non-assaultive women offenders admitted to abusing animals. Thus, even within samples of criminals, animal abuse appears to be associated with more generalized violent behavior toward other human beings. And animal abuse clearly is not a behavior confined only to male perpetrators.

In the past few years, a number of researchers have re-examined criminal populations and shown that the earlier results obtained by Felthous and others still ring true. In the United States, Miller and Knutson (1997) tabulated animal abuse self-reported by 299 prison inmates, most of whom were men (84%). A small percentage of the inmates were between 15 and 19 years of age (11.9%) but the remaining inmates were older than 19. These prisoners had been incarcerated for a variety of felony offenses and were compared with 308 introductory psychology class undergraduates (57.1% female). The percentages of inmates versus undergraduates, respectively, reporting the following types of animal abuse was:

- "Hurt an animal?" 16.4% vs. 9.7%,
- "Killed a stray?" 32.8% vs. 14.3%,
- "Killed a pet?" 12% vs. 3.2%.

Although the difference between inmates and college students was not substantial for hurting animals, the differences for more significant abuse were substantial. Inmates were more than two times as likely to have killed a stray animal and nearly four times as likely to have killed a family pet.

More recently, my colleagues in South Africa and I (Schiff, Louw, and Ascione 1999) surveyed 117 men incarcerated in a South African prison about their childhood animal abuse. We used a questionnaire based on the interview protocol that Felthous developed. Some of the men resided in maximum security because their crimes had been violent in nature. The remaining men had been incarcerated for primarily "white collar" types of offences. For the 58 men who had committed crimes of aggression, 63.3% admitted to cruelty to animals; for the 59 non-aggressive inmates, the percentage was 10.5%.

In a study of 28 convicted, incarcerated sexual homicide perpetrators (all men), Ressler, Burgess, and Douglas (Ressler, Burgess, and Douglas 1988) assessed their self-reports of cruelty to animals in childhood, adolescence, and adulthood. This was part of a larger study, by the Federal Bureau of Investigation, that was searching for patterns in the backgrounds of serial murderers in an effort to develop profiles of such individuals. Childhood animal abuse was reported by 36% of the perpetrators and 46% admitted to abusing animals as adolescents. Thirty-six percent of these men said they had also abused animals in adulthood.

Finally, in a study of 64 male convicted sex offenders conducted by Tingle, Barnard, Robbins, Newman, and Hutchinson (1986), animal abuse in childhood or adolescence was reported by 48% of the rapists and 30% of the child molesters.

Taken together, these studies suggest that animal abuse may be characteristic of the developmental histories of between 1 in 4 to nearly 2 in 3 violent adult offenders. This is clearly a significantly higher rate than what we would find in the general population of non-offending adults. But we must remember that not all criminals, even those who are violent to people, are animal abusers. As observed by Stanton E. Samenow in *Inside the Criminal Mind*, "Some are so fond of animals that they will bring home a lost, injured animal and treat it more tenderly than their own children. Furthermore, these animal lovers will chew out and even assault anyone whom they find abusing an animal. Other criminals abuse animals or are completely indifferent to them" (1984, p. 167).

Let me illustrate how our conclusions about the relation between animal abuse and interpersonal violence are influenced by the way the research is conducted. As I have mentioned, most of the research in this are has been retrospective, that is, usually asking adults about their behavior in childhood and adolescence. The following two diagrams show this strategy. First we identify a group of indi-

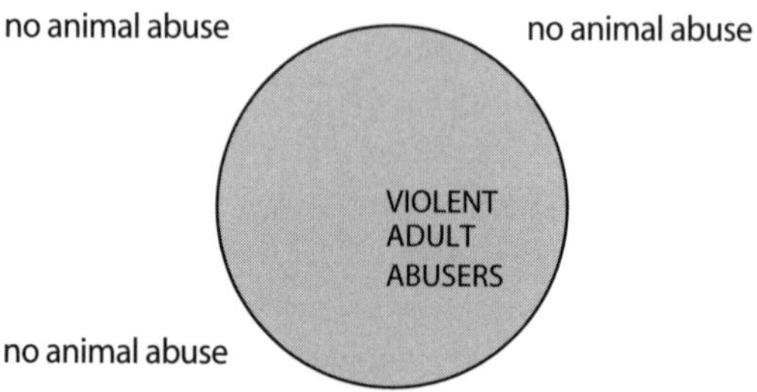

viduals who are violent adults. Then we interview them about their early years and discover that a significant proportion of them have a history of abusing animals. The proportion here is hypothetical but not that different from what has been actually found in research. One study found that 56% of incarcerated adult violent of-

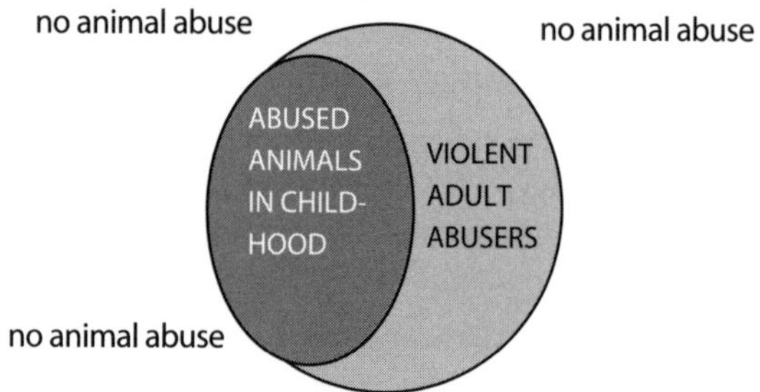

fenders had abused animals in the past (Merz-Perez, Heide, and Silvereman 2001; for a more detailed examination, see Merz-Perez and Heide 2004). This was true for 20% of a comparison group of nonviolent offenders The conclusion from this retrospective strategy is that most violent adults have a history of abusing animals.

An alternative strategy is prospective or longitudinal. We begin with a group of children who have been identified as cruel or abusive toward animals. After gath-

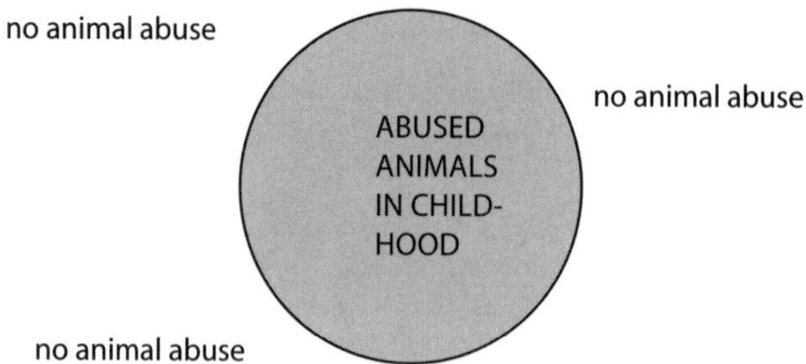

ering these data, we follow up this group of children for a number of years until they have become adults. At this point, we assess whether violence has become part of their behavior pattern.

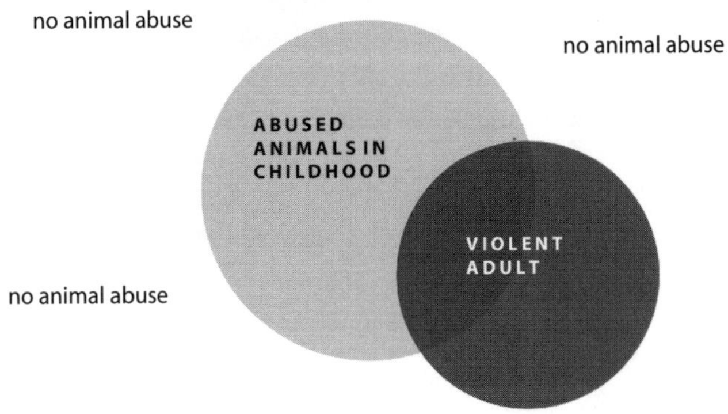

As you can see, using the prospective strategy, a much smaller proportion of children with a history of animal abuse go on to become violent adults. This is the dilemma of predicting or forecasting future behavior. How we differentiate children who are on a path toward adult violence and those whose acting out ends in childhood or adolescence is one of the most challenging tasks for child clinicians.

Conduct Disorder. As I noted in chapter 3, the mental health professions, especially psychiatry and psychology, have developed a standardized listing of mental disorders in children and adults to facilitate diagnosis and to provide basic information on the form and course of these disorders. The Diagnostic and Statistical Manual of Mental Disorders, fourth edition (DSM-IV 1994) defines Conduct Disorder (CD) as ". . . a repetitive and persistent pattern of behavior in which the basic rights of others or major age-appropriate societal norms or rules are violated" (p. 90). and requires that at least three of 15 separate symptoms be present in the past year. Among the symptoms listed are those categorized under "deceitfulness or theft," "destruction of property"—which encompasses fire setting and vandalism, and "aggression to people and animals"—which includes cruelty to people or to animals, stealing with confrontation of the victim, and forced sexual activity. There is a great deal of overlap between the symptoms of CD and behaviors used to characterize serious violent juvenile offenders (see Loeber, Farrington, and Waschbusch (1998, pp. 14–15).

Cruelty to animals has only recently been included in the symptom list for CD, appearing for the first time in *DSM-III-R* (1987). When it first appeared, the psychiatric community was apparently uncertain whether cruelty to animals should be viewed as a type of destructiveness (against inanimate objects) or as a type of aggression (against living victims). After all, in most jurisdictions, animals are legally considered property. If a child abuses an animal, is this more comparable to vandalism or to attacking a human being? This confusion was eliminated in the *DSM-IV* (1994) since cruelty to animals is now specifically included under the heading "aggression to people and animals," which is distinct from property destruction. Cruelty to animals, however, does not specifically appear in any of the categories under which juvenile offenders are categorized in national crime reporting systems (i.e., person, property, drug, and public order offenses; see Snyder and Sickmund's [1999] *Juvenile Offenders and Victims: 1999 National Report*) despite law enforcement acknowledgement of the link between animal abuse and human violence (Lockwood and Church 1996; Ponder and Lockwood 2000; Schlueter 1999; Turner 2000).

Including cruelty to animals in the *DSM-IV* (1994) is a very significant development in our understanding of this problem. What this means is that when a clinician is evaluating a child or adolescent, he or she is much more likely to ask the question, "Has this client abused or been cruel to animals?" Before cruelty to animals was listed as a Conduct Disorder symptom, clinicians might or might not ask about this behavior, perhaps based on their own judgment of its significance.

Animal abuse may vary in frequency, severity, and how chronic it is (for example, has this been going on for just the past week or for the past two years?). It can range from the developmentally immature teasing of animals (e.g., a toddler pulling a kitten along by the tail) to serious animal torture (e.g., stealing neighborhood pets and setting them on fire). Unfortunately, most assessments of cruelty to animals lack measures of these important differences. One exception is the Interview for Antisocial Behavior (IAB) developed by Kazdin and Esveldt-Dawson (Kazdin and Esveldt-Dawson 1986).

Although it was created before the 1987 revision of the *DSM*, this instrument assesses 30 forms of antisocial behavior in childhood and adolescence, a number of which reflect the current (1994) Conduct Disorder symptom listings. The IAB has a number of positive features including both parent- and self-report forms and ratings of problem severity and chronicity. Kazdin and Esveldt-Dawson report that responses to the cruelty to animals item were positively correlated with the IAB Total score (the higher the cruelty score, the more overall antisocial behavior) and this item significantly differentiated samples of CD-diagnosed from non-CD-diagnosed boys and girls, ages 6–13, who were all inpatients at a psychiatric facility. Children with Conduct Disorder were much more likely to be cruel to animals that children with other psychiatric diagnoses.

Patterns of chronic behavior may be more significant than isolated incidents as illustrated in a study by Loeber, Keenan, Lahey, Green, and Thomas (1993) with psychiatric outpatient referrals. Three, yearly assessments that included a question about cruelty to animals were completed with 177 boys, ages 7–12 years, some of whom (40.1%) were diagnosed with oppositional defiant disorder (ODD), which includes negativistic and hostile behavior, and others with CD (38.4%). Single-year assessment of cruelty to animals did not differentiate boys with ODD from those with CD diagnoses, but a significant differentiation emerged when scores on this item were aggregated over a three-year period. What this study suggests is that cruelty to animals displayed over 12 months may not reveal a child's disturbance; but if this behavior has persisted over 36 months, there is greater cause for concern. As an analogy, each of us may experience days when we are affected by depression, but depressive episodes that last for weeks and months warn of a more serious mental health problem.

Given interest in the early identification of children at-risk for later violent offending, it should be noted that cruelty to animals may be one of the earliest CD symptom to appear in the early lives of some children. Frick and his colleagues (Frick, Van Horn, Lahey, Christ, Loeber, Hart, et al. 1993) indicated that parental reports on the emergence of CD symptoms in their children mark 6.5 years as the median age of onset for "hurting animals," earlier than bullying, cruelty to people, vandalism, or setting fires. This study reinforces the importance of considering animal abuse a significant "red flag" for identifying a potential for receiving a CD diagnosis.

In an Australian and New Zealand journal, Luk, Staiger, Wong, and Mathai (1999) reported a reanalysis of case data for a sample of children (N=141) referred to mental health services for "symptoms suggestive of oppositional defiant/conduct disorder" (p. 30) and a sample of community children (N=37). The clinic-referred children were subdivided into two groups based on Child Behavior Checklist (CBC) assessments: cruelty to animals present (N=40) or absent (N=101). Therefore, 28.4% of the clinic-referred children displayed animal abuse. (A similar finding was reported in Burns, Landsverk, Kelleher, Faw, Hazen and Keeler 2001.) The community children were selected only if cruelty to animals was absent in their CBC assessments.

Luk et al. demonstrated that differentiating the clinic-referred subgroups on the basis of cruelty to animals was related to scores on a measure of childhood behavior problems that, unlike the CBC, does not assess cruelty to animals—the Eyberg Child Behavior Inventory (Eyberg and Ross 1978). The authors found that clinic children with cruelty to animals had significantly higher mean problem and problem severity scores on the Eyberg than the means for either clinic children without cruelty to animals or community children. Another disconcerting finding was that children who were cruel to animals had levels of self-esteem comparable to children in the other two groups suggesting, perhaps, that cruelty may bolster a child's sense of power and efficacy, albeit through harmful actions. Therefore, in an already disturbed group of children, the presence of cruelty to animals predicts even greater psychological impairment, at least, as measured in standard assessments of behavioral problems.

Members of this Australian research group recently published an article that, I believe, represents a significant advance in the way we assess animal abuse perpetrated by young people. Guymer, Mellor, Luk, and Pearse (2001) also lamented the fact that most of our information about animal abuse is derived from single items taken from instruments like the Child Behavior Checklist. In fact, they refer to an unpublished master's thesis by one of the authors (Pearse 1999) in which she reported that the Child Behavior Checklist missed identifying half of the children who were reported to be cruel to animals in a more in depth clinical interview with parents. Although the authors were familiar with the Children and Animals Assessment Instrument (CAAI) I had developed (described earlier in the chapter on motivations) and the dimensions of animal abuse that it taps, they correctly observed that this instrument is too lengthy to be used as an easily administered screening device for community and clinic samples of children.

Therefore, using the CAAI as the basis for their instrument development, Guymer and her associates constructed a 13-item test designed as a parent-report measure and tested with children at least 4 years of age. As with the CAAI, the Children's Attitudes and Behaviors Toward Animals (CABTA) questionnaire that resulted assessed the following dimensions of animal abuse: severity, frequency, duration, recency, diversity of animals harmed, intention to cause harm, covertness of the abuse, whether it was performed with others or in isolation, and whether the child displayed empathy for animals who were harmed. Because I believe this is an important development in our ability to identify children with potentially significant levels of animal abuse, I reproduce the individual items of the CABTA below. Although I caution the reader that this is a research instrument, those of you who are parents, teachers, or others who work with children may find value in seeing the types of questions relevant for assessing animal abuse.

CABTA (Guymer, Mellor, Luk, and Pearse 2001)

Some children may be rough with animals. We are interested in a range of behaviours, which may or may not apply to your child. Please answer the following questions.

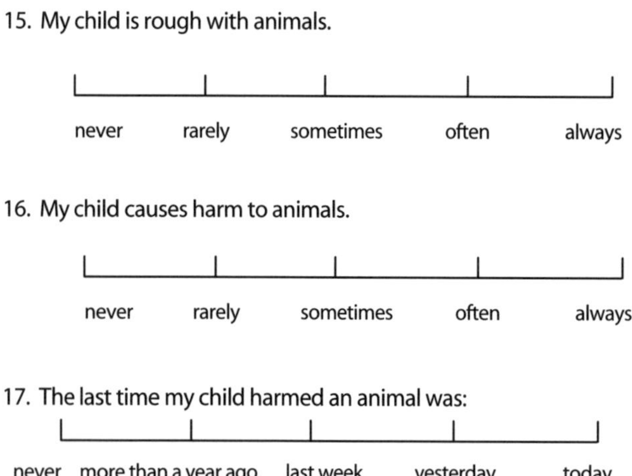

15. My child is rough with animals.

never rarely sometimes often always

16. My child causes harm to animals.

never rarely sometimes often always

17. The last time my child harmed an animal was:

never more than a year ago last week yesterday today

18. My child has harmed

	Yes	No
a. Small insects	☐	☐
b. Other non domestic animals	☐	☐
c. Other people's pets	☐	☐
d. His or her own pets	☐	☐

19. My child has harmed animals alone:

never rarely sometimes often always

20. My child has harmed animals when he was with another person or in a group

never rarely sometimes often always

21. My child has harmed animals

never accidentally in curiosity maybe intentionally definitely intentionally

22. My child has shown concern over the suffering of animals

never rarely sometimes often always

23. I believe that my child has secretly harmed animals:

never rarely sometimes often always

24. My child has shown pleasure when harming animals:

never rarely sometimes often always

Numerical ratings are assigned to each of these items (excluding 18b, 18c, and 22 which were statistically unstable items) so scores on the CABTA can range from 0–21 for what the authors refer to as Typical Cruelty (items 15, 16, 17, 18d, 19, and 21) and 0–17 for Malicious Cruelty (items 18a, 20, 21, 23, and 24). A community sample, not a clinical sample of disturbed children, was drawn from local elementary schools and included 192 boys and 168 girls whose parents completed the CABTA. The mean or average scores for these children were calculated and served as a comparison for a later part of the study. One important question that must be asked of a newly developed test is whether the scores it generates are reliable. In this study, reliability was assessed by having a small subsample of parents complete the CABTA twice, separated by two-weeks; they found the two sets of score to be virtually identical, indicating excellent test-retest reliability.

The last phase of this project involved the administration of the CABTA to parents of 19 children, 5 to 12 years of age, who had been diagnosed with a disruptive behavior disorder at mental health clinics (disruptive behavior disorders include cases of oppositional and defiant behavior and Conduct Disorder). An in depth clinical interview was also conducted and the results used to classify children into either a "cruel to animals" or a "not cruel to animals" group. The authors found that the CABTA scores (using a stringent minimum cruelty score) correctly classified 89% of the children with reference to the presence or absence of cruelty. Recall that the Child Behavior Checklist only achieved a 50% correct classification rate (Pease 1999). It appears that the CABTA holds real promise as a reliable, relatively quickly administered, and valid assessment of childhood animal abuse. One recommendation I would make is that a parallel self-report version of the CABTA be developed since we know that parents may not be the best informants for this particular behavior. A future study could determine the consistency, or lack thereof, between parent/caregiver reports and child/adolescent self-reports of animal maltreatment.

I must also remind you that animal abuse is only one of 15 potential symptoms of Conduct Disorder (CD), with only 3 of 15 required for a diagnosis. Are there different types of CD? (For an excellent discussion of this issue, see Tremblay 2003.) The *DSM-IV* (1994) differentiates childhood-onset (symptoms appear before 10 years of age) and adolescent-onset forms (no symptoms prior to age 10). In addition, since there are 15 symptoms, there are literally hundreds of combinations of the minimum of 3 required symptoms. However, attempting to identify hundreds of subtypes of CD would be cumbersome and unproductive. A recent attempt at examining possible subtypes of CD is the work of Paul J. Frick and his colleagues (Frick, O'Brien, Wootton, and McBurnett 1994; Frick and Ellis 1999). His description of a "callous-unemotional" subtype of CD may fit some children who abuse animals and who display no emotion, guilt, empathy, or concern for their victims.

Related research with adults also appears to support this relationship. Gleyzer, Felthous, and Holzer (2002) studied 96 adult criminal defendants. Half of this group had a history of "substantial animal cruelty" and the other half did not. The authors found that men with a history of animal cruelty were more likely (37.5%) to receive a diagnosis of Antisocial Personality Disorder than men without this history (8.3%). Antisocial Personality Disorder is the new term for what was referred to as psychopathic or sociopathic personality and the adult diagnosis requires, in part, that the patient received a diagnosis of Conduct Disorder in childhood or adolescence

Thus, there is substantial evidence for the value of assessing cruelty to animals as a specific symptom of CD and as a correlate of other forms of antisocial behavior in both childhood and adulthood. One additional study will be described to illustrate this conclusion.

Arluke, Levin, Luke, and Ascione (1999) located the records of 153 individuals (146 males and 7 females, age range 11–76 years) who had been prosecuted for intentional physical cruelty to animals (not passive forms of cruelty such as neglect) in the files of the Massachusetts Society for the Prevention of Cruelty to Animals. Usually, animal abuse cases are only prosecuted criminally if the abuse has resulted in serious injury to or the death of an animal (this is also generally true for child maltreatment cases). After selecting the "animal abusers," a comparison group of 153 other individuals was formed. They were matched to the animal abusers on age, gender, and socioeconomic status and were selected from the same neighborhoods in which those who had been prosecuted resided. However, none of the members of the comparison group had any record of cruelty to animal complaints.

Following the formation of these two groups, the state's criminal records were reviewed for each individual, noting any adult arrests for violent, property, drug, or public order offenses. These are the four main categories of offense that are tracked in national crime statistics. As shown in Figure 7.1, individuals prosecuted for animal abuse were more likely to have an adult arrest in each of the four crime categories than the comparison group members. The differences between percentages for abusers and non-abusers were highly significant for all four types of offenses. These results make it clear that animal abusers are not only dangerous to their animal victims but that they may jeopardize human welfare as well.

One limitation of this study is related to the use of official records. The records only tell us when the offenders were *detected and caught*, not when they first engaged in these abusive or criminal acts. Without using self-reports, we do not know if the individuals began abusing animals and then progressed to human-related crimes, began with human-related crimes and then progressed to animal abuse, or began their offending toward both types of victims roughly at the same time. Answers to these questions must await longitudinal research that follows the lives of children into their adolescence and adulthood.

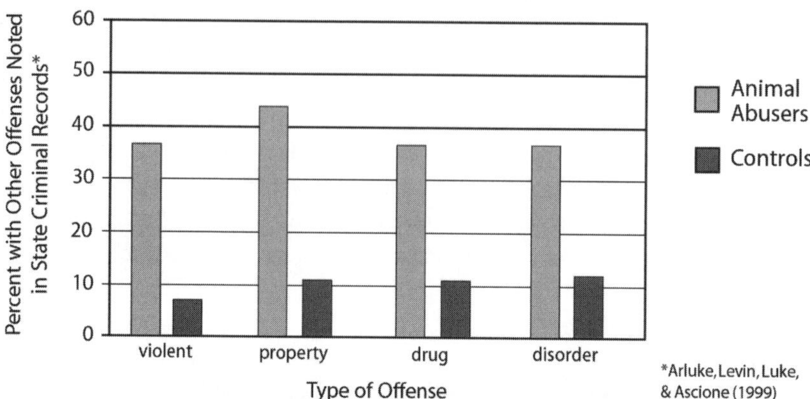

FIGURE 7.1. All chi square comparisons between abusers and controls significant at p<.0001.

IN THIS CHAPTER, I have focused primarily on individual characteristics that may be related to animal abuse. The next three chapters examine the environmental contexts more likely to be tainted by animal abuse, environments that may predispose individuals to animal cruelty.

CHAPTER 8

Child physical and emotional maltreatment and animal abuse

> **A**nimal cruelty conviction preceded murder charge. A Draper man charged with killing his 4-year-old son by bubbling Freon into the boy's bathtub last year was prosecuted five years ago for animal cruelty because he shot and skinned his pet dog. (Hunt 2000, p. D2)

> **W**e are tested and sometimes we fail. The maltreated child cries, 'I hurt'. Unheard or unheeded, that cry becomes prophesy. (A. H. Vachss 1993, p. 21)

Although "bad seed" interpretations of youth violence have waxed and waned throughout history (Garbarino 1999; Kellerman 1999), it is clear that attention to the family, social, and community contexts of children's lives is critical for understanding violent behavior. This holds true for the special case of animal abuse. As Widom (1989) has demonstrated, a history of child abuse and neglect places individuals at risk for later delinquency, adult criminal offending, and violent criminal activity. Other researchers have also noted that damaging prenatal environments and head injuries may also be related to violent behavior, including its most extreme form—murder (this topic is beyond the scope of this book but I refer the reader to the following sources: D. O. Lewis (1998), *Guilty by Reason of Insanity: A Psychiatrist Explores the Minds of Killers;* J. H. Pincus (2001), *Base Instincts: What Makes Killers Kill;* and A. Raine (1993), *The Psychopathology of Crime: Criminal Behavior as a Clinical Disorder*). This chapter and the two that follow address factors in children's lives that have been associated with increased levels of animal abuse. The factors range from negative but relatively normative experiences (e.g., corporal punishment) to potentially more devastating circumstances (e.g., child maltreatment, domestic violence).

Corporal punishment. Evidence continues to mount on the ineffectiveness and deleterious consequences of corporal punishment as a child-rearing technique (Straus 1991) and two recent studies tie this evidence to animal abuse. In a survey of 267 undergraduates, 68.4% of whom were women, Clifton Flynn (Flynn 1999a) asked participants about their history of abusing animals (e.g., hurting, torturing, or killing pets or stray animals, sex acts with animals). Students then responded to items assessing attitudes toward spanking and husband-on-wife abuse. Thirty-four point five percent of the men and 9.3% of the women reported at least one childhood incident of animal abuse. Participants (regardless of gender) admitting to animal abuse were significantly more likely to endorse the use of corporal punishment and to approve of a husband slapping his wife.

In a follow-up report with this same sample of undergraduates, Flynn (1999b) found that, for men, perpetrating animal abuse was positively correlated with the frequency of their fathers' use of corporal punishment in adolescence (spanking, slapping, or hitting). Self-reports of animal abuse by men experiencing paternal corporal punishment in adolescence were 2.4 times higher than for men not physically disciplined (57.1% vs. 23.1%, respectively).

Because this was a correlational study, we must use some caution in interpreting these findings. For example, it is unclear whether corporal punishment *causes* children to be angry and aggressive, taking out their distress on animal victims *or* the alternative possibility that animal abuse perpetrated by the child is only one of a constellation of acting out behaviors that elicit more coercive and physically punitive behavior from the caregiver. Longitudinal studies that trace the emergence of both animal abuse and the use of corporal punishment have not been conducted but will be necessary for disentangling the direction of the relation between these two factors.

Physical abuse. The latest statistics on national estimates of the incidence of child physical abuse in out country were reported for 1993 by Andrea J. Sedlak and Diane D. Broadhurst in the *Third National Incidence Study of Child Abuse and Neglect* (1996). Using what is referred to as the "harm standard," a stringent criterion that identifies cases where there has been demonstrable harm to a child as a result of the abuse, there were 381,700 young people who were substantiated victims of physical abuse in 1993. Physically neglected youth numbered 338, 900.

Physical abuse has been related to heightened aggression in children (Reidy 1977). In this study with children whose average age was 6 years, physical abuse was defined by cases where a physical injury had occurred more than once and where a referral had been made from family services. Physically abused children showed more aggression than comparison groups of neglected children or children for whom no maltreatment was assumed. Research specifically designed to assess the relation between animal abuse and child maltreatment is meager yet compelling in its implications. One example is the 1983 study I referred to earlier by DeViney, Dickert, and Lockwood of 53 New Jersey families meeting state criteria for substantiated child abuse and neglect. All families selected had pets in their homes. Home observations revealed that in 60% of these families, pets were also abused or neglected. Animal abuse was significantly higher (88%) in families where child physical abuse was present than cases where other forms of child maltreatment occurred (34%). One or both parents and their children were responsible for abusing the families' pets.

In a study conducted *before* cruelty to animals was added to the list of symptoms for Conduct Disorder in the *DSM*, Rogeness and his colleagues (Rogeness, Amrung, Macedo, Harris, and Fisher 1986) studied 539 four- to sixteen-year-olds who had been admitted to a psychiatric hospital for diagnosis. Children were categorized into a group that had been abused (physical abuse appeared to be the focus in this study) and neglected, a group that was only neglected, and a group without evidence of either form of maltreatment. The authors found a relation between abuse history and cruelty to animals (most likely scored from chart and record reviews) for boys but not for girls. For the 395 boys, 17% in the abused only and the abused and neglected group were cruel to animals. In contrast, 4% of the neglected only boys and 9% of the boys without maltreatment were reported to be cruel to animals.

The data from studies such as these suggest that there is a greater likelihood that abused children may abuse animals. But we must also remember that many children who are victims of abuse do not strike out at others, either human or animal. For example, in a study of 238 institutionalized juveniles who had been abused, Michael Robin, Robert W. ten Bensel, Joseph Quigley, and Robert K. Anderson (1984) found that "91 percent indicated that they had had a special pet, and of these 72 percent said they loved their pet very much" (p. 113). The authors also report that the pets of abused children were accidentally or intentionally killed nearly three times more often (34%) than the pets of non-abused children (12%) (pp. 114–115). Pets were also reported to have been mistreated: 17% were abused by the juveniles but 21% by others. But these data suggest that pets were not mistreated by 83% of these abused young people.

In chapter 7, I referred to a study by Miller and Knutson (1997) that reported on the relation between prison inmates' early experiences and histories of animal abuse. The respondents were also asked whether they had used physical or sexual coercion in their relationships with intimate partners, for example, dating partners or spouses. The authors assessed physical punishment experienced in childhood with a 12-item scale with questions ranging from spanking to being punched, kicked, or choked. Some of the items clearly relate to physical abuse definitions since they include being hit with objects and sustaining physical injuries.

As might be expected, for this group of inmates, both childhood experiences of punitive and abusive discipline tended toward the high range as did experience with animal abuse. Because of this lack of spread in the scores, statistically significant relations between factors are more difficult to demonstrate. Nevertheless, Miller and Knutson found that animal abuse experience was positively correlated with physical punishment received and with the inmates' use of physical and sexual coercion in their intimate relationships.

When these authors conducted a similar analysis with a group of 308 college students, they found once again that animal abuse experiences were positively related to physical punishment histories (in this sample, the authors did not report the results for the measures of physical and sexual coercion with intimate partners). Thus, these relations are not unique to criminal samples. But I also caution overextending these findings. Again, I quote VanLeeuwen (1981): ". . . it should be remembered that in many cases child abuse and cruelty to animals are not related because the dynamics are different . . . the existence of child abuse in a family does not automatically mean that animals are also abused" (p. 182).

One of the limitations of this study was that the assessment of animal abuse included items related to the respondent hurting or killing animals as well as items related to the respondent witnessing or being forced to engage in acts of animal abuse (one item also asked about being controlled by another person via threats to hurt or kill an animal), which can be considered forms of emotional abuse (see section below). Therefore, it is difficult to determine whether high scores on the animal abuse survey indicate that the respondent intentionally hurt or killed animals, whether they primarily were exposed to animal abuse perpetrated by others, or some combination of such experiences.

Emotional and psychological maltreatment

> . . . psychological maltreatment is a concerted attack by an adult on a child's development of self and social competence, a *pattern* of psychically destructive behavior . . . (Garbarino et al. 1986, p. 8)

All of us, at one time, have experienced the sting of rejection, the loneliness of isolation from others, the shame of being exploited, or, perhaps, even the immobilizing effect of being terrorized. For most of us, these experiences may be isolated events, infrequent, and embedded within an overall life history of acceptance, nurturing interactions, and abiding security. Unfortunately, for some children, psychological maltreatment may be an everyday experience, a devastating backdrop against which children attempt to survive and cope. Recall the case of Mary Ellen described at the beginning of this book. Yes, she was a victim of extreme physical abuse. But she was also isolated, neglected, rejected, and terrorized. As we will see, emotional abuse can occur in families with or without pets. However, when pets are in a home, threats against them or their actual mistreatment can be one more vehicle by which a child is psychologically abused.

My colleague Dr. Barbara Boat, quoting a psychiatrist, provides a vivid example: "That reminds me of a patient I had who is a Vietnam vet. He said that he went through hell in the war and can deal with that. But what he cannot deal with is his father killing his dog when he was a kid" (1999, p. 83).

As you might imagine, defining and detecting emotional and psychological maltreatment is challenging since such abuse may not leave physically visible signs. Despite this challenge, researchers and clinicians have done their best to define the various ways that children may be psychologically abused. One of the clearest treatments of this topic is N.J. Binggeli, S.N. Hart, and M.R. Brassard's *Psychological maltreatment of children* (2001). They elaborate on what has become a standard set of categories that capture the range of psychologically abusive caregiving practices (pp. 6–7). I will briefly describe a number of these, quoting Binggeli, Hart, and Brassard's definitions, and illustrate ways that pets may be implicated.

Spurning reflects a pattern of caretaker behavior that represents hostilely rejecting and degrading a child. One form of spurning is "shaming and/or ridiculing a child for showing normal emotions such as affection, grief , or sorrow." In Michael Mewshaw's *Life for Death* (1980), the author describes a father's (Pat Dresbach) insensitivity to the attachment his young son, Wayne, has developed for a litter of kittens (pp. 109–110) and his complete insensitivity to and discounting of his son's fear and grief related to the fate of the kittens:

> But one weekend morning his father scooped the kittens into a paper sack, picked up the .22, and headed out the back door. Worried, Wayne went with him.
>
> Wayne: "I thought we were going to give them away."
>
> Pat: "I'm tired of waiting. Tired of them whining all night and stinking up the house."
>
> At the creek Dresbach rolled the top of the bag tight, then tossed it into the shallow water. While the kittens screeched and pawed to get out, and Wayne sobbed for him not to do it, his father took aim and emptied the rifle. At that range he couldn't miss. The slugs tore the sack to pieces, and blood poured out in trickles, then in a great rush as the bottom gave way.
>
> Wayne wanted to bury the kittens, but Pat told him not to bother. Dogs and buzzards would take care of them.

Terrorizing is a form of psychological maltreatment that includes placing a child in dangerous situations, threatening the child with physical harm and/or abandonment, and threatening to harm or actually harming a child's loved ones or objects.

Although Binggeli and his colleagues do not specifically refer to animals in their definition, it is clear that, especially if a child is attached to pets, animals may be among the "loved ones" threatened. Richard Gelles and Murray Straus (1988) recount a case: "Bill (the father) rarely spanked Cindy. When he did, it was rather mild. But his other punishments were extraordinarily cruel. Cindy's clearest childhood memory was of her father shooting her pet cat" (p. 119). In the example of Wayne Dresbach and the kittens I described in the previous paragraph, not only were Wayne's empathy and sympathy for the kittens belittled, we could also assume that seeing one's father commit such a horrible attack would be terrorizing.

One other relevant form of psychological maltreatment is *exploiting and corrupting* a child. These forms of abuse include modeling and encouraging antisocial behavior and forcing developmentally inappropriate responsibilities on a child. A parent who beats a dog into submission and then requires his or her child to implement the same form of "discipline" corrupts that child. In the next chapter, I describe the case of the Thompson family and the father's forcing his daughters to kill a cat. I will also discuss forced bestiality and note that in some cases, caregivers may photograph, film, or make videos of such exploitation to sell as pornography.

Psychological abuse involving animals can also take a symbolic form. Dr. Barbara Boat describes a young woman who reported being terrorized by her brother when she was a child. Once, upon entering her bedroom one afternoon after returning from school, she found that her brother had tied a noose around the necks of her stuffed animals and suspended them from the ceiling.

Adult caregivers are not the only family members who may be psychologically abusive. Vernon R. Wiehe, perhaps best known for calling the professional community's attention to the significance of sibling abuse, describes a number of examples of children and adolescents using pets as a vehicle for psychologically maltreating their siblings (1997b, p. 54):

> "My second oldest brother shot my little dog that I loved dearly. It loved me—only me. I cried by its grave for several days. Twenty years passed before I could care for another dog."
>
> "My older brother would come to my room and tear up my toys. He would beat my dog after tying his legs together and wrapping a cloth around its mouth to tie it shut. My brother would tell me I was stupid and say, 'Why me, why me? Why did I get a sister so stupid and dumb?'"
>
> "He took my pet frog and stabbed it to death in front of me while I begged him not to. Then he just laughed!"

The abuse of animals as a form of psychological maltreatment may be more common than we know. And children who have the strongest attachments to their pets may be those most devastated by their injury or death. In contrast, Celia Doyle has described the buffering and supportive role that pets may play for victims of emotional abuse (2001). Five of the fourteen adults she interviewed reported that pets were a source of comfort during the time these adults were emotionally abused.

A form of abuse reported less frequently than physical or emotional maltreatment is sexual abuse. The next chapter examines this equally disturbing form of maltreatment and the way that animal abuse may be implicated.

CHAPTER 9

Sexual abuse and animal abuse

No other topic seems as capable of capturing our attention and concern than the sexual molestation and abuse of children and adolescents. Sexual abuse encompasses a variety of practices that are judged morally wrong in our culture and that may lead to severe physical and psychological injury in young people. What follows is only a partial listing of the types of sexual behavior to which children may be subjected:

- Fondling an infant's genitals (as distinct from appropriate hygienic practices)
- Intrusive "care taking" practices that may result in injury to an infant's or older child's genital or anal areas (e.g., unneeded enemas, digital inspection of a child's vagina)
- Exhibitionism in which an adult derives sexual gratification from exposing their genitals to another
- Female genital mutilation in which a girl's clitoris is partially or completely cut away and/or her labia are cut and sewn together
- Oral stimulation of a child's genitals or forcing a child to orally stimulate an adult's
- Exposing a child to pornographic media
- Anal intercourse
- Vaginal intercourse
- Forcing a child into sexual activity with animals

I could also add to this list new forms of sexual abuse that have resulted from advances in computer-based technologies. For example, the internet and world wide web are remarkable sources of information, communication, and entertainment for children and adults alike. Yet, as with other technologies, the potential for their misuse and abuse always lurks behind the next keystroke.

In 1997, we learned about 15-year-old Sam Manzie, who met a convicted pedophile in an internet chat room, later having a number of sexual encounters with this 43-year-old man (Bellafante 1997). Eventually, the police learned of the abuse and enlisted Manzie as an informant to obtain evidence on the abuser. Although there were signs of psychological disturbance in this adolescent—his parents attempted to have him committed to a residential treatment facility—it would have been difficult to predict the violence he eventually perpetrated. An 11-year-old, Edward Werner, trying to sell candy and wrapping paper for a school fund-raiser, knocked on Manzie's door. Two days later, Edward's body was found in nearby woods. He had been sexually assaulted and strangled to death.

This is obviously an extreme example of the potential dangers of the internet and, I should emphasize, the sexual assault of children existed long before computers became common household appliances. Less dramatic and severe computer-based dangers may be much more common. Children may be sexually harassed when they participate in internet chat rooms (Finkelhor, Mitchell, and Wolak 2000) and typing in seemingly benign or incorrect search terms can take a child to disturbing adult pornographic websites. Let me give an example of the latter.

In a college class I teach on abuse and family violence, I have the luxury of a classroom equipped with a computer and university internet connection. As a class demonstration, I have asked my students to imagine that they are 6 years old and preparing for a show-and-tell opportunity for school tomorrow. This 6-year-old, not surprisingly, loves animals and decides it would be a great idea to take pictures of his favorite types of animals to share with classmates. Again, not surprisingly, this child is already a computer and internet aficionado and his or her parents have a color printer to boot. After logging on, the child accesses a search engine and types in "*animal pictures.*" Although a number of legitimate nature, zoological, pet or companion animal, and photography websites will be listed, it is not uncommon for these innocent search terms to yield websites that contain X-rated adult pornography that includes depictions of bestiality. And if the child's curiosity prompts him or her to enter one of these sites, it may be difficult to escape direction to additional pornographic sites without ending the internet session or rebooting the computer! The challenges for parents to provide appropriate supervision for their children seem to get more and more complex and demanding.

Although a recent report indicates that the incidence of substantiated cases of child sexual abuse declined during the 1990s (from a high of 149,800 in 1992), there were still 103,600 cases of child sexual maltreatment in 1998 (Jones and Finkelhor

2001). While this is encouraging news, far too many young people in our society continue to be victims of inappropriate sexual activity.

Children and sexual behavior—what's normal? I use the term "inappropriate" purposely because children may engage in sexual behavior *with other children*, behavior that is often related to curiosity and exploration and very different from the coercive and exploitive sexual interactions that significantly older children or adults may force, however gently, on young children. A parent may ask, "But how do I tell if what my child (or a neighbor's) is doing sexually is normal or something I should be worried about?" Thankfully, research and clinical experience with children are providing answers to this understandable and complex question.

Toni Cavanagh Johnson is a highly respected clinician who has worked for decades with young victims of sexual abuse and with children who act out in sexually inappropriate ways. In 1999, she published *Understanding Your Child's Sexual Behavior: What's Natural and Healthy*, which provides guidelines, for parents and other caregivers, by which to judge the normalcy of sexual behavior for children at various developmental stages. In a series of charts (pp. 52–57) divided into two age groups (preschoolers and children in kindergarten through fourth grade), Johnson gives specific examples of behaviors that may be considered normal or typical for children of a certain age, those that should raise parental concern, and, finally, behaviors that should prompt parents to seek professional assessment of their children. As I will discuss in more detail below, sexual behavior with animals is listed by Johnson as one of a number of behaviors warranting professional intervention.

We now know that children are more likely to be sexually abused by people they know or members of their own family than by strangers lurking at bus stops or parks. As we learn more about sexual abuse in families and in the other settings in which children spend much of their time, for example, day care facilities, we find that animal abuse may sometimes be an element of these abusive scenarios. Let me illustrate with two cases.

The Thompson family. In Alexandra Artley's book *Murder in the Heart* (1993), we are introduced to the Thompson family—Mrs. Thompson (Hilda) and Tommy Thompson, the mother and father, and their two daughters, June and Hilda. In 1988, the daughters were convicted of killing their father with a shotgun. Through extensive interviews with this family, their relatives, and neighbors, Artley constructs a picture of the terror-filled and abusive context in which this murder takes place, a picture whose elements include domestic violence, physical and sexual abuse, and the torture and killing of animals.

Tommy and Hilda became Mr. and Mrs. Thompson in 1951 and his physical and emotional assaults on his wife began just days after their honeymoon and continued throughout their marriage. Tommy was obsessed with order and control and often used violence to insure that his demands and expectations were met. In 1952, their first daughter, June, was born, followed soon after by daughter Hilda.

As the girls grew up, they obviously witnessed the abuse their mother was subjected to, sometimes ". . . standing on either side of their mother to prevent her from falling when their father put his boots on to kick her in the shin or punch her in the face" (p. x). The girls quickly learned that if they protested or tried to intervene, their mother would be even more viciously abused. The girls themselves were not immune from their father's violence. He once held daughter Hilda's hand next to a coal fire until she screamed. Hilda described how her dad would "head butt us on the back of the head where he knew the bruises wouldn't show" (p. 6). In describing the various forms of abuse to which Tommy Thompson subjected his wife and daughters, Artley observes, "cruelty, rather than brutality, is a form of human endeavor which is capable of almost infinite refinement" (p. 94).

Animals were not safe in the Thompson home either. Tommy trained their pet dog, Beauty, to perform typical animal tricks but also to run to him, on command, across a busy road. After almost being hit by a car one night, Beauty was relinquished to a pet shop by Mrs. Thompson, who feared for the dog's life (pp. 145–146). Even more bizarre and sadistic was his nearly killing the girls' goldfish by dumping them in the sink, letting them thrash about for awhile, then returning them to their bowl. Or the time he held a canary under a gas vent and when it began to lose consciousness, would wave it back and forth in the fresh air of an open window to revive it (p. 147). Artley notes that this was reminiscent of the times Tommy would strangle his wife and then release her.

Family pets were not only tortured, they were killed. On one occasion, Tommy was upset with the family cat, made his wife fill a pottery container with water, and stuffed the cat into an empty flour sack. June and Hilda were called to watch the lesson their father was about to teach. He then plunged the sack into the water. Not satisfied with this, he next commanded his terrified daughter Hilda to put the lid on the container and hold it against the cat's futile attempts to escape (pp. 149–150).

When June Thompson was 12 years old, Mr. Thompson raped her. His sexual assaults continued each week until June was a 36-year-old woman (p. 152). June's silence about her abuse was guaranteed by Tommy's threats to shoot everyone in the family (p. 168) if they ever revealed the nature of their family life. When young Hilda reached the age at which June had been first assaulted, Mr. Thompson attempted to rape her as well but, for reasons that are unclear, did not pursue her sexually ever again. Artley suggests that June's "compliance" with her father's rapes was to divert his attention from her younger sister, a not uncommon phenomenon in families where incest is present.

After killing their father and calling the police, June and Hilda were arrested and charged with murder. Mrs. Thompson was charged with conspiracy to murder, a charge of which she was later acquitted. The daughters pled guilty to manslaughter and were sentenced to two years in prison. The judge suspended the sentence, and June and Hilda returned home to their mother (p. 247).

The life of Mary Bell. In 1968 in Newcastle, England, within the space of three months, 4-year-old Martin Brown and 3-year-old Brian Howe were murdered. The perpetrators were apprehended, charged, and their trial began in December of that same year. The defendants were unrelated girls who shared the same surname—13-year-old Norma Bell and 10-year-old Mary Bell. In a chilling narrative (*The Case of Mary Bell*—I'll refer to this book as CMB) provided by well-known writer and biographer Gitta Sereny (1972), we eventually learn that Norma was found not guilty but Mary, judged the leader of the two, was convicted and sentenced to detention for life.

Murder by strangulation, murder of a child, murder by a child. The accumulation of these three phrases shatters our beliefs and expectations about the innocence of childhood, a time when children should be playmates, not perpetrators and victims. In the face of crimes so vicious, victims so vulnerable, and a perpetrator so young, we are often quick to demonize a child like Mary Bell, label her a "bad seed," and move on to less disturbing issues. Describing her as suffering from a psychopathic personality, the psychiatric diagnosis she received during her trial, helps to categorize her but does little to help us understand how a child becomes capable of murder. But, as Sereny asks in her first book on this case, "Are we still not beyond the point where we call sick children monsters and believe in evil birth?" (1972, p. xv).

During the trial, while Mary Bell was in custody, an animal abuse incident again emerges as an indicator of this child's serious disturbance. Although Mary had a pet dog she reportedly loved, her devotion to animals may not have extended to other species. During her detention and while supervised by a policewoman, Mary watched a cat outside her window and asked the policewoman if she could entice it into the room. The policewoman agreed, the cat was brought in, and Mary began to play with it. But play soon changed into behavior more ominous. As the policewoman relates, ". . . I realized she was holding the cat so tight it could not breathe and its tongue was lolling." After the woman rescued the cat from Mary's hands, telling her that the cat could be injured, Mary's response was, "Oh, she doesn't feel that, and, anyway, I like hurting little things that can't fight back" (1972, p. 84).

In her first book on this tragedy, *The Case of Mary Bell,* Sereny provides detailed coverage of the trial and laments that the circumstances of Mary Bell's birth and early childhood were never addressed in the testimony that led to her conviction and sentencing. Sereny was able to glean some information about Mary Bell's history for her first book and supplemented this extensively in *Cries Unheard. Why Children Kill: The Story of Mary Bell* (Sereny 1998). The more recent book is, in part, based on personal interviews Sereny conducted with the adult Mary Bell. The material that follows is derived from both these sources.

Mary Flora Bell was born to her mother Betty on May 26, 1957. When her newborn daughter was first brought to her bedside, Betty said, "Take the 'thing' away from me," refusing to touch her child (1972, p. 193). Betty married her boyfriend, Billy, within a year of Mary's birth.

During her first few years of life, Mary would "accidentally" ingest her mother's medications on two separate occasions, was nearly dropped out of a window by her mother, and at one point was nearly given up for adoption by her mother. Betty was also a victim of domestic violence at the hands of Billy, a factor that may have further overwhelmed her capacity to care for Mary. Mary's interactions with her own peers were no better. She would attack other children, on occasion trying to strangle them, and once did this to a newborn baby she saw in a carriage. And Mary's aunt Audrey reported that Mary ". . . killed pigeons by throttling them" (1972, p. 214). (After the trial, and during her incarceration at one facility, hamsters would die of neck injuries while she was "caring" for them [1972, p. 241].)

In hindsight, Mary's early childhood appeared to be an accumulation of risk factors, stresses that a child may be exposed to which, individually, may not seriously affect a child's development. But when the individual risks are combined, there comes a point where a child may no longer be able to cope. Mary was born to an adolescent mom (Betty may have had serious psychological problems already), there appeared to be no healthy attachment between mother and daughter, domestic violence may have further impaired Betty's caregiving abilities, poor supervision or intentional neglect almost killed Mary on at least two occasions, and, as we will soon learn, Mary was the victim of even more insidious forms of abuse. Her lashing out at other children and at animals should have been a clear signal of a child in distress. But as the title of Sereny's second book suggests, the cries for help were unheard.

In 1980, after 12 years in detention facilities, one benevolent and focused on therapeutic intervention and rehabilitation, the other a maximum security prison for women, Mary Bell, by that time 23 years of age, was released. Four years after her release, Mary gave birth to a daughter but the relationship that brought forth this child ended for a number of reasons. including domestic violence by Mary's partner. Mary held her daughter right after she was born and protested when the newborn had to be temporarily taken away for cleaning and other routine medical procedures. The daughter was allowed to be raised by Mary and her partner but was considered a ward of the court. Governmental supervision of Mary's daughter was lifted in 1992 when her daughter was 8 years old. Mary, her partner Jim, and Mary's daughter continue to live in England.

Sereny interviewed Mary Bell when she was 41 years old, her daughter an adolescent. Eventually, Mary revealed parts of her childhood history that never saw the light of scrutiny decades earlier during her trial. What Sereny learned was that the dysfunction in Mary's relationship with her mother, Betty, was even more malignant than a poor attachment and neglect would suggest. Betty was a prostitute during Mary's preschool years and Mary was not only present to watch her mother's activities with her clients, which included sadomasochistic beatings, but was forced to be an unwilling participant. Betty would pull Mary's head back by her hair, restrain her arms behind her back, and then allow her male clients to have oral sex with her, ejaculating into her mouth. Sometimes restrained by the neck, Mary would lose consciousness. (Mary later admitted that she had attempted, unsuccessfully, to cut off the penis of one of the boys she had killed.) She was also anally penetrated with objects, again with her mother helping to restrain her. Mary remembered being four or five years old when these episodes occurred. Her mother would give her candies as a reward.

The severity of the sexual abuse endured by June Thompson and Mary Bell strains our credulity. The early lives of these two women read like a gothic horror novel or a story penned by Charles Dickens. But the abuse they experienced occurred not in the distant past of Hogarth's England but just a few decades ago. For those of us who are middle aged, June and Mary are our contemporaries. And as any examination of a daily newspaper or weekly news magazine will show, children continue to be misused sexually in ways too horrible to describe.

Less than two years ago, in Salt Lake City, Andrew Fedorowicz and Ferosa Bluff were convicted of first-degree felony murder, child abuse, and sexual abuse of Bluff's 3-year-old daughter, Rebecca. Injuries on the child's body matched those that would be inflicted by a leather strap and belt buckle as well as a cat-o'-nine-tails whip found at the couple's residence. In addition to injuries on her face, arms, legs, and soles of her feet, Rebecca had bruising around her genitals and buttocks. Fedorowicz was also shown engaging in sadomasochistic sex with his wife in a videotape seized from their home (Hunt 1999).

The stories about June Thompson and Mary Bell are case histories. They are detailed, informative, and allow us an intimate look at the lives of two people over a significant part of their history of development. Case histories, because of these qualities, are part of the research process, the attempt to explain the phenomena of interest. But case histories suffer from questions about whether the findings derived from a small number of individuals can be generalized to larger samples of children.

Beyond case studies. Is there research on the relation between sexual abuse and animal abuse? Recall the data that I presented in chapter 4 that were collected by Friedrich (W. Friedrich, personal communication, April 1992). He and his colleagues were able to study a group of 880 two- to twelve-year-old children who had no history of sexual abuse. These children were typical of those you would find in the waiting rooms of local pediatricians' offices. In addition, 276 children, in the same age range, were recruited but every one of these children was a substantiated victim of sexual abuse. In the majority of cases, the most recent incident of abuse had occurred in the past year. Data from the Child Behavior Checklist (CBC) were available for all these children and had been provided by their mothers or a primary female care giver (e.g., a foster mother). The women who completed the CBC for children in the sexually abused group were *not* the perpetrators of the abuse. This is important to note, since perpetrators might be expected to portray their victims as being more psychologically disturbed and, therefore, as potentially less reliable and trustworthy informants. Or perpetrators might suggest that these "disturbed" children actually initiated the sexual encounters.

Friedrich reported that less than 5% of the non-abused boys and girls were reported to be sometimes or often cruel to animals. In contrast, cruelty to animals was present for 34.8% of the sexually abused boys and 27.5% of the sexually abused girls, rates that are *7 and 8 times higher* than the rates for non-abused children. Clearly, being a victim of sexual abuse places some children at risk for behavioral disturbances that include animal abuse. This heightened risk must, however, be viewed in the context of the significant proportion of sexually abused children who were *not* reported to be cruel to animals.

In some cases, sexually abused children may seek out pets as a source of solace and support (Barker, Barker, Dawson, and Knisely 1997). One example of the power that animals may have to reduce the terror experienced by abused children is provided in Alice Vachss's book *Sex Crimes* (1993b). Vachss, as a prosecutor and chief of a special victims unit in New York City, decided that the unit needed a child-friendly area in which to conduct interviews with victimized children. One of her personal touches was acquiring a retired guide dog, named Sheba, and allowing her to become a part of the interviewing environment. One young girl who had been victimized found Sheba so comforting that she refused to testify unless Sheba was nearby. "With Sheba there to make her feel safe enough, the little girl was able to tell what had been done to her" (p. 172). The strong attachments some abused children have to their pets help us understand how threats against pets could be used to coerce a child into compliance and silence. Roland Summit (1983) mentions this issue in his analysis of the factors that might prevent children from revealing that they have been victimized or prompt them to recant earlier disclosures about their having been abused.

Some children are so seriously debilitated by their experiences of abuse that they may require hospitalization at psychiatric facilities that can provide 24-hour care. Jon McClellan and his colleagues (McClellan, Adams, Douglas, McCurry, and Storck 1995) reviewed the records of 499 patients at one such facility in Washington State. These children ranged in age from 5 to 18 years and suffered from a variety of psychiatric disturbances. Fifty-five percent of these young people also had histories of sexual abuse and 45 percent did not. Being sexually abused was associated with a significantly higher rate of cruelty to animals among these children and adolescents. Put another way, within this large sample of seriously, psychologically impaired children, knowing that a child abused animals helped predict that the child was a victim of sexual abuse.

These relations may eventually help predict adult behavior. In a recent prospective study of 224 men who had been sexually abused as children, Salter and colleagues (Salter et al. 2003) discovered that 26 (12%) of these men, as adults, sexually abused children. Information on histories of animal abuse was available for 21 of these 26 men. Cruelty to animals was present for 29% of the child abusers but only 5% of the men with no evidence of child abuse.

When young people act out sexually. Unfortunately, although some young people may be assaulted sexually, other young people may also be capable of sexually abusing others. The research on juvenile sex offending or children and adolescents who act out sexually is becoming extensive and I refer the reader to Toni Cavanagh Johnson's work mentioned earlier. Comprehensive treatments of this topic can also be found in Gail Ryan and Sandy Lane's *Juvenile Sexual Offending: Causes, Consequences, and Correction* (1997), William Breer's *The Adolescent Molester* (1996), and Howard E. Barbaree, William L. Marshall, and Stephen M. Hudson's *The Juvenile Sex Offender* (1993). Here, I will focus on the implication of animal abuse in cases of juvenile sex offending.

Michelle E. Ford and Jean Ann Linney (1995) studied boys who were juvenile sex offenders and were incarcerated or in residential treatment facilities. Fourteen were considered rapists and had sexually assaulted a peer or adult and 21 were child molesters, sexually assaulting a child or adolescent 5 or more years younger than the perpetrator. The average age of these 35 offenders was between 15 and 16 years. Although the CBC was not used to gather information about behavior problems, offenders were asked to describe their first or earliest childhood experience or memory. Examining the spontaneous recollections that were provided, the researchers found that 1 in 10 of the offenders mentioned being cruel to animals and 17% mentioned a family member killing a pet as one of their earliest memories.

In 1998, Monique Frazier, a former graduate student and current colleague, completed her dissertation on abuse histories and juvenile offending (Frazier 1998). As part of this study of juvenile offenders (whose average age was 15.7 years), she was able to interview 30 sexually violent young people who were either incarcerated in juvenile detention or were in residential treatment programs. When asked if they had ever abused animals, 90% replied that they had and 37% admitted to sexually hurting animals.

A caveat. Children as young as preschool age may act out sexually in inappropriate ways but I do not think that any of us are ready to label them as "juvenile sex offenders." I want to call the reader's attention to efforts that are being made to distinguish children in need of clinical intervention from those whose behavior warrants the involvement of the law enforcement community. Toni Cavanagh Johnson's book deals with this issue by stressing the importance of comprehensive evaluations of children who act out sexually before any decisions are made about therapy or placement. Jan Hindman, well known for her clinical work with sex offenders as well as with child victims of sexual abuse, has developed the *Juvenile Culpability Assessment* (1992). This is a comprehensive assessment of a child's intellectual, social, and sexual characteristics and includes assessment of a child's capacity for empathy, towards both humans and animals. The goal of the assessment is to determine how "criminally" culpable or responsible children can be considered if they have acted out sexually in inappropriate ways against other children. Hindman stresses that we need to determine whether children know that the behavior they are engaging in is wrong *and* what the consequences of their behavior could be; without both of these elements, criminal intent will be difficult to judge. One could wish that Hindman's assessment had been used to evaluate Mary Bell before she was brought to trial.

Much more information is available if we widen our scope to include adult sex offenders. Recall, for example, Tingle et al.'s (1986) study of 64 men who were incarcerated sex offenders (rapists and child molesters). When asked about their early development, 48% of the rapists and 30% of the child molesters admitted to being cruel to animals. In the landmark study conducted as part of the FBI's efforts to develop criminal profiles, Ressler, Burgess, and Douglas (1988) were able to interview 28 men who had been convicted and were incarcerated for serial sexual homicide, perhaps the most chilling form of sex offending. As part of their extensive interviews with these men, the researchers asked about their perpetrating animal abuse in childhood, adolescence, and adulthood. Childhood animal abuse was admitted by 36% of the men, adolescent animal abuse by 46%, and adult animal abuse by 36%. The level of animal abuse in adulthood reminds us again that cruelty to animals is not necessarily a symptom that disappears in adulthood.

Bradley Johnson and Judith Becker recently reported on nine adolescents referred to them for evaluation because they had fantasized about perpetrating serial killings (1997). The adolescents ranged in age from 14–18 years and 8 of the 9 young people were boys. Nearly 50% (4 out of 9) admitted to abusing animals or killing them. Some of the examples these adolescents shared were:

- Shooting animals with a BB gun and then drowning, stabbing, or setting them on fire while still alive.
- Strangling or stabbing animals and keeping their skulls in his room. This boy also admitted to masturbating into the open wound of an animal he had killed.
- Killing dogs by snapping their necks.
- Killing snakes and rabbits with a knife and searching for dead animals and road kill he would later dissect.

Although it is clear that not all children who are cruel to animals will grow up to be the Ted Bundys and Jeffrey Dahmers of the world, animal abuse, especially when severe, seems to be a fairly common feature of young people and adults who are capable of sadistic violence against other human beings.

Sexual behavior with animals. In 1993, when I had just published my first review paper on the issue of cruelty to animals in childhood and adolescence, I opened the morning paper to find an article entitled "Boy; 13, Beats Two Birds to Death at Aviary" (Horiuchi 1993). As I read the article, I learned that this young man, who was in counseling and taking medication, beat an adult female pink flamingo to death on one night and decapitated a 5-week-old Black Neck swan the next night.

In 1989, four years before this incident, the aviary, a usually tranquil facility in a local park, was the scene of another attack (Burton 1999). A rare female breeding crane had been sexually assaulted and killed by a 22-year-old man, Marty Trujillo. He was apprehended but could only be charged with property damage because sexual abuse of animals, or bestiality, had been dropped from Utah's criminal codes when they were revised in 1973. Also, at the time the crane was killed, cruelty to animals in Utah was a Class C misdemeanor, the least serious form of an offense. As a result, in part, of the Trujillo case and the accumulating evidence on the significance of sexual abuse of animals, Utah reinstated bestiality as an offence against "public order and decency" in the Criminal code under the cruelty to animals statutes. In 1994, it became a Class B misdemeanor to have sexual activity with an animal.

Ten years after Marty Trujillo sexually abused and killed the crane, his name was in the news again (Burton 1999). Now he was charged with four counts of first-degree felony sexual assault and one count of first-degree felony aggravated kidnapping in the rape of an 18-year-old woman and the attempted rape of a 16-year-old girl. Found guilty in May of 2000, Trujillo was sentenced to 6 years to life in prison.

The sexual abuse of animals is one form of cruelty that has not received very much attention in the literature. Bestiality may range from touching or fondling the genitals of animals to sexual intercourse and violent sexual abuse. It may be a form of behavior that an individual may actually prefer to sex with humans (Earls and Lalumière 2002) or it may co-occur with the sexual abuse of children (Hill 2000). Some species of animal may be seriously injured or die as a result of the abuse inflicted (e.g., penetration that damages internal organs—[Kattolinsky 1937]), as in the case of the crane described above.

Dr. Jane Gilgun (J. Gilgun, personal communication, August 20, 1996), who is well known for her research on therapeutic work with sex offenders, describes one individual who derived sexual gratification by penetrating chickens. As he penetrated an animal, he would hold the animal's head against the door jamb and slam the door. The chicken, in the throes of death, apparently experienced contractions in its anus and alimentary canal. This gave the man intense sexual pleasure. Imagine the pathological sexual arousal and gratification patterns created by the association of dominance and control of a living creature, sexual assault, and the death of the victim. This individual also had a history of molesting a number of boys and girls. Beetz (2002), Beirne (1997), and Miletski (2002) provide excellent theoretical overviews of the issue of bestiality, but empirical studies, especially with children, are rare. However, we can turn to cases studies for examples, and, in this section, I will limit my discussion to case studies of children.

Sandra Hewitt, well known for her work with young sexual abuse victims (e.g., *Assessing Allegations of Sexual Abuse in Preschool Children: Understanding Small Voices* [1999]), described the case of a 29-month-old boy being evaluated for suspected sexual abuse. Hewitt describes the sexualized behavior displayed by this young child (Hewitt 1990).

> His masturbation would leave him red and raw . . . he was observed holding the dog's head against his crotch so the dog would lick his exposed penis. (pp. 227–228)

Hewitt suggests that though this child's speech was delayed and difficult to understand, his behavior, so unusual for a child this age, was a window on the abuse he most likely had experienced.

Barbara Boat, another respected clinician with expertise on the assessment of traumatized children, provides another case study of a 3½-year-old girl (1991). Allegations of physical and sexual abuse of this child dated from her second birthday. Placed with a foster family that had a pet dog, this child was frightened of being licked and would attack the animal. Later in therapy, when she was about 5 years old, she told the therapist that when she lived with her birth mother and stepfather, a dog had licked her "bottom" and that she had been forced to suck the dog's penis (p. 16). This recollection emerged together with this child's description of the many pets she had lost before her foster placement and a kitten who was mutilated by her stepfather while she watched.

These two case studies illustrate that bestiality may emerge at a very young age—in the first case, as a probable re-enactment of the child's own victimization and, in the second case, as a coerced activity orchestrated by the child's adult perpetrator. And bestiality may not be confined to the traumatic play of preschoolers.

In a case study from Germany, Wiegand, Schmidt, and Kleiber (1999) reported on an 11-year-old boy hospitalized with anal injuries. The boy had himself called emergency services saying he had fallen down while playing and his pants had been pulled down in the process. According to the boy, his "German Shepherd dog mounted him and penetrated him with his penis" (p. 324). Understandably, the police suspected the boy may have been sexually abused by two of his male relatives. Lab tests of the boy at the hospital and a veterinary test of the dog confirmed that the boy had actually been penetrated by the animal. The police could not confirm any involvement of the suspected male relatives and weeks later, the boy admitted to a psychologist that he had manually aroused the dog and "caused the animal to penetrate him" (p. 325). No further clinical information was provided about this child's history.

Some might suggest that bestiality committed without injury of or violence to the animal might be considered a distasteful but harmless activity. However, I judge that animals, just as is the case with children, cannot give consent to sexual activity to humans. We could compare an animal being sexually abused to a nonverbal infant or young toddler being fondled—neither is capable of understanding their victimization or of disclosing it to a third party.

At times, adult human "participants" in bestiality may have been coerced. Holly Rice (H. Rice, personal communication, October 28, 1999; Montminy-Danna and Rice 1999) related the case of a man who forced his wife to have sex with a dog, videotaped the interactions, and then used the videotape as a threat. If she ever considered telling anyone about being a victim of battering, he threatened that he would show their children the video.

Lane (1997) notes that juvenile sex offending may include bestiality, sometimes combined with other violent behavior toward animal victims. Adolescent sexual offenders may also use threats of harm to pets as a way of gaining compliance from their human victims (Kaufman, Hilliker, and Daleiden 1996). Such threats have also been reported in studies of sexual abuse in day care settings (Finkelhor, Williams, and Burns 1988; Waterman, Kelly, Oliveri, and McCord 1993). In the study, cited earlier (Ressler et al. 1988), with serial sexual homicide perpetrators, 40% of the men who said they had been sexually abused in childhood or adolescence reported having sexual contact with animals. Itzin (1998) reports anecdotal case material in which bestiality was forced on children who were also sexually abused by adults and involved in the production of child pornography. One of the victims, now an adult, was devastated by the thought that such photographic and video depictions of her as a child might surface and be seen by people she now knew as an adult.

Although it is challenging to obtain information about sexual behavior from children and adolescents, especially sexual behavior with animals, William Friedrich (1997) provides some information on this issue with data obtained with his Child Sexual Behavior Inventory (CSBI). The CSBI was designed to survey caregivers about a number of sexual behaviors that might be displayed by children of varying ages. One of the goals of developing this assessment instrument was to differentiate children's sexual behavior that could be considered normal and behavior that could be judged abnormal, given the age of the child. Caregivers of 1,114 non-abused (normative group) and 512 sexually abused children reported on a variety of sexual or sexualized behaviors in their 2- to 12-year-old children, including one item asking about whether the child "touches animal's sex parts." The CSBI has been shown to differentiate groups of children who have been sexually abused from those with no history of sexual abuse.

Caregivers' (who were *not* the perpetrators for the sexually abused group) responses to the "touches animal's sex part" item are shown in Figure 9.1. Although this behavior is most common among preschool age children, it is relatively infrequent overall (it is reported for less than 12% of children). However, it is clear that, for the two older age groupings (children 6–9 and 10–12 years old), sexually abused children are more likely to display this behavior than non-abused children, And although it appears that "touches animal's sex parts" declines for sexually abused 10–12 year olds, we might speculate that the decrease is accounted for, in part, by a greater secretiveness in acting out sexually with animals in older children. The decrease may also be related to older children moving from animal to human victims of inappropriate sexual activity. We could test whether these explanations are valid by asking young people to report on their own behavior. As you might imagine, because of the obviously sensitive nature of the topic, trying to obtain young children's *self-reports* about sexual behavior presents ethical and other challenges (e.g., securing parental permission).

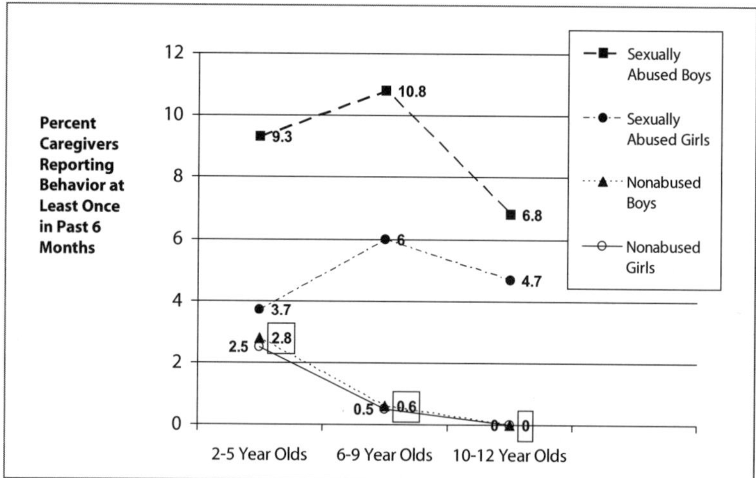

FIGURE 9.1. Responses to item 14, "Touches Animal's Sex Parts" from Friedrich (1997) Child Sexual Behavior Inventory.

Further evidence for the sexual abuse/bestiality relation is provided by Wherry, Jolly, Feldman, Adam, and Manjanatha (1995). They administered the CSBI to caregivers of 24 six- to twelve-year-old boys who were psychiatric inpatients. Eight of these boys had been sexually abused. "Touches animal's sex parts" was reported for 50% of abused boys but for none of non-abused boys. Although this study involved a small sample of children, it illustrates how the incidence of this behavior may be substantially higher in some clinically disturbed groups of children. It's also likely that since the children studied by Wherry et al. were *inpatients,* that is, had actually been hospitalized, they may represent a more disturbed sample than the sexually abused children in Friedrich's (1997) report on the CSBI.

Studying the self-reports of 381 institutionalized, juvenile male offenders whose average age was 16.9 years, Fleming, Jory, and Burton (2002) found that 6% admitted to bestiality, 42% admitted to sex offenses against humans, and 51% denied either type of offending. Twenty-three of the 24 offenders admitting to bestiality also reported offending against humans.

A study by Zolondek, Abel, Northey, and Jordan (2001) of 11- to 17-year-old juvenile sex offenders specifically asked them if they had engaged in sexual behavior with animals. The authors also included a measure of "social desirability" in the study, which taps the respondent's willingness to admit to violations of social norms and morals. The participants with the lowest social desirability scores (that is, the ones most willing to admit to violating social norms) had the highest rate of admitting to bestiality—12.8%. Although this is higher than the rates reported in Friedrich's study, it should be remembered that Friedrich's sample included sexual abuse victims, not necessarily perpetrators, that the Zolondek et al. sample was older than Friedrich's, and Zolondek and colleagues gathered self-reports, not caregiver reports. This may be another example of caregivers underestimating a problem behavior in their children.

I add one caution about the interpretation of these self-report data based on a recent study. English, Jones, Patrick, and Paini-Hill (2003) interviewed 180 adult sex offenders most of whom had been convicted of crimes against children. Information derived from case records was compared with information provided by the men *after treatment programs that included the use of polygraphs ("lie detectors").* Case records revealed that 4.4% of the men had engaged in bestiality but 36.1% admitted to bestiality when polygraphs were used. Twenty-seven percent of men who *only* committed offenses against family members or relatives admitted to bestiality; 56.7% of men whose victims included both family and non-family members reported engaging in bestiality. Offenders may not always be willing to provide accurate information about this behavior.

Perhaps it would be wise, at this point, to emphasize that children's natural curiosity about their own sexuality and that of others may sometimes lead them to explore the sexual parts of animals. These could be considered "teachable moments" for talking with young children about genitals and inappropriate and respectful touch. We should remember that touching animals' sex parts may be common and normative for some infants and toddlers, as is interest in animals' sexual anatomy and behavior (Sandnabba, Santtila, Wannäs, and Krook 2003). As a colleague once mentioned, when children at this age encounter an orifice, they often try to stick something into it! However, if this behavior continues beyond the preschool years, if it is accompanied by physical harm or injury to the animal, or if it persists despite a parent's efforts to educate the child about the behavior's unacceptability, professional consultation may be the wisest step to take. Bestiality may be associated with a history of victimization but it may also be related to exposure to bestiality in computer-based images (Mehta 2001) or bestiality practiced by adults in the child's home (Sandnabba et al. 2002).

ALTHOUGH THE READER MAY JUDGE I have already devoted too much attention to this unpleasant and disturbing topic, I must warn you that this issue will emerge again when we turn our attention to domestic violence in the next chapter.

Children who suffer stressful life circumstances may be especially vulnerable to abusing animals. The nonchalance of the child observing this animal abuse is equally disturbing. Photograph © Kari René Hall, *Beyond the Killing Fields,* Aperture and Asia 2000 Ltd., New York, 1992.

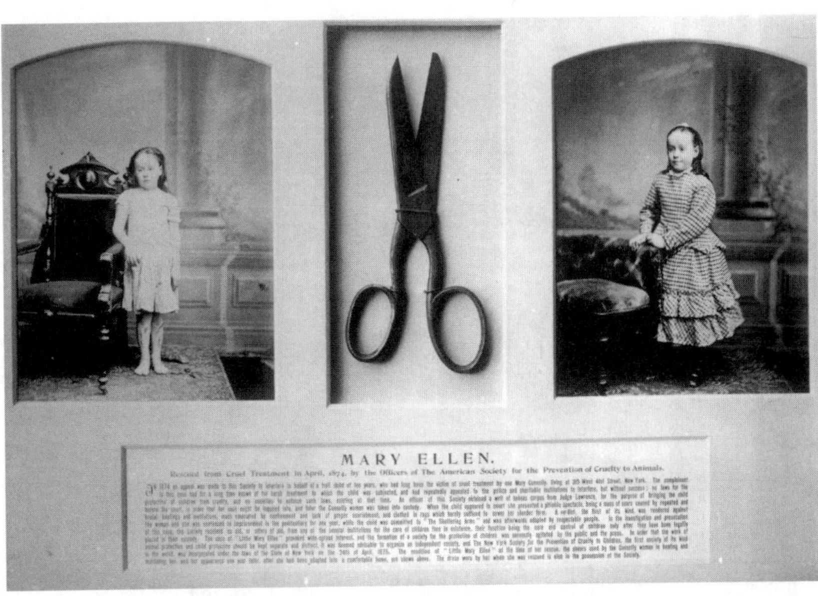

The Mary Ellen case is legendary in the history of social work and represented one of the earliest collaborations between animal welfare and child welfare organizations.

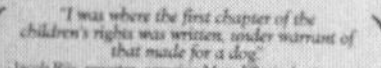

HER PARENTS TREATED HER LIKE AN ANIMAL. TO SAVE HER, SO DID HER RESCUERS.

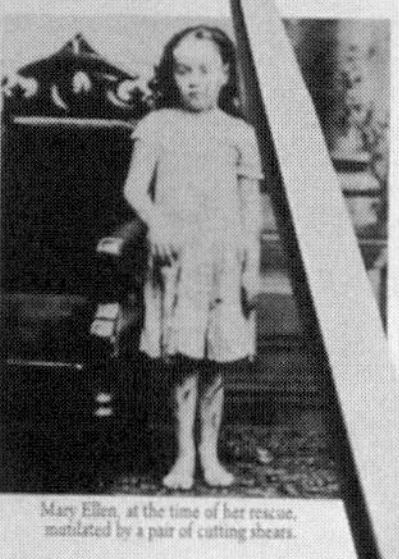

Mary Ellen, at the time of her rescue, mutilated by a pair of cutting shears.

She was beaten, whipped, starved and slashed from head to toe with a pair of cutting shears.

Yes, she was treated like an animal. And to save her, she had to be treated as if she were an animal.

Let us explain.

In 1875, there were laws against animal abuse. There were, however, no laws against child abuse.

Which meant, in effect, it was okay to beat a child to death, but not a dog.

Unbelieveable, isn't it?

Therefore, to rescue this poor child, Henry Bergh, the founder of the New York Society for the Prevention of Cruelty to Animals, acted as if she was, literally, an animal.

As he remarked, "Since there is no justice for her as a human being, she shall have the rights of a cat on the streets."

It was the beginning of the children's rights movement, and the catalyst for the formation of the first child protection agencies—agencies which eventually became part of our organization.

And who are we? We're the American Humane Association, the first and only national organization committed to protecting children and animals.

And one of the many, many things we do is work aggressively to protect children from such cruelty and neglect.

Specifically, through our child protection division, we work to build effective response systems in every community in the country.

We continually push for more effective public policies to protect children.

We provide formalized training for child welfare professionals.

We publish *the* most widely used training manual for child protective services.

We act as a clearinghouse for any question about child abuse.

We will, in short, do anything and everything we can to make the world a safer place for children.

For more information on what we do to make sure neither children nor animals are treated cruelly, or to make a contribution, call 1-800-227-5242.

Or write: The American Humane Association, 63 Inverness Drive East, Englewood, CO 80112-5117.

1877
AHA established the first national organization to protect animals.

1885
AHA also dedicated its effort to child welfare.

1914
Originated "Be Kind To Animals Week."

1916
Emergency Animal Relief Fund established, the only one of its kind.

1939
The first to protect animals in the entertainment industry.

1990
First with National Cruelty Investigations School.

Mary Ellen, one year after she was rescued.

AMERICAN HUMANE ASSOCIATION

Photograph of Mary Ellen exhibit and poster courtesy of American Humane.

CHAPTER 10

The family: Safe haven or landscape of terror?

> **W**omen are more likely to be permanently injured, scarred, or even killed by their husbands in societies in which animals are treated cruelly, criminals are subjected to physical punishment, enemy captives are tortured, men and women solve conflicts violently, girls are subjected to painful initiation ceremonies, and military glory is a source of male pride. (Levinson 1989, p. 45)

Pets were terribly important to her, they were her only source of comfort and affection. One afternoon, Billy said he had had it with her damn cats and started screaming that he was going to kill them. Kim didn't take it too seriously." (Browne 1997, p. 154)

Aubrey got angry with the family dog for straying outside their yard. He loaded one of his nine guns, then shot and killed it. The kids began to sob, devastated. He grabbed [one child's] hair . . . slapped another of the kids, then began crying himself. Joyce tried to comfort them all. But her feelings of anger were mixed with genuine terror: in a moment of rage, she knew, Aubrey could kill any one of them and cry about it afterward. (Walker 1989, pp. 20–21)

A vivid example of the confluence of spouse battering, child abuse (emotional and physical), and cruelty to animals is provided in recent

> reports of a murder trial in Salt Lake City. 'Peggy Sue Brown was acquitted Thursday of fatally shooting her husband—the first time a defendant has used battered women's syndrome as a defense in a Utah murder case" (Hunt 1996). "Brown testified she killed her husband after he beat, raped and locked her in a closet for days without food or water during their seven-year marriage. She said Bradley Brown, 23, had made her a virtual prisoner in their home. He also beat and terrorized their young children" (p. B8). One of Ms. Brown's children testified that Mr. Brown had on one occasion kicked her one year old brother into a wall.
>
> The level of terror Mr. Brown apparently instilled in his family members is illustrated by another incident noted during the trial. "(He) hung a pet rabbit in the garage and summoned his wife. When she came with the baby on her shoulder, her husband began skinning the animal alive. Then he held the boy next to the screaming rabbit. 'See how easy it would be?' Bradley said" (Ascione 1998, pp. 129–130).

The domestic violence literature is filled with stories, anecdotes, and case studies similar to those you just read. Animal abuse seems to be the rule rather than the exception in families where men seriously abuse and maltreat their intimate partners. Research on this issue, however, is still in its infancy, with most studies appearing in the past 7 years.

How common is domestic violence? The results of a variety of recent surveys suggest that "at least 1.8 million women are severely beaten by their intimate partners every year in the United States" (Mahoney, Williams, and West 2001, p. 143). And "as many as half a million children may be encountered by police during domestic violence arrests each year" (Jacobsen 2000, p. 7). We do not know how many other children are exposed to domestic violence in cases where there is no police involvement. The terrible effects of seeing or hearing parents come to blows are captured in a memory of childhood shared by the late Philip Hallie: "During their almost nightly battles my younger brother and I cowered in a corner. We were afraid that they might kill each other, or that he might leave us and we would starve to death. The feeling my brother and I shared was fear. We seemed to be part of a war to the death, a war whose purpose we did not understand" (Hallie 1997, pp. 9–10).

Humans and pets in danger. Although my search through the domestic violence literature revealed many anecdotes about the abuse of family pets, I could only fine one study that addressed this as a research issue. In 1992, Claire M. Renzetti published *Violent Betrayal: Partner Abuse in Lesbian Relationships.* Of the 100 women who voluntarily completed questionnaires for Renzetti, 38% of those with pets reported that their partner had abused the animals. Renzetti also noted that increases in women's desire for greater independence and the relationship conflict this created was associated with increased pet abuse (Renzetti 1992). And Lenore E. Walker, in her classic book, *The Battered Woman Syndrome,* had written, ". . . the best predictor of future violence was a history of past violent behavior. This included . . . violent acts toward pets" (Walker 1984, pp. 10–11).

I also found that checklists used by researchers and domestic violence agencies to estimate how dangerous a batterer might be sometimes included questions about animal or pet abuse, but other times did not. The most current federal guidelines for research on domestic violence still do not include any questions about batterers abusing pets or other animals (Salzman, Fanslow, McMahon, and Shelley 1999). And only one questionnaire, that I am aware of, includes a specific question about whether a woman was "required to be involved with an animal in a sexual way" (Dutton 1992), an issue also noted by Angela Browne in her book *When Battered Women Kill* (1997).

In 1997, Claudia Weber, David Wood, and I surveyed one of the largest domestic violence shelters in each of the 50 states, except Utah, and the District of Columbia. The shelters we selected had to have residential facilities that could house women and children and they also had to provide some form of services for children (e.g., day care, play groups, therapy). We were fortunate that 96% of the shelter directors or staff members familiar with shelter programs whom we contacted agreed to complete our questionnaire.

We found that the vast majority (85.4%) of the respondents reported that they had encountered women who talked about pet abuse incidents and 63% reported that children accompanying their mothers also described incidents where their fathers, stepfathers, or mothers' boyfriends had abused animals. Despite the fact that 83.3% of the respondents believed that domestic violence and animal abuse often co-occur in the same family, only 27.1% of the respondents reported that the shelter included in its intake interviews questions about pets and their treatment. Given the chaos that women fleeing violence are experiencing and shelter staff's focus on women's safety, it is understandable that questions about animal abuse may be neglected. However, I also suspect that another reason for failing to ask women about their pets is that many shelters may feel ill-equipped to deal with this further complication. It's difficult to ask someone a question when you are not sure how you can respond to their answer.

Beyond anecdotes. Because of my interest in these issues and the lack of information about how common pet abuse is in the context of domestic violence, I decided to conduct a pilot study with colleagues who operated a shelter for women who were battered. And because I knew that women entering shelter are in crisis, I purposely designed a simple questionnaire and asked shelter staff to be the judge of when to best approach women about completing it. The questionnaire and pilot study had already been approved by a research ethics committee at my university but we also stressed the voluntary nature of participation to women and secured their informed consent before proceeding.

I approached this project with two primary questions. First of all, how common is keeping pets among women who flee to domestic violence shelters? I had a preconceived notion that being able to care for pets might be too stressful in the chaos of a violent home and expected pet ownership to be low. Second, if women did have pets, how common were threats of harm and actual cases of abuse or killing of pets? Threats to hurt or kill animals should be considered a significant form of psychological abuse (Brassard, Hart, and Hardy 1993). Given Renzetti's research and the anecdotal reports, I expected a significant minority of women would report that their partners abused pets.

In 1998, I reported the results of this interview study of 38 women volunteers who were battered and had sought shelter at a facility in Utah designed to house and provide support for women fleeing a violent partner (Ascione 1998). Fifty-eight percent of the women had children and 74% had pets. My first preconception about pet ownership had been wrong. Pet ownership for these women was comparable to the level for typical samples of women in the United States who have families with school-aged children (Albert and Bulcroft 1988).

When the women were asked whether their adult partners had ever threatened or actually hurt of killed one or more of their pets, 71% of women with pets responded "yes." Thirty-two percent of women with children reported that their children had hurt or killed one or more family pets. Note that this rate of cruelty to animals is higher than the estimates I described in chapter 3 on Child Behavior Checklist data for children referred to mental health clinics. My expectation that threatened or actual abuse of pets would be present for a minority of these women was also disconfirmed. In fact, when I examined the rate of actual hurting or killing of pets, aside from threats, 57% of the women reported their partners injured or killed animals

More recently, Claudia Weber, then a graduate student at Utah State University, and I completed a follow-up study that involved a larger number of women, five different shelter sites, and a comparison group of women who did not report being victims of domestic violence. Since pet ownership in the pilot study was so high, in this study we selected only women who currently had a pet or had had pets in the past year. Shelter staff completed interviews with 101 women who were battered and had entered a shelter (SHELTER) and a comparison group of 120 nonbattered women (NONSHELTER). The NONSHELTER women reported that they had not experienced violence in their relationship(s) with intimate partners.

We found that 54% of SHELTER women in comparison with 5% of NONSHELTER women reported that their partners had hurt or killed pets (see Figure 10.1) (Ascione 2000b).

Again, nearly one in three of the SHELTER women with children reported that at least one of their children also abused animals. Children's exposure to their partners' animal abuse was reported by 62% of SHELTER women. The word "exposure" does not really capture the intensity of the terror some children must experience when they see or hear or find the remains of abused animals.

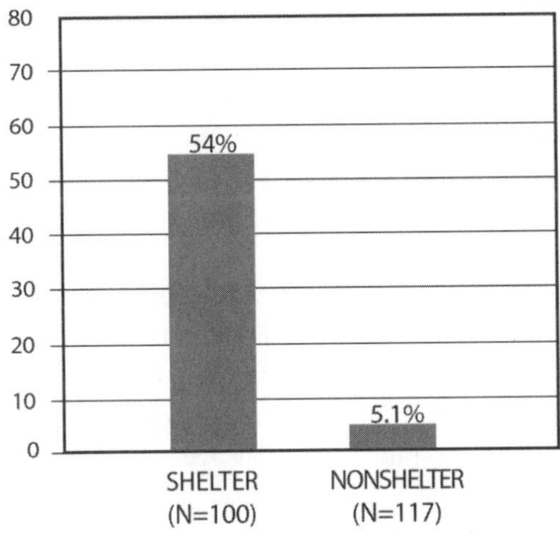

FIGURE 10.1. Women's reports of their partners' actual hurting or killing pets (percent responding "yes").

"Children who see too much." At a domestic violence conference I attended in Vancouver, BC, a domestic violence professional shared an example with me (A. Henderson, personal communication, October 27, 1999). The father of a 4-year-old girl bludgeoned the family's kitten in front of his daughter and wife. He then put his daughter in her bedroom with the remains of the kitten, unscrewed the light bulb from the ceiling, and locked his daughter in the darkened room for the night. The next morning, he forced this child to clean up the remains of the kitten. It is very difficult to conceive how horrifying that night must have been to that child but it would not be surprising if the memory of that episode haunts that little girl for the rest of her life.

The traumatic effects of violent pet loss are poignantly captured in a poem written by a fifth-grader named Sasha (Raphael, Colman, and Loar 1999, p. 25):

> I had too many pets that died.
> I really don't want to write about it.
> I can't tell you about them either.
> I just don't want to.
> It makes me too sad.
> The door is closed.
> Don't ask me anymore.
> I will cry into the ocean.

There is another disturbing aspect to this issue. Let me share the experience of Jane Ann Quinlisk, a social worker and director of a domestic violence program:

> My first day as a newly hired, freshly graduated, starry-eyed counselor at the local battered women's shelter almost made me run home crying… What I wasn't prepared for were the pictures my first client brought to show me, apologetically, to explain why she had to return home. The pictures were of her 'loving' husband cutting her beloved dog's ears off with a pair of garden shears. He had sent the ears along, too, but her mother thankfully neglected to forward them.
>
> As I started ranting about calling the police and animal shelter, my client calmed me down and with tears in her eyes, explained that in her county there was no humane society, and that the local sheriff was her husband's cousin, and that if she went home she could take care of the dog and the other animals on the farm and thank you very much for all the help but couldn't I please understand that it was best that she just go back? I felt horrified and helpless because I had no answers for her in my rattled brain. She returned home and we never heard from her again. Her face and those pictures still turn up in my nightmares. (1999, p. 168)

The fear of leaving animals behind. In my follow-up study with 101 women who were battered, nearly one in four women reported that concern for their pets' welfare had prevented them from seeking shelter sooner (in my first, 1998, study, this figure was 18%). Thus, some domestic violence victims and their children may remain with a batterer because they have no one to care for their pets if the victim and children decide to enter a domestic violence shelter or seek safety with friends or relatives who do not permit pets in their homes. Programs to remove this obstacle (by sheltering pets of domestic violence victims) have been and continue to be established across the United States and Canada (Ascione 2000b). And helping mothers achieve safety may be one of the best ways to insure the safety of their children (Jacobsen 2000).

Different samples of women, similar results. To demonstrate that this phenomenon is not confined to women in Utah, South Carolina sociologist Clifton Flynn (2000) reported similar findings in a study of 43 women with pets who had entered a South Carolina domestic violence shelter (28 were accompanied by children). For these women, 46.5% reported threats to (N=9) or harm (N=11) of their pets. Although only 7% of children were reported to be cruel to animals, 33.3% of women whose pets were abused reported that their children had also been abused. For women whose pets were not abused, 15.8% reported child abuse (the figure was 10.5% for women with no pets). Flynn reported that 19% of the women in his sample said worry over their pets' welfare kept them from seeking shelter sooner, *in some cases delaying their leaving their partners for more than two months.*

In Tennessee, Faver and Strand (2003b) surveyed 41 pet-owning women who were using domestic violence services. Forty-six percent reported that their partners had hurt or killed pets and 26.8 percent shared that concern for their pets' welfare affected their decision making about leaving or staying with their partners.

Two additional studies conducted in Canada provide further evidence of the prevalence of animal abuse in samples of women who have sought shelter at domestic violence sanctuaries. The Ontario, Canada Society for the Prevention of Cruelty to Animals reported the results of a survey of 111 women who were battered and who had sought shelter at one of 21 different "transition" houses, the term for domestic violence shelters in Canada. All of these women had or had had pets during the past year and 44% reported that their partner had abused or killed one or more of their pets (Daniell 2001).

Another study conducted in Calgary, Canada with 65 sheltered women who had pets currently or in the past year found that 47% of the women reported that their partner had hurt or killed a family pet (Thomas and McIntosh 2001). The authors of this study also noted that 64.5% of the mothers believed that their children were aware of the threats to and/or abuse of family pets, a figure very similar to what Claudia Weber and I reported in our research (62% of our participants reported that their children had witnessed pet abuse perpetrated by the women's partners). The Calgary study also reported that 23.3% of the women who had both children and pets said they were concerned that their children may have treated animals roughly and 16.4% that their children may have hurt or killed animals.

I urge the reader to consider that, despite the violent home environment in which they live, the majority of children in my research and that of others were not reported to be cruel to animals. In fact, when we interviewed children at Utah domestic violence shelters, 50% reported that they had tried to intervene to protect their pets when violence erupted in their homes. This finding echoes the results of a study showing that children may also intervene to protect their mothers from being battered (Edleson, Mbilinyi, Beeman, and Hagemeister 2003).

Both the Canadian studies reported that women (43% in Ontario and 25.4% in Calgary) said they had delayed entering a shelter due to concern for the safety of their pets, a concern that was probably well founded. For example, Thomas and McIntosh report that one of the Calgary study participants told the researchers "that once she entered the shelter, her cat disappeared, and that she has since been sent pictures in which the cat looks dead. Another participant told us that her partner killed a whole hobby farm full of animals when his last wife left him—and told his kids that their Mom did it" (p. 14).

A domestic violence professional in New Hampshire shared a case where a woman had ultimately made the decision to leave her partner and enter a domestic violence shelter. However, since the shelter could not accept pets, she had had to leave her dog behind. Within days, her partner managed to have an audiotape delivered to her. When the woman played the audiotape it was a recording of her partner torturing her dog. The woman packed her belongings, left the shelter, and the staff said she never returned.

Thus far, all of the studies of animal abuse and domestic violence have derived information exclusively from the reports of women who are battered and, in some cases, from their children. How might the data from these studies compare with the reports of batterers themselves? Dr. Harold Blakelock, a colleague of mine who is a psychologist with the Utah Department of Corrections, and I completed a study of 42 men incarcerated in the Utah prison system (Ascione and Blakelock 2003). These men were either incarcerated because of a domestic violence offense or for some other crime but also admitted to engaging in domestic violence. For the 38 men who said they had pets while living with an adult intimate partner, 55.3% reported actually hurting or killing pets. Thus, the reports of animal abuse by batterers themselves correspond well with the reports of victims of battering.

Much remains to be discovered about animal abuse in the context of domestic violence. For example, all the studies conducted to date have surveyed women at domestic violence shelters (Faver and Strand did include some women who were not residing in shelters but they did not conduct separate analyses for these participants). Is pet abuse more or less common among women who are battered but who, for whatever reasons, have not left their abusive partner? Is pet abuse a component of dating or courtship violence? Is it related to the socioeconomic status of the victim or rural/suburban/urban differences? Are the pets of abused women who are elderly subjected to violence and, if so, how common is this? Do victims of domestic violence who have a disability also experience the abuse of their pets? I close this section with a case reported to me by a domestic violence shelter worker in the course of assembling material for my book, *Safe Havens for Pets: Guidelines for Programs Sheltering Pets for Women who are Battered.*

A woman who was blind and had an assistance dog was a victim of domestic violence. She was married to a man who was also blind and had his own assistance dog. The woman reported that her husband abused her, beat her assistance dog, and would prompt his assistance dog to attack hers. The woman found that her dog was no longer functioning effectively and would now lead her into traffic, obstacles, or other dangerous situations. The abuse in this family took its toll on both the human and animal victims.

These studies make it clear that in families challenged by child maltreatment and domestic violence, there is ample opportunity for children to be exposed to the abuse of animals. It is encouraging that researchers in the area of domestic violence are now more likely to include questions about animal abuse in their studies of victims who are battered (Graham-Kevan and Archer 2003; McCloskey 2001; McCloskey and Lichter 2003). Even if adult family members do not abuse animals, some children may express the pain of their own victimization by abusing vulnerable family pets. Just as we are beginning to understand the overlap between child abuse and neglect and violence between intimate adult partners (Gayford 1975; Ross 1996), we must now consider the overlap of these forms of abuse with animal maltreatment (see Figure 10.2).

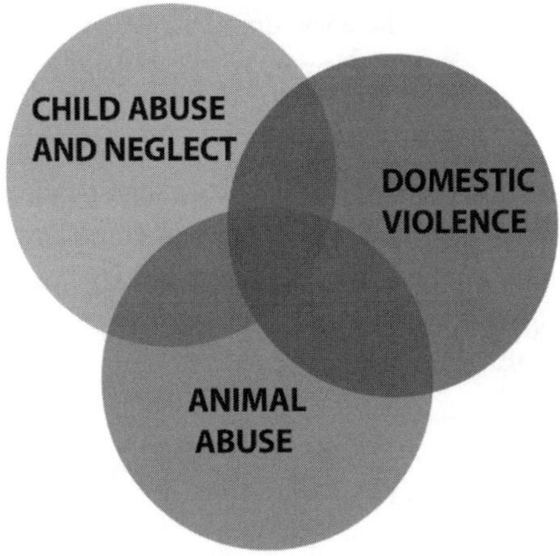

FIGURE 10.2. From Ascione and Arkow 1999.

Multiple victimization in childhood and adolescence

Each form of maltreatment we have discussed so far—physical abuse, sexual abuse, and domestic violence—can be devastating in its own right. But as you, the reader, already know or have probably anticipated, children and adolescents may be subjected to multiple forms of abuse. In the past decade, there have been concerted efforts to examine multiple victimization with the underlying assumption that, as forms of abuse accumulate, so too will their deleterious effects (Dong et al. 2003; Saunders 2003; Whitfield et al. 2003). Children who might be able to cope with being beaten may be overwhelmed when they are also sexually assaulted.

The type of overlap that is currently being studied most intensively is that between child maltreatment and exposure to domestic violence. Unfortunately, only one study thus far has examined animal abuse in this context. Recently, William Friedrich was again kind enough to make available data related to animal abuse from a larger study he and his colleagues have published (Friedrich et al. 2001). Using these data, colleagues and I were able to examine the prevalence of animal abuse in three samples of 6–12-year-old children (Ascione, Friedrich, Heath, and Hayashi 2003). One group was composed of 540 children being seen at pediatric and medical clinics and was considered a normative sample. A second group included 481 children who were substantiated victims of sexual abuse and a third group included 412 children who were psychiatric clinic outpatients. I should emphasize that the normative and psychiatric group children were only included if they had *not* been sexually abused, to the best of anyone's knowledge.

In addition to the categorization of children into these three groups, we had questionnaire data on whether children had been physically abused and whether they came from homes where there was domestic violence, here defined as parental physical fighting. Animal abuse information was available from caregivers' completion of the Child Behavior Checklist.

Let me first address the issue of overlapping forms of maltreatment. With regard to the normative group of children, the presence and overlap of abuse forms were minimal. For example, only 0.2% had experienced physical abuse and 5.9% lived in homes with domestic violence. This picture is more encouraging than the more disturbing findings for the other two groups.

In the tables below, I have indicated the percentages of children in the sexually abused and psychiatric samples who 1) were neither physically abused nor from homes with domestic violence, 2) were *either* physically abused *or* from homes with domestic violence, and 3) were *both* physically abused *and* from homes with domestic violence.

As you can see by examining these tables, 52.6% of the sexually abused children and 24.9% of the psychiatric group children also experienced additional forms of maltreatment—that is, physical abuse and/or parental physical fighting. Multiple forms of maltreatment were more likely for children in the sexually abused sample.

Sexually Abused—SEXAB (data available for 462 children)

		PARENTAL PHYSICAL FIGHTING	
		NO	**YES**
PHYSICAL ABUSE	NO	47.4%	**15.4%**
	YES	**16.9%**	**20.3%**

Psychiatric Outpatients—PSY (data available for 410 children)

		PARENTAL PHYSICAL FIGHTING	
		NO	**YES**
PHYSICAL ABUSE	NO	75.1%	**13.4%**
	YES	**6.3%**	**5.1%**

Now let's examine the prevalence of animal abuse in these three samples. First of all, if we look at data for overall reports of the presence of cruelty to animals, 3.1% of the normative group, 17.9% of the sexually abused group, and 15.6% of the psychiatric group were reported to be cruel. But the picture becomes more complex when we examine the last two groups—sexually abused and psychiatric outpatients—in terms of their additional experiences of physical abuse and domestic violence (these factors were too rare in the normative group for meaningful analysis).

The results for the *sexually abused children* are presented in the figure below (Figure 10.3) separately for boys and girls (complete data were available for 341 children). Remember, all these children were substantiated victims of sexual abuse. (I've included the data for the normative group as a dashed line, for purposes of comparison.) When we look at the data for children who were not physically abused or from families with domestic violence, we find that 25% of the boys but only 6.1% of the girls were cruel to animals. Therefore, among sexually abused children, this cruelty symptom seems more likely to be expressed in boys than girls. If we now add physical abuse to the picture (the second pair of bars), cruelty prevalence for boys is 36% and for girls, 17.1%. Parental physical fighting alone (the third pair of bars) does not seem to be related higher levels of boys' cruelty but yields a level of cruelty for girls (20%) similar to the their level for physical abuse. When these sexually abused children have been physically abused *and* come from homes where there is domestic violence, the highest rates of animal abuse emerge—36.8% for boys and 29.4% for girls.

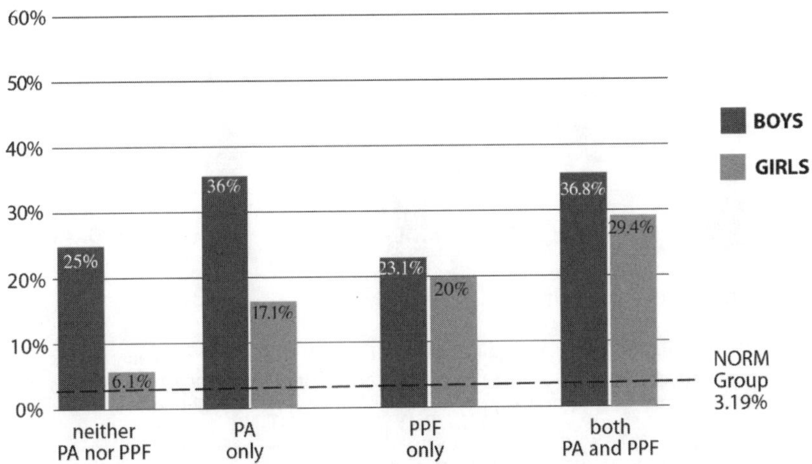

FIGURE 10.3. Mother/Caregiver Reports of "Cruel to Animals," Sexually Abused Group — N = 341. Percent reporting "sometimes" or "often" present. PA = physically abused; PPF = parents physical fighting.

An equally complicated picture emerges when we examine the results for the *psychiatric group* in the figure below (Figure 10.4) in which we had complete data for 351 children. For children with neither physical abuse nor domestic violence, 15% of boys and 10.7% of girls were reported to be cruel to animals. These rates are 5 and 3 times higher than the rates for boys and girls in the normative group.

What happens when we add physical abuse to the mix (the second pair of bars)? Rates of cruelty are somewhat higher for both boys, 26.3%, and girls, 16.71%. But when children come from homes with domestic violence (the third pair of bars), an interesting sex difference emerges. Boys' rate of cruelty is 12.1%, comparable to the rate when neither physical abuse nor domestic violence are present. But for girls, the rate drops to zero when parental physical fighting is present. This sex difference is magnified when we look at the data for children with physical abuse who come from homes with domestic violence (the fourth pair of bars). Now, the boys' rate of cruelty to animals is 60% while for girls it is zero. The reasons for the absence of cruelty to animals for girls who come from families with domestic violence are not yet clear. It may be that girls exposed to domestic violence experience increased fear and anxiety in the presence of their parents and this heightened wariness reduces girls' likelihood of acting out.

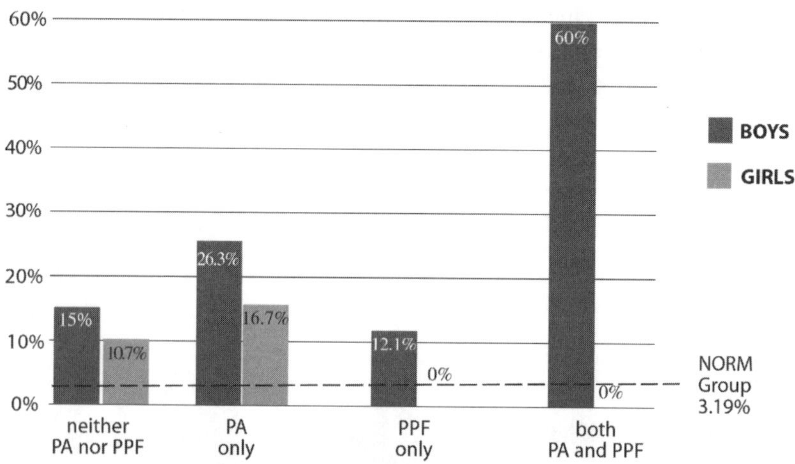

FIGURE 10.4. Mother/Caregiver Reports of "Cruel to Animals," Outpatient Psychiatric Group — N = 351. Percent reporting "sometimes" or "often" present. PA = physically abused; PPF = parents physical fighting.

The complex sex differences we found when examining rates of cruelty to animals and single or multiple forms of victimization suggest that further studies are needed. The high rate of cruelty to animals for boys who were psychiatric inpatients, physical abuse victims, *and* living in families with parental physical fighting is especially disturbing. At least for the case of boys with psychiatric problems, domestic violence coupled with physical maltreatment seems to exacerbate their problems.

Reducing risk factors: One piece of the puzzle. The past two decades have witnessed an increase in programs to prevent child maltreatment and to provide intervention and treatment for victims and perpetrators in families who have already abused their children (Lutzker 1998; Myers, Berliner, Briere, Hendrix, Jenny, and Reid 2002). Preventing and intervening in cases of domestic violence have a shorter history. One fact is clear: helping women and children to escape a violent intimate relationship is one of the highest priorities. In fact, some suggest that recent decreases in the number of *men* who are killed by their intimate female partners can, in part, be attributed to better services and options for women who have been battered, including the increased availability of shelters and safe houses. In the next chapter (11) on prevention and intervention, I will describe the "pet connection" for helping women find safety—and when women are safe, if children are present, children will benefit. So, too, will families' pets.

> "Just as social justice is the route to genuine political peace, domestic justice and democracy is the path to nonviolence in the family. Peaceful families will help build the social foundation for peaceful societies. (Garbarino 1993, p. 791)

CHAPTER 11

Prevention and intervention: Promising programs and persistent challenges

In this chapter, I describe how far we have come in understanding animal abuse and directions for additional study and analysis. The chapter includes a discussion of the ways we assess animal abuse and the importance of assessment for effective intervention and therapy. Innovative programs that use animals to facilitate prevention and therapy with children at risk for behavioral and psychological problems will be illustrated. I will describe a recent trend to consider animal welfare as a vehicle for assisting some women who are victims of domestic violence and will end with a discussion of issues related to professional training in a variety of areas that directly or indirectly touch on the welfare of animals in our society.

Assessing animal abuse. Assessing and intervening in cases of animal abuse perpetrated by young people should not involve reinventing the wheel. Randy Lockwood and I (2001) recently proposed one model that could be used to develop an animal abuse assessment strategy based on the approach that has been taken to assess juvenile fire setting. Fire setting shares many features with animal abuse: both are CD symptoms, may show developmental changes, may share causal factors, may often be performed covertly (Stickle and Belechman 2002), and may be early sentinels for later psychological problems.

Some disturbed children may present with both problem behaviors, as may some adults (Langevin 2003). Wooden and Berkey (1984) note the co-occurrence of cruelty to animals in a sample of 69 four- to seventeen-year-old fire setters: cruelty to animals was reported for 46% of four- to eight-year-olds, 9% of nine- to twelve-year-olds, and 12% of thirteen- to seventeen-year-olds. The authors caution that the lower rates for older children and adolescents may be related to the covert nature of this behavior as children experience greater independence and venture farther from home for more prolonged periods. Sakheim and Osborne (1994) report similar results with samples of children who set fires (N=100) and those who did not (N=55). Their assessment included a question about "cruelty to children or animals." This item was endorsed for 50% of fire setters but for only 9% of children not setting fires.

Animal abuse in the context of fire setting may also have predictive value. Rice and Harris (1996) studied 243 fire setters who had resided in a maximum-security psychiatric facility and were later released. In a follow up of recidivism for 208 of these men, Rice and Harris found that a childhood history of cruelty to animals (coded from patient records) predicted violent offense re-offending, or recidivism, and non-violent offense recidivism but not fire setting recidivism. It is interesting to note that enuresis (bed-wetting) was not significantly related to any of the three forms of recidivism. Bedwetting has been included in the so-called "triad" of symptoms (with cruelty to animals and fire setting) as a possible predictor of serious violence. As I noted earlier, research has been inconclusive about the triad's predictive value (Barnett and Spitzer 1994; Lockwood and Ascione 1998, pp. 245–246).

How assessment can inform intervention. The U.S. Department of Justice funded the development of the Salt Lake City Area Juvenile Firesetter/Arson Control and Prevention Program (1992). The program is based on a categorization or typology of juvenile fire setters that may be relevant for developing a typology of children who abuse animals (M. Chappuis, personal communication, March 23, 1998). The typology of juvenile fire setters is as follows:

- **Normal Curiosity Fire Setters,** mean age 5 years (range 3–7 years), who often share the characteristics of poor parental supervision, a lack of fire education, and no fear of fire.
- **"Plea-for-Help" Fire Setters,** mean age 9 years (range 7–13 years), whose fire setting is often symptomatic of more deep-seated psychological disturbance. These individuals usually have had adequate fire education.
- **Delinquent Fire Setters,** mean age 14 years (range 13 years to adulthood), whose fire setting may be one of a host of adolescent-onset antisocial behaviors including gang-related activities.

The program has developed a series of assessment scales that is geared to each age group of fire setters and that can be administered to the child's parent/guardian *and* to the child. In addition to questions about fire education and the fire setting incident(s), questions about general behavior problems (similar to those on the CBCL) are included. It is noteworthy that among these questions is an item about cruelty to animals (there is also a direct question about whether the fire setting incident involved the burning of an animal). Responses to these assessments are then used to direct the selection on an intervention strategy. Children who fall into the Normal Curiosity group are often enrolled in a fire education program and attempts may also be made to educate parents about fire safety and the need for supervising young children. Children who fall into the other two groups are referred to mental health services since fire departments are not prepared to deal with the psychological problems these young people may present. A local version of this program reduced the percentage of arson incidents started by juveniles from 80% to 50% (Lyon 1993, p. 2).

It might be possible to develop a similar typology for children who present with the problem of animal abuse. Although there is not a great deal of empirical information on which to rely, the study by Ascione, Thompson, and Black (1997) suggests the varied motivations that may underlie child and adolescent animal abuse. Together with the extensive experience of animal control and animal welfare professionals, one could develop a typology mirroring that for juvenile fire setters. A sketch of such a typology might approximate the following:

- **Exploratory/Curious Animal Abuse**—children in this category would likely be of preschool or early elementary school age, poorly supervised, and lacking training on the physical care and humane treatment of a variety of animals, especially family pets and/or stray animals and neighborhood wildlife. Humane education interventions (teaching children to be kind, caring, and nurturing toward animals) by parents, childcare providers, and teachers are likely to be sufficient to produce desistence of animal abuse in these children. It should be noted that age alone should not be the determining factor in including children in this category. For example, CD symptoms may have an early developmental onset and, as noted earlier, cruelty to animals is one of the earliest CD symptoms to be noted by caregivers.
- **Pathological Animal Abuse**—children in this category are more likely to be older (though, as noted above, not necessarily) than children in the Exploratory/Curious group. Rather than a lack of education about the humane treatment of animals, these children's animal abuse may be symptomatic of psychological disturbances varying in severity. For example, studies have tied childhood animal abuse to childhood histories of physical abuse, sexual abuse, and exposure to domestic violence (see chapters 8, 9, and 10). Here, professional, clinical intervention is warranted.
- **Delinquent Animal Abuse**—youth in this category are most likely to be adolescents whose animal abuse may be but one of a number of antisocial activities. In some cases, the animal abuse may be a component of gang/cult-related activities (e.g., initiation rites) or

> less formal group violence and destructiveness. The associated use of alcohol and other substances may be implicated with these youth. These youth may require both judicial and clinical interventions.

The value of this typology, or others that may be proposed, for helping select intervention strategies is, of course, a topic that needs study. Human behavior is complex and children and adolescents may not fit neatly into the "boxes" in which psychologists and others try to place them. Jon Katz (2003) describes the case of Jamal, a young adolescent isolated from his peers and somewhat of a loner. Jamal was also enduring various forms of bullying from a group of neighborhood children from whom he wished he could be protected. Jamal asked his mother to let him get a dog and she agreed. Jamal then proceeded to "train" his pit bull, Dre, by beating him violently each day after Jamal returned from school. This "training" was mixed with nurturing and affectionate care. As you might expect, Dre became a frightening (and no doubt frightened) dog and helped Jamal keep those who had taunted him at a distance. Does Jamal's cruelty fit into any of the three categories I described above? I don't think so, It is clear we face serious challenges in understanding the phenomenon of animal abuse. Animal abuse may be the symptom but it may not be the problem.

Although the development of methods to assess animal abuse has a shorter history than methods to assess fire setting, promising approaches have emerged in the past few years. Guymer, Mellor, Luk, and Pearse's (2001) screening questionnaire for cruelty to animals, described in chapter 7, is an excellent example of an easily administered assessment, using caregiver reports, that goes beyond the typical approach of asking parents the vague and rarely clarified question, "Is your child cruel to animals?" Just as this book was going into production, I discovered that Mark Dadds and his colleagues in Australia developed parent-report and self-report versions of a cruelty assessment that appears equally promising (Dadds et al. 2004). Their measure was also shown to correlate with observations of children's actual cruel or nurturing behavior with a live animal. Kelly Thompson and Eleonora Gullone (2003) introduced an assessment focusing on children's positive behaviors toward animals (using self reports) that would be a useful adjunct to Guymer et al.'s assessment of cruelty. Remember, interventions with children who abuse animals are more likely to be successful if they not only teach children to be *less* cruel but, at the same time, to be *more* compassionate toward animals. We need to gather information about both these propensities in children who are psychologically distressed. It would also be helpful if these two questionnaires used assessments by other informants (for example, asking *children* to self-report on the cruelty measure and asking *caregivers* to report on their children's positive behavior with animals).

"Safe Havens for Pets"

As I noted in chapter 11, the few studies of animal abuse in the context of domestic violence were consistent in their findings that substantial minorities of women reported delaying leaving a violent partner, in part, because of concern for their pets' welfare. The dilemma for many of these women is that, in some cases, their social isolation and lack of economic resources may preclude leaving pets with family, friends, or at a commercial kennel. When pets are left behind, they may become prey for the batterer. If women take their pets with them, they will usually discover that domestic violence shelters are not equipped or willing to house pets. As one woman ("Linda") lamented, "Where was I going to go? I couldn't go to a shelter because they wouldn't take my dog. I've had this dog for thirteen years and I wasn't going to leave her. So I felt I had nowhere to go, I felt trapped" (Anderson 1997, p. 32). Is there a solution to this bind some women, attempting to escape violence, may encounter?

As my research and that of others on this issue received attention, I would often receive a call, electronic mail message, or note asking me about programs to shelter pets in these circumstances and how to establish them. As an academic, I clearly was not an expert on this topic but I also realized advice was needed. I knew that many informal pet sheltering programs existed and there were a few well-developed, highly organized programs I had encountered in my travels and research. Rather than each domestic violence or animal welfare program having to "reinvent the wheel" to establish pet sheltering for victims of domestic violence, I judged that published guidelines could benefit agencies considering offering such a service.

With a grant from the Geraldine R. Dodge Foundation, I was able to interview 41 domestic violence and animal welfare professionals across the U.S. whose agencies were already offering or about to offer pet sheltering for victims of domestic violence. After completing these interviews and analyzing the responses to my many questions, I distilled the collective wisdom of these professionals in a book entitled *Safe Havens for Pets: Guidelines for Programs Sheltering Pets for Women Who Are Battered* (2000a). The Dodge Foundation funded the production of 3,000 copies as well as the costs of disseminating the book, free of charge, to any animal welfare, domestic violence, child welfare, law enforcement, or related agency that wanted a copy. Four years later, all of the hard copies have been distributed and I have learned of literally hundreds of programs being developed in the U.S., Canada, the United Kingdom, and Australia. If you are interested in examining this book, I provide instructions for accessing a full copy, via the Internet, in the resources section at the end of this chapter.

The beauty of these programs is that they remove *one* of the obstacles that may be preventing women, often with children, from seeking safety and nonviolence. Knowing that their pets are safe, well cared for, and can later be retrieved allows both women and children to focus on other aspects of their immediate safety and planning for the future (Kogan, McConnell, Schoenfeld-Tacher, and Jansen-Lock 2004). The message for these women is, "don't let caring for your pet keep you from caring for yourself and your children." Safe Havens Programs have not been formally evaluated but the testimonials from both professionals and victims suggest that they can be instrumental in facilitating some women's escape to safety.

I close this section with a description of one of these programs that was developed in Baltimore, Maryland (Col. M. Patten, personal communication, June 3, 1998). In the late 1990s, Colonel Margaret Patten, Chief of the Research and Development Bureau of the Baltimore, MD Police Department noted that her Department handled over 23,000 domestic-related incidents in 1997. Knowing that, in some cases, family pets were endangered during these incidents, Colonel Patten and her Department helped initiate a collaborative intervention for domestic violence cases with the Snyder Foundation for Animals, the House of Ruth (a domestic violence agency), and Second Step (a mental health agency). In cases where police were called to a domestic violence incident, a House of Ruth representative could provide assistance and advice to the victim and describe the availability of shelter if the victim so desired. If children were present in the home, a child welfare professional addressed the children's safety and welfare. And if pets were present, a representative of the Snyder Foundation offered to shelter the pets if victims decided to enter a safe house and could not find other accommodations for their pets. When both children and pets were present and when the victim decided to check into the shelter, the Baltimore team added one more component to their services. Using a Polaroid™ camera, a member of the team photographed the pet(s) and gave the photo to the children. The children were told that the shelter would keep them and their mother safe and that other members of the team would keep their pets safe as well. The photo would serve to remind the children that their pets were okay and not to worry.

This inexpensive yet exquisitely sensitive response to the needs of children caught up in domestic violence should be a model for all programs of this type. When mothers and children enter a domestic violence shelter, their lives, especially those of their children, undergo upheaval. Children must leave their place of residence, their neighborhood, their peers and playmates, their schools and church communities, and, to add further distress, they often have to leave their beloved pets behind, pet who may have been one of their few remaining sources of nurturance and affection. The Baltimore program acknowledges the importance of the bond between children and their pets and affirms children's need to know that their pets will not be in danger.

Policy implications

Cruelty to animals is all too often a part of the landscape of violence in which youth participate and to which they are exposed. The number of animals who are victims of such abuse is, at present, difficult to estimate as is the number of young people who perpetrate such abuse. In an ideal world, national data would be available on the yearly incidence of animal abuse, data that could be used to track trends and serve as a baseline against which the effectiveness of interventions could be assessed. Our existing national data collection systems in the area of child abuse and neglect (Sedlak and Broadhurst 1996) illustrate the value of such archival records. Currently, it is not clear how animal abuse offenses could be incorporated into the existing person-property-drug-public order categorization of juvenile arrests.

Only two states (Minnesota and West Virginia) *mandate* that veterinarians report suspected cases of animal abuse (Frasch, Otto, Olsen, and Ernest 1999), although other states recommend that veterinarians report suspected animal abuse in certain cases (a sequence of unexplained injuries to animals). Only a handful of states formally protect veterinarians from lawsuits for good faith reporting of animal abuse. Ironically, two states, California and Colorado, include veterinarians among other mandated reporters of *child* (but not animal) abuse (Lawrie 2002). Until such a system of monitoring and reporting animal abuse incidents becomes nation-wide, more circumscribed approaches to recording cases of animal abuse are recommended.

For example, local humane societies, societies for the prevention of cruelty to animals, and animal control agencies should routinely refer cases of serious, juvenile-perpetrated animal abuse to social welfare and law enforcement agencies and should maintain systematic records that could be available for archival review (Ascione and Barnard 1998; Ascione, Kaufmann, and Brooks 2000). Once such record keeping is in place, agencies would be able to monitor the incidence of animal abuse from year to year and share this information with the public. These records will also permit description of changes in the incidence of animal abuse and serve as a baseline for assessing changes that might be related to the implementation of new laws on animal abuse (e.g., including some forms of animal abuse as a felony-level offense) or to public education campaigns.

We need to inform parents, childcare providers, teachers, others who play care giving roles for children (e.g., clergy, coaches), and young people themselves that animal abuse may be a significant sign of a propensity to violence and psychological disturbance and should not be ignored. Efforts in this area are already emerging and mention of animal abuse as a warning sign for interpersonal violence is included in the U.S. Department of Education's *Early Warning, Timely Response: A Guide to Safe Schools* (Dwyer, Osher, and Warger 1998), the collaborative MTV-Music Television™ and American Psychological Association (1999) guide disseminated as part of their "Fight for your rights: Take a stand against violence" campaign, and Seifert's (2003) *Care, Child and Adolescent Risk Evaluation—A Measure of the Risk for Violent Behavior* (manual). The American Humane Association's (1996), *Growing up Humane in a Violent World: A Parent's Guide,* provides developmentally sensitive information about children and animals and the significance of animal abuse. The guide also includes educational strategies appropriate for preschoolers as well as those designed for elementary and secondary school students.

Because animals may often be abused in secret, parents and other adults may not be the best informants about this behavior problem. Youth surveys of violent behavior should include self-report items such as "Have you hurt an animal on purpose?" "Have you made an animal suffer for no reason?" to obtain a better estimate of animal abuse incidence. Likewise, *exposure* to animal abuse is a form of violence exposure that should be routinely assessed (Baldry 2003; Boat 1999) since it may have significant effects on young people. Children are often deeply attached to their pets and witnessing their violent abuse or death at the hands of others may be emotionally devastating.

Assessment and treatment

As part of the search for effective youth violence prevention and intervention programs, animal welfare organizations have been developing educational and therapeutic efforts that incorporate "animal-assisted" or "animal-facilitated" components (Duel 2000). The underlying theme for many of these programs is that teaching young people to train, care for, and interact in a nurturing manner with creatures who are also vulnerable will reduce young people's propensity for aggression and violence. These programs also assume that animal abuse is enabled when children's capacity for empathy has been undermined or compromised—for example, by years of neglect or maltreatment (Bavolek 2000). Developing a sense of empathy for animals is assumed to be a bridge to greater empathy for fellow human beings, making violence toward them less likely (Fawcett and Gullone 2001).

Although formal protocols for the clinical assessment of animal abuse (Lewchanin and Zimmerman 2000) and treatment (Jory and Randour 1999; Randour, Krinsk, and Wolf 2002; Zimmerman and Lewchanin 2000) are beginning to emerge, they are still at a formative stage of development and their effectiveness is difficult to evaluate.

As I noted earlier, attempts to create typologies of animal abuse, similar to typologies for fire setters, have face validity but their utility has not been empirically assessed. We need to determine if using the purported categories of animal abusers can facilitate the selection of appropriate therapeutic interventions.

Mental health professionals need to be more consistent in querying clients about their current and past histories of animal abuse. In a recent survey of 203 licensed psychologists, Nelson (2002) found that 94% believed that animal abuse could be related to other psychological disturbances but only 14% routinely asked clients questions about animal abuse. Bell (2001) reported similar results in a survey of 164 child welfare and mental health agencies in the U.K.

Given the challenges of incorporating animals in the therapeutic process (Fine 2000), evaluation of animal-facilitated therapy programs must move beyond anecdotal evidence (Fawcett and Gullone 2001). Katcher and Wilkins (2000) provide a model of such evaluation in a study of animal-facilitated therapy for children with attention disorders. The model should be expanded to programs for youth with conduct disorders (Gullone 2003).

Evaluation of intervention effectiveness will continue to grow in importance since courts, in some jurisdictions (e.g., California, Colorado), may recommend or mandate assessment and treatment of individuals convicted of certain forms of animal abuse (Frasch et al., 1999). The effects of such programs on recidivism have not been examined.

Professional training

Professional training on the issue of animal abuse and its overlap with other forms of family and community violence needs greater emphasis at both pre-professional and in-service education levels. These efforts have already emerged for veterinary education (Ascione and Barnard 1998), the legal profession (Davidson 1998), and law enforcement (Lockwood 1989) and should be expanded to include mental health and other human health professions (e.g., psychology, psychiatry, social work, child welfare, and pediatrics) and elementary and secondary education. Recently, Muscari (2004) addressed this issue for pediatric nurse practitioners, and Faver and Strand (2003a) provided an excellent overview of professional training in the field of social work that could be a model for other mental health professions.

Professional cross training (Ascione, Kaufmann, and Brooks 2000) where, for example, animal control officers are trained to identify signs of child maltreatment and child protection workers are trained to identify animal abuse, should be expanded. The National Crime Prevention Council (2002) recently published a book entitled *50 Strategies to Prevent Violent Domestic Crimes* and included a model cross-training program being implemented in Boston ("LINK-UP to animal abuse: Screening animal cruelty cases for domestic violence," pp. 100–102). The underlying theme of such training should be that animal abuse is a significant form of violence that not only harms animals but may be a red flag for a child who is psychologically disturbed or in danger of maltreatment (Arkow 2003b). March 2003 marked the beginning of a national cross-training and cross-reporting program in England involving collaboration between the Royal Society for the Prevention of Cruelty to Animals and the National Society for the Prevention of Cruelty to Children (Carvel 2003). A strong advocate of this approach is a remarkable person who has devoted her entire professional life (as well as most of her childhood and adolescence!) to the welfare of animals and vulnerable humans (S. Schlueter, personal communication, December 29, 2002). Lieutenant Sherry Schlueter is Section Supervisor for the Special Victims and Family Crimes Section for the Broward County (Florida) Sheriff's Office and has been instrumental in highlighting the value of both cross-training and cross-reporting to law enforcement professionals (Schlueter 1999). Her work takes her to cases of animal abuse, child maltreatment, and abuse of the elderly (Boat and Knight 2000) and is a model of professional attention to the issue of animal abuse.

Law enforcement is only one part of the process. Training and continuing education is also needed for prosecutors and judges and should include current information on the associations among animal abuse, domestic violence, and child maltreatment. Decisions about child custody and foster placements should be informed by research showing adults who abuse animals are potentially dangerous to humans.

Cross training could also enhance the success of foster placements for maltreated children who may be physically or sexually abusing animals. Foster care providers, especially those with family pets, should be alerted to the potential for animal abuse to occur.

THE IMPLICATIONS OF THE RELATION between animal abuse and human violence will, no doubt, continue to expand as we study this phenomenon in more detail. The studies and incidents I have described throughout this book attest to the maltreatment endured by animals who share their lives with human families, cases where a usually beautiful bond has broken. The stories have been difficult to describe and, no doubt, equally difficult for you to read. But I hope that illuminating this dark side of human-animal relationships will encourage efforts to prevent and intervene in cases where animals may suffer.

Animals, sharing so many qualities with humans, express their distress when they have been abused and their distress calls out for our attention. This book has provided an overview of the under-reported and under-studied phenomenon of animal abuse in childhood and adolescence. Perhaps by addressing cruelty to animals as a significant form of aggressive and anti-social behavior, we will add one more piece to the puzzle of understanding and preventing violence and fostering peace in the family and community.

AFTERWORD

EVERY MORNING FOR A DECADE I awoke to the soulful eyes of Abby—a yellow Labrador retriever. She closed her eyes and died in my arms a few years ago, euthanized by a kind vet who came to the house when Abby grew too weak even to walk and eat, from the tumors that grew mysteriously in her body. Her picture sits on my desk—on the porch of the lake house where she spent her first and last summers, and every summer in between. Abby was a puppy when I gave my first public lecture on the links between animal abuse and child maltreatment (to a conference sponsored by the American Humane Association), and she is a memory now. And I cannot think of these issues without my eyes tearing up from the loss of Abby.

Frank Ascione has long struggled to bring the professional communities of psychologists and child welfare specialists to a deeper, higher, and more encompassing awareness and understanding of the crucial linking of caring for animals and children in human experience. In this book he has brought his work to a new fruition. Careful research, documentation, and compelling narrative accounts are blended into a rich resource to help professionals and concerned citizens and parents understand how the ethics of caring are not bounded by species.

Of course, the fields of child and animal welfare have shared historical roots. The classic tale of the New York City abused child who could only be rescued by the efforts of the Society for the Prevention of Cruelty to Animals is but one often quoted example. Now, as much as ever before, we need to harness the joint protective energies of these two threads of the ethic of caring. Practically speaking, in a time of diminished public resources for protecting the well-being of both children and animals, there is a natural synergy and efficiency in mobilizing all those who care for the one group to care for the other. Animal protection workers and child protection works should share a brief, with each group looking out for the interests of the other's primary clients. Preliminary work along these line is encouraging The cost-effectiveness here parallels the moral imperative of empowering the protectors of the animals to be attentive to children on the scene, and vice versa.

Beyond even this, there is a crying need for increased awareness and knowledge about the conjoined issues of cruelty to children and cruelty to animals among the many front-line professionals whose lives naturally touch those of children. Here I speak of educators, clergy, coaches, law enforcement, and mental health workers. Each group should do more to recognize the multi-dimensional nature of cruelty. Often there are opportunities for preventive intervention evident in one domain (animal or child) that come from disturbing findings in the other. This book offers guidance for all those professional groups.

What is more, the book speaks to parents (perhaps most probably through parent educators). As in every developmental issue, parents are typically the first line of defense (and harm, if truth be told) when it comes to children. With very rare exceptions, parents care for their children and want the best for them. When I lecture to parents I often begin with this question: "If you could choose between giving your child good character or a million dollars, which would you choose?" No parents (at least in public) have ever hesitated, and always choose "good character." But translating these good intentions into good outcomes is another matter. This was the theme of my book (with Claire Bedard), *Parents Under Siege.* In this it echoed a second theme of my work, namely that the "social toxicity" of American life works against the desires of parents to produce caring children of good character. Focusing on the interplay of caring for animals and children is one important path for parents to take in both strengthening children against social toxicity and detoxifying the social environment. I think it is clear that when social and physical environments degrade it is the most vulnerable who show the effects first and worst. Children and animals are always at heightened risk in such times, and often share a common fate: exploitation, suffering, diminished well-being, and shortened life expectancy.

There is a third important agenda for this book. Students of developmental science have grossly neglected the links between children and animals as a topic of research and theory. There are amply tantalizing indications in the research of the importance of this issue. I recall reviewing a manuscript thirty years ago reporting that when children were asked to identify the key elements of their social networks (friends and confidants), their pets ranked as high as any human group. When children were followed around on a "neighborhood walk," their interactions with animals were a common and often central feature of the experience. One hopes that this book will stimulate a new generation of researchers to sign on for studies of the multiple links between children and animals, in all its aspects, "positive" and "negative."

For me, one of the most important elements of the book—and indeed, the entire field—is the issue of how caring transposes across species lines. In Chapter 6 Frank writes of "the circle of compassion." In my own thinking, this idea appears as "the circle of caring." I was drawn to this concept through my work with violent boys (as reported in my 1999 book *Lost Boys: Why Our Sons Turn Violent and How We Can Save Them*). When people learned that I spent time talking with boys and young men who kill, they often asked, "Don't they know the difference between right and wrong?" Eventually I realized that this was not the only or best question to be asking, for in fact many of these boys had very strong ideas of right and wrong—and sometimes were even moralistic and judgmental. Often the problem was not one of having moral values but of applying them.

I came to see that one of the important limiting factors on their moral lives was that they had very small and/or distorted "circles of caring." By circle of caring I meant (and mean) the domain within which they apply moral values. Outside of this circle the decisions to be made are essentially "logistical"—in the sense that they refer to simply managing cause and effect in the material world. They often said of their violent behavior, "I did what I had to do." They said this with the same sense that someone might speak of taking a crowbar to a boarded up-door. Missing was a sense that there was a moral concern here that transcended the material issues of making things happen or conform to one's will.

The more I heard, the more I realized we all have limited circles of caring. This is why it is possible to believe that "thou shalt not kill" and yet support the death penalty or abortion. In both cases, the respondent maintains the value but defines the case in point as outside the scope of that value—"justice" in the case of the death penalty and "a medical procedure reflecting control of a woman's body" in the other. I choose these two examples, of course, because they rarely seem to overlap in the same person (most people who favor the death penalty being "pro-life" and most death penalty opponents being "pro-choice"). The larger point is that each of us should feel some humility on this score.

How does one enlarge the circle of caring? I think we find answers implicit in Frank Ascione's work. We do so through some combination of emotional openness—empathy—coupled with philosophical development—an ethic of caring. Some people have such a large circle of caring that it essentially extends to all beings—such that killing a mosquito or a worm is as much a moral consideration as killing a puppy, such that eating meat becomes a moral dilemma just as the death penalty is (albeit perhaps of diminished moral hierarchy). Bravo for this. Callousness comes with a diminished circle of caring, be it the boys I interviewed in prison, the industrial farmers and ranchers who brutalize animals for profit, the explosive child or adult who tortures pets, or the researchers who inflict agony on animals in testing for narrow human benefits.

I believe the more we work towards an ever-expanding circle of caring we will supplant cruelty to children and animals. War is unhealthy for children—and animals. The battlefields of the world are littered with the bodies of both. The more we refuse the "logistical" models of decision making for both children and animals, the more we will see a clearer path away from making war at home and abroad.

—James Garbarino, Ph.D.
Cornell University

RESOURCES

AMERICAN HUMANE (AH), established in 1877, includes both child protection and animal protection divisions. AH operates the National Resource Center on the Link between Violence to People and Animals, provides training to professional groups across the country, and has available brochures, fact sheets, and special issues of Protecting Children, devoted to the link.

American Humane
63 Inverness Drive East
Englewood, CO 80112-5117
Voice [303] 792-9900 FAX [303] 792-5333
www.americanhumane.org

The National Resource Center on the Link between Violence to People and Animals
63 Inverness Drive East
Englewood, CO 80112-5117
Toll free 1-877-LINK-222 (1-877-546-5222)
Email: Link@americanhumane.org

THE HUMANE SOCIETY OF THE UNITED STATES (HSUS) launched the First Strike™ Campaign in 1997 to raise public and professional awareness about the connection between animal abuse and human violence. The Campaign provides training for law enforcement officers, prosecutors, social service workers, veterinarians, mental health professionals, educators, and the general public on the importance of treating animal abuse as a serious crime and an indicator of other forms of violence. A complete list of resources available through the HSUS First Strike™ Campaign is available at the website listed below and can also be obtained by calling the toll free number also listed below. Resources include a free campaign kit, with brochures and fact sheets in English and Spanish for law enforcement, social workers, and educators, the First Strike Campaign video and PSAs, articles addressing the animal abuse/human violence connection, and Violence prevention and intervention: A directory of animal-related programs (Duel, 2000), an 82-page listing of prevention and intervention programs.

The Humane Society of the United States
First Strike Campaign
2100 L Street, NW
Washington, DC 20037
Voice [202] 452-1100 Toll free 1-888-213-0956
www.hsus.org/firststrike/

ESTABLISHED IN 1918, THE LATHAM FOUNDATION was founded to promote respect for all life through education and publishes a quarterly periodical, *The Latham Letter.* The Latham Foundation maintains a number of print and video resources related to animal abuse, child maltreatment, and humane education. These include:

> *Breaking the cycles of violence: A video and training manual* (Set)—Authored by Phil Arkow and available in a new 2003 edition, the video and 64-page manual are ideal for cross training professionals on animal and human abuse issues.
>
> *Teaching compassion: A guide for humane educators, teachers, and parents.* Written by Pamela Raphael with Libby Coleman, Ph.D. and Lynn Loar, Ph.D., this 130-page guide includes a teacher's narrative and lesson plans to encourage respect, responsibility, compassion, and empathy. The guide is especially sensitive to working with children who have been maltreated or exposed to violence in their homes. A variety of lesson plans are included. These were designed for school settings but could easily be adapted for use in the home by parents and other caretakers.

The Latham Foundation for the Promotion of Humane Education
1826 Clement Avenue
Alameda, CA 94501
Voice [510] 521-0920 FAX [510] 521-9861
www.Latham.org

> *Child Abuse, Domestic Violence, and Animal Abuse: Linking the Circles of Compassion for Prevention and Intervention.* Produced with the assistance of the Latham Foundation and published by Purdue University Press, this book, edited by Frank R. Ascione, Ph.D., and Phil Arkow, includes original chapters written by authorities from each of these three areas of professional focus and chapters written by victims of abuse and domestic violence.

Safe Havens for Pets: Guidelines for Programs Sheltering Pets for Women Who Are Battered, by Frank R. Ascione (Logan, UT: Author, 2000) is based on in-depth interviews with 41 domestic violence and animal welfare agencies, explores the development and operation of programs that shelter pets for women and children who are escaping violent homes. This project was funded by the Geraldine R. Dodge Foundation and provided for the free dissemination of the book to interested agencies. Printed copies have been exhausted but the entire book, in pdf format, is available at the following Internet site (courtesy of Andrew Vachss): http://www.vachss.com/guest_dispatches/safe_havens.html.

REFERENCES

Achenbach, T. M. (1991). *Manual for the Child Behavior Checklist/4-18 and 1991 Profile.* Burlington, VT: University of Vermont Department of Psychiatry.

Achenbach, T. M. (1992). *Manual for the Child Behavior Checklist/2-3 and 1992 Profile.* Burlington, VT: University of Vermont Department of Psychiatry.

Achenbach, T. M., Howell, C. T., Quay, H. C., and Conners, C. K. (1991). *National survey of problems and competencies among four- to sixteen-year-olds.* Monographs of the Society for Research in Child Development, 56, Serial No. 225.

Albert, A., and Bulcroft, K. (1988). Pets, families, and the life course. *Journal of Marriage and the Family, 50,* 543–552.

Allen, K. (2003). Are pets a healthy pleasure? The influence of pets on blood pressure. *Current Directions in Psychological Science, 12,* 236–239.

American Psychiatric Association. (1987). *Diagnostic and statistical manual of mental disorders* (3rd ed., revised). Washington, DC: Author.

American Psychiatric Association. (1994). *Diagnostic and statistical manual of mental disorders* (4th ed.). Washington, DC: Author.

Anderson, V. (1997). A woman like you: The face of domestic violence. Seattle: Seal Press.

Angell, G. (1884, February 14). *The new order of mercy; or, crime and its prevention.* Presentation before the annual meeting of the National Association of Superintendents of Public Instruction. Washington, DC: National Bureau of Education.

Arkow, P. (1987). *The loving bond: Companion animals in the helping professions.* Saratoga, CA: R and E Publishers.

Arkow, P. (1992). The correlation between cruelty to animals and child abuse and the implications for veterinary medicine. *Canadian Veterinary Journal, 33,* 518–521.

Arkow, P. (1994). Child abuse, animal abuse, and the veterinarian. *Journal of the American Veterinary Medical Association, 204,* p. 1004–1007.

Arkow, P. (2003a). *Breaking the cycles of violence: A video and training manual.* Alameda, CA: Latham Foundation Publication.

Arkow, P. (2003b). Groundbreaking legislation in Great Britain: British vets take major step forward in reporting suspected family violence. *Latham Letter, 24,* 12–13.

Arluke, A., Levin, J., Luke, C., and Ascione, F. (1999). The relationship of animal abuse to violence and other forms of antisocial behavior. *Journal of Interpersonal Violence, 14,* 963–975.

Artley, A. (1993). *Murder in the heart.* Middlesex, England: Penguin Books.

Ascione, F.R. (1993). Children who are cruel to animals: A review of research and implications for developmental psychopathology. *Anthrozoös, 6,* 226–247.

Ascione, F.R. (1997). Humane education research: Evaluating efforts to encourage children's kindness and caring toward animals. *Genetic, Social and General Psychology Monographs, 123* [1], 57–77.

Ascione, F.R. (1998). Battered women's reports of their partners' and their children's cruelty to animals. *Journal of Emotional Abuse, 1,* 119–133.

Ascione, F.R. (1999). The abuse of animals and human interpersonal violence: Making the connection. In F. R. Ascione and P. Arkow (eds.), *Child abuse, domestic violence, and animal abuse: Linking the circles of compassion for prevention and intervention* (pp. 50–61). West Lafayette, IN: Purdue University Press.

Ascione, F.R. (2000a). *Safe Havens for Pets: Guidelines for programs sheltering pets for women who are battered.* Logan, UT: Author.

Ascione, F.R. (2000b). *What veterinarians need to know about the link between animal abuse and interpersonal violence.* Proceedings of the 137th Annual Meeting of the American Veterinary Medical Association (CD-ROM records #316–317).

Ascione, F.R., and Barnard, S. (1998). The link between animal abuse and violence to humans: Why veterinarians should care. In P. Olson (ed.), *Recognizing and reporting animal abuse: A veterinarian's guide* (pp. 4–10). Englewood, CA: American Humane Association.

Ascione, F.R., and Blakelock, H.H. (2003, July 14). *Incarcerated men's reports of animal abuse: A study of the perpetrator's perspective.* Presentation at the 8th International Family Violence Conference. Portsmouth, NH.

Ascione, F.R., and Lockwood, R. (2001). "Cruelty to animals: Changing psychological, social, and legislative perspectives." In D. J. Samen and A. N. Rowan (eds.), *The state of the animals, 2001.* Washington, D.C. : Humane Society Press.

Ascione, F.R., Friedrich, W.N., Heath, J., and Hayashi, K. (2003). Cruelty to animals in normative, sexually abused, and outpatient psychiatric samples of 6- to 12-year-old children: Relations to maltreatment and exposure to domestic violence. *Anthrozoös, 16,* 194–212.

Ascione, F.R., Kaufmann, M.E., and Brooks, S.M. (2000). Animal abuse and developmental psychopathology: Recent research, programmatic, and therapeutic issues and challenges for the future. In A. Fine (ed.), *Handbook on animal-assisted therapy: Theoretical foundations and guidelines for practice* (pp. 325–354). New York: Academic Press.

Ascione, F.R., Thompson, T.M., and Black, T. (1997). Childhood cruelty to animals: Assessing cruelty dimensions and motivations. *Anthrozoös, 10,* 170–177.

Ascione, F.R., Weber, C., and Wood, D. (1997). The abuse of animals and domestic violence: A national survey of shelters for women who are battered. *Society and Animals, 5,* 205–218.

Azar, B. (1997). Defining the trait that makes us human. *APA Monitor, 28,* 1, 15.

Baldry, A.C. (2003). Animal abuse and exposure to interparental violence in Italian youth. *Journal of Interpersonal Violence, 18,* 258–281.

Bandura, A., Grusec, J.E., and Menlove, F.L. (1967). Vicarious extinction of avoidance behavior. *Journal of Personality and Social Psychology, 5,* 16–23.

Barbaree, H.E., Marshall, W.L., and Hudson, S.M. (1993). *The juvenile sex offender.* New York: Guilford Press.

Barker, R.G., and Wright, H.F. (1954). *Midwest and its children: The psychological ecology of an American town.* Evanston, IL: Row, Peterson and Company.

Barker, S.B., Barker, R.T., Dawson, K.S., and Knisely, J.S. (1997). The use of Family Life Space Diagram in establishing interconnectedness: A preliminary study of sexual abuse survivors, their significant others, and pets. *Individual Psychology, 53,* 435–450.

Barnett, W., and Spitzer, M. (1994). Pathological fire-setting 1951–1991: A review. *Medical Science and the Law, 34,* 4–20.

Baruch, D.W. (1943). *You, your children, and war.* New York: D. Appleton-Century Company.

Battistich, V., Watson, M., Solomon, D., Schaps, E., and Solomon, J. (1991). The Child Development Project: A comprehensive program for the development of prosocial character. In W. M. Kurtines and J. L. Gewirtz (eds.), *Handbook of moral behavior and development* (Vol. 3: Application). Hillsdale, NJ: Erlbaum.

Baumeister, R.F. (1997). *Evil: Inside human violence and cruelty.* New York: W.H. Freeman.

Bavolek, S.J. (2000, November). The Nurturing parent programs. *Juvenile Justice Bulletin.* Washington, DC: Office of Juvenile Justice and Delinquency Prevention.

Beetz, A. (2002). *Love, violence, and sexuality in relationships between humans and animals.* Aachen, Germany: Shaker Verlag.

Beirne, P. (1997). Rethinking bestiality: Towards a sociology of interspecies sexual assault. *Theoretical Criminology, 1,* 317–340.

Bell, L. (2001). Abusing children—abusing animals. *Journal of Social Work, 1,* 223–234.

Bellafante, G. (1997, October 13). Finding trauma next door. *Time,* pp. 41–42.

Beston. H. (1992). *The outermost house.* New York: Henry Holt. (Original work published 1928)

Beyer, K.R., and Beasley, J.O. (2003). Nonfamily child abductors who murder their victims. *Journal of Interpersonal Violence, 18,* 1167–1188.

Binggeli, N.J., Hart, S.N., and Brassard, M.R. (2001). *Psychological maltreatment of children.* Thousand Oaks, CA: Sage.

Boat, B. (1991). Caregivers as surrogate therapists in the treatment of a ritualistically abused child. In W. N. Friedrich (ed.), *Casebook of sexual abuse treatment* (pp. 1–26). New York: W.W. Norton.

Boat, B. (1999). Abuse of children and abuse of animals: Using the links to inform child assessment and protection. In F. R. Ascione and P. Arkow (eds.), *Child abuse, domestic violence, and animal abuse* (pp. 83–100). West Lafayette, IN: Purdue University Press.

Boat, B.W., and Knight, J.C. (2000). Experiences and needs of adult protective services case managers when assisting clients who have companion animals. *Journal of Elder Abuse and Neglect, 12,* 145–155.

Boglioli, L.R., Taff, M.L., Turkel, S.J., Taylor, J.V., and Peterson, C.D. (2000). Unusual infant death: Dog attack or postmortem mutilation after child abuse? *American Journal of Forensic Medicine and Pathology, 21,* 389–394.

Bossard, J.H.S. (1944). The mental hygiene of owning a dog. *Mental Hygiene, 28,* 408.

Bossard, J.H.S. (1950). I wrote about dogs. *Mental Hygiene, 34,* 385–390.

Bossard, J.H.S., and Boll, E.S. (1966). *The Sociology of Child Development* (4th ed). New York: Harper and Row.

Bowlby, J. (1953). *Child care and the growth of love.* Baltimore: Pelican Books.

Boy sentenced for disfiguring dog. A 13-year-old boy convicted of cutting the eyes out of a dog. (2001, January 4). *Herald Journal,* p. 2.

Boyer, E. (1950). *The secret game.* New York: Harcourt Brace and Co.

Brassard, M.R., Hart, S.M., and Hardy, D.B. (1993). The Psychological Maltreatment Rating Scales. *Child Abuse and Neglect, 17,* 715–729.

Brazelton, T.B. (1992). *Touchpoints: Your child's emotional and behavioral development.* New York: Addison-Wesley Publishing Company.

Breer, W. (1996). *The adolescent molester.* Springfield, IL: Charles C. Thomas.

Bronfenbrenner, U., and Morris, P.A. (1998). The ecology of developmental processes. In W. Damon (ed.), *Handbook of child pPsychology* (5th ed.), (pp. 993–1028). New York: Wiley.

Browne, A. (1997). *When battered women kill.* New York: Free Press.

Bryant, B.K. (1985). *The neighborhood walk: Sources of support in middle childhood.* Monographs of the Society for Research in Child Development, no. 50. Chicago: Child Development Publications, University of Illinois Press.

Bryant, B. K. (1990). The richness of the child-pet relationship: A consideration of both benefits and costs of pets to children. *Anthrozoös, 3,* 253–261.

Buchta, R. (1988). Deliberate intoxication of young children and pets with drugs: A survey of an adolescent population in a private practice. *American Journal of the Diseases of Children, 142,* 701–702.

Burk, W. F. (1897). Teasing and bullying. *Pedagogical Seminary, 4,* 336–371.

Burney, M. (1997, June 21). Jury orders Megan's killer put to death; life without parole rejected. *Chicago Sun-Times*, p. 10.

Burns, B. J., Landsverk, J. Kelleher, K., Faw, L., Hazen, A., and Keeler, G. (2001). Mental health, education, child welfare, and juvenile justice service use. In R. Loeber and D. P. Farrington (eds.), *Child delinquents: Development, intervention, and service needs* (pp. 273–303). Thousand Oaks, CA: Sage Publications.

Burt, C. (1925). *The young delinquent*. New York: D. Appleton and Company.

Burton, G. (1999, July 3). Sex Offender Held in New Assault Case. *Salt Lake Tribune*, pp. D1, D3.

Carey, S. (1987). *Conceptual change in childhood*. Cambridge, MA: MIT Press.

Carmichael, L. (1954). *Manual of Child Psychology*. New York: Wiley.

Carvel, J. (2003, March 5). Child and animal cruelty linked. *The Guardian*. Retrieved from the World Wide Web: http://www.guardian.co.uk/uk_news/story/0,3604,907511,00.html.

Cavanagh Johnson, T. (1999). *Understanding your child's sexual behavior: What's natural and healthy*. Oakland, CA: New Harbinger Publications.

Cavanaugh, K., Kaufmann, M., and Moulton, C. (1998). *Humane education at the crossroads: Visions for the future*. Englewood, CO: American Humane Association.

Centers for Disease Control. (1997). Dog-bite-related fatalities—United States, 1995–1996. *Morbidity and Mortality Weekly Report, 46, no. 21*, 463–467.

Chapman, S. Cornwall, J., Righetti, J., and Sung, L. (2000). Preventing dog bites in children: Randomized controlled trial of an educational intervention. *Western Journal of Medicine, 173*, 233–234.

Child Abuse Prevention and Treatment Act. U.S. Code Citation: 42 USC 5101 et seq; 42 USC 5116 et seq; ACF Regulations: 45 CFR 1340.

Church of the Lukumi Babalu Aye, Inc., et al. v. City of Hialeah. 508 U.S. 520 (1993).

Clément, R. (Director). (1952). *Forbidden Games (Jeux interdits)* [Motion picture]. (France) United States: Home Vision Entertainment.

Cole, M., and Cole, S.R. (2001). *The Development of Children* (5th ed.). New York: Worth Publishers.

Coles, R. (1997). *The moral intelligence of children*. New York: Random House.

Compayré, G. (1902).*Development of the child in later infancy*. New York: D. Appleton and Company.

Costin, L.B. (1991). Unraveling the Mary Ellen legend: Origins of the "cruelty" movement. *Social Science Review, 65*, 203–223.

Courier Chronicle [Humboldt, TN]. 1993. Humboldt children face animal cruelty and burglary charges. *Courier Chronicle*, Feb. 10, p. 1A.

Cover Jones, M. (1924). A laboratory study of fear: The case of Peter. *Pedagogical Seminary, 31*, 308–315.

Dadds, M. R., Whiting, C., Bunn, P., Fraser, J. A., Charlson, J. H., and Pirola-Merlo, A. (2004). Measurement of cruelty in children: The Cruelty to Animals Inventory. *Journal of Abnormal Child Psychology, 32,* 321–334.

Daniell, C. (2001). Ontario SPCA's women's shelter survey shows staggering results. *The Latham Letter, XXII,* (2) 16–17.

Darwin, C. (1965). *The expression of emotions in man and animals.* Chicago: The University of Chicago Press. (Original work published 1872.)

Davidson, H. (1998). What lawyers and judges should know about the link between child abuse and animal cruelty. *American Bar Association Child Law Practice, 17,* 60–63.

de Las Casas, B. (1992). *The devastation of the Indies: A brief account.* Baltimore: Johns Hopkins University Press. (Original work published 1552.)

de Waal, F. (1996). *Good natured: The origins of right and wrong in humans and other animals.* Cambridge, MA: Harvard University Press.

de Waal, F. (2001). *The ape and the sushi master.* New York: Basic Books.

Delk, J.L. (1977). Use of EMG biofeedback in behavioral treatment of an obsessive-phobic-depressive syndrome. *Diseases of the Nervous System, 38,* 938–939.

DeViney, E., Dicket, J., and Lockwood, R. (1983). The care of pets within child abusing families. *International Journal for the Study of Animal Problems, 4,* 321–329.

Dogs bite 4.5 million each year. (1998, January 7). *Salt Lake Tribune,* p. A6.

Dong, M., Anda, R.F., Dube, S.R., Giles, W.H., and Felitti, V.J. (2003). The relationship of exposure to childhood sexual abuse to other forms of abuse, neglect, and household dysfunction during childhood. *Child Abuse and Neglect, 27,* 625–639.

Doyle, C. (2001). Surviving and coping with emotional abuse in childhood. *Clinical Child Psychology and Psychiatry, 6,* 387–402.

Drews, C. (2001a). Wild animals and other pets kept in Costa Rican households: Incidence, species, and numbers. *Society and Animals, 9,* 107–126.

Drews, C. (2001b, September 12). *Attitudes towards animals in the neotropics: When positive feelings backfire.* Plenary address at the 9th International Conference on Human-Animal Interactions, Rio de Janeiro, Brazil.

Duel, D.K. (2000). *Violence prevention and intervention: A directory of animal-related programs.* Washington, DC: The Humane Society of the United States.

Dutton, M.A. (1992). *Empowering and healing the battered woman.* New York: Springer.

Dwyer, K., Osher, D., and Warger, C. (1998). *Early warning, timely response: A guide to safe schools.* Washington, DC: U.S. Department of Education.

Earls, C.M., and Lalumière, M.L. (2002). A case study of preferential bestiality (zoophilia). *Sexual Abuse: A Journal of Research and Treatment, 14,* 83–88.

Eckstein, D. (2000). The pet-relationship impact inventory. *The Family Journal: Counseling and Therapy for Couples and Families, 8,* 192–198.

Eddy, S. (1899). *Friends and helpers.* Boston: Ginn and Company.

Edgerton, R.B. (1992). *Sick societies: Challenging the myth of primitive harmony.* New York: Free Press.

Edleson, J.L., Mbilinyi, L.F., Beeman, S.K., and Hagemeister, A.K. (2003). How children are involved in domestic violence: Results from a four-city telephone survey. *Journal of Interpersonal Violence, 18,* 18–32.

Edwards, C.P. (1986). Another style of competence: The caregiving child. In A. Fogel and G.F. Melson (eds.), *Origins of nurturance* (pp. 95–121). Hillsdale, NJ: Lawrence Erlbaum Associates.

Eisenberg, N. (1988). Empathy and sympathy: A brief review of the concepts and empirical literature. *Anthrozoös, 2,* 15–17.

Eisenberg, N. (1992). *The caring child.* Cambridge, MA: Harvard University Press.

Eisenberg, N., and Fabes, R.(1998). Prosocial development. In W. Damon (ed.), *Handbook of child psychology* (5th ed.) (vol. 3, pp. 705–707). New York: Wiley.

English, K., Jones, L., Patrick, D., and Paini-Hill, D. (2003). Sexual offender containment: Use of postconviction polygraph. *Annals of the New York Academy of Sciences, 989,* 411–427.

Eyberg, S. M., and Ross, A. W. (1978). Assessment of child behavior problems: The validation of a new inventory. *Journal of Clinical Psychology, 7,* 113–116.

Faver, C.A., and Strand, E.B. (2003a). Domestic violence and animal cruelty: Untangling the web of abuse. *Journal of Social Work Education, 39,* 237–253.

Faver, C.A., and Strand, E.B. (2003b). To leave or to stay? Battered women's concern for vulnerable pets. *Journal of Interpersonal Violence, 18,* 1367–1377.

Fawcett, N.R., and Gullone, E. (2001). Cute and cuddly and a whole lot more? A call for empirical investigation into the therapeutic benefits of human-animal interaction for children. *Behaviour Change,* 18, 124–133.

Feldman, M.C. (1997). Canine variant of factitious disorder by proxy. *American Journal of Psychiatry, 154,* 1316–1317.

Felthous, A.R., and Yudowitz, B. (1977). Approaching a comparative typology of assaultive female offenders. *Psychiatry, 40,* 270–276.

Ferrato, D. (1991). *Living with the enemy.* New York: Aperture.

Field, T. (2001). *Touch.* Cambridge, MA: MIT Press.

Finch, P. (1989). Learning from the past. In D. Paterson and M. Palmer (eds.), *The status of animals: Ethics, education and welfare* (pp. 64–72). Wallingford, UK: C-A-B International.

Fine, A. (ed). (2000). *Handbook on animal-assisted therapy: Theoretical foundations and guidelines for practice.* San Diego: Academic Press.

Finkelhor, D., Mitchell, K.J., and Wolak, J. (2000). *Online victimization: A report on the nation's youth.* Alexandria, VA: National Center for Missing and Exploited Children.

Finkelhor, D., Williams, L.M., and Burns, N. (1988). *Nursery crimes: Sexual abuse in day care.* Newbury Park, CA: Sage.

Fleming, W.M., Jory, B., and Burton, D.L. (2002). Characteristics of juvenile offenders admitting to sexual activity with nonhuman animals. *Society and Animals, 10,* 31–45.

Flexner, S.B. (ed.). (1987). *The Random House dictionary of the English language* (2nd ed.). New York: Random House.

Flynn, C. (2000). Woman's best friend: Pet abuse and the role of companion animals in the lives of battered women. *Violence against Women, 6,* 162–177.

Flynn, C.F. (1999a). Animal abuse in childhood and later support for interpersonal violence in families. *Society and Animals, 7,* 161–171.

Flynn, C.P. (1999b). Exploring the link between corporal punishment and children's cruelty to animals. *Journal of Marriage and the Family, 61,* 971–981.

Ford, M.E., and Linney, J.A. (1995). Comparative analysis of juvenile sex offenders, violent nonsexual offenders, and status offenders. *Journal of Interpersonal Violence, 10,* 56–70.

Fox, M. (1999). Treating serious animal abuse as a serious crime. In F.R. Ascione and P. Arkow (eds.), *Child abuse, domestic violence, and animal abuse: Linking the circles of compassion for prevention and intervention* (pp. 306–315). West Lafayette, IN: Purdue University Press.

Frasch, P.D., Otto, S.K., Olsen, K.M., and Ernest, P.A. (1999). State animal anticruelty statutes: An overview. *Animal Law, 5,* 69–80.

Frazier, M.R. (1998). *Physically and sexually violent juvenile offenders: A comparative study of victimization history variables.* Unpublished doctoral dissertation, Department of Psychology, Utah State University, Logan, UT.

Freud, S. (1938). Totem and Taboo. In A.A. Brill (ed.), *The basic writings of Sigmund Freud* (p. 905). New York: The Modern Library.

Frick, P.J., and Ellis, M. (1999). Callous-unemotional traits and subtypes of Conduct Disorder. *Clinical Child and Family Psychology Review, 2,* 149–168.

Frick, P.J., O'Brien, B.S., Wootton, J.M., and McBurnett, K. (1994). Psychopathy and conduct problems in children. *Journal of Abnormal Psychology, 103,* 700–707.

Frick, P.J., Van Horn, Y., Lahey, B.B., Christ, M.A.G., Loeber, R., Hart, E.A., et al. (1993). Oppositional Defiant Disorder and Conduct Disorder: A meta-analytic review of factor analyses and cross-validation in a clinical sample. *Clinical Psychology Review, 13,* 319–340.

Friedman, E., and Thomas, S.A. (1998). Pet-ownership, social support, and one-year survival after acute myocardial infarction in the Cardiac Arrhythmia Suppression Trial (CAST). In C.C. Wilson and D.C. Turner (eds.), *Companion animals in human health* (pp. 187–201). Thousand Oaks, CA: Sage.

Friedmann, E., Katcher, A.H., Thomas, S.A., Lynch, J.J., and Messent, P.R. (1983). Social interaction and blood pressure: Influence of animal companions. *Journal of Mental and Nervous Disease, 171,* 461–465.

Friedrich, W.N. (1997). *Child sexual behavior inventory: Professional manual.* Odessa, FL: Psychological Assessment Resources.

Friedrich, W.N., Fisher, J.L., Acton, R., Berliner, L., Butler, J., Damon, L., et al. (2001). Child Sexual Behavior Inventory: Normative, psychiatric, and sexual abuse comparisons. *Child Maltreatment, 6,* 37–49.

Frost, R. (2000, April). People who hoard animals. *Psychiatric Times, 17,* Issue 4. Retrieved from the World Wide Web: http://www.mhsource.com/pt/p000425.html.

Garbarino, J. (1993). Challengers we face in understanding children and war: A personal essay. *Child Abuse and Neglect, 17,* 787–793.

Garbarino, J. (1999). *Lost boys: Why our sons turn violent and how we can save them.* New York: Free Press.

Garbarino, J., Guttmann, E., and Seeley, J.W. (1986). *The psychologically battered child.* San Francisco: Jossey-Bass Publishers.

Garbarino, J., Kostelny, K., and Dubrow, N. (1991). *No place to be a child: Growing up in a war zone.* Lexington, MA: Lexington Books.

Garza, J. (1999, March 19). Teens charged with torturing and killing dogs, pups. *Milwaukee Journal-Sentinel.* Retrieved from the World Wide Web: http://www.jsonline.com/news/mar99/0319teens.asp

Gayford, J.J. (1975). Wife battering: A preliminary survey of 100 cases. *British Medical Journal, 1,* 195–197.

Gelles, R., and Straus, M. (1988). *Intimate violence.* New York: Simon and Schuster.

Gilligan, J. (1996). *Violence: Our deadly epidemic and its causes.* New York: G.P. Putnam's Sons.

Glaspell, S. (1996). A jury of her peers. In S. Koppelman. *Women in the trees: U.S. Women's short stories about battering and resistance,* 1839–1999 (pp. 76–93). Boston: Beacon Press.

Gleyzer, R., Felthous, A.R., and Holzer, C.E., III (2002). Animal cruelty and psychiatric disorders. *Journal of the American Academy of Psychiatry and the Law, 30,* 257–265.

Golden, J. (1992). Humane education elementary school. In M.E. Kaufmann (ed.), *Progress in humane education* (pp. 10–11). Englewood, CO: American Humane Association.

Goldstein, A.P. (1999). *Low-level aggression: First steps on the ladder to violence.* Champaign, IL: Research Press.

Goleman, D. (1995). *Emotional intelligence: Why it can matter more than IQ.* New York: Bantam Books.

Gomes, C.M., Ribeiro-Filho, L., Giron, A.M., Mitre, A.I., Figueira, E.R.R., and Arap, S. (2000). Genital trauma due to animal bites. *Journal of Urology, 165,* 80–83.

Gompertz, L. (1997). Moral inquiries on the situation of man and of brutes . . . on the crime of committing cruelty on brutes . . . In C. Magel (ed.), *Moral inquiries on the situation of man and the brutes.* Lewiston, NY: The Edwin Mellen Press. (Original work published 1824)

Gordon, L. (1988). *Heroes of their own lives: The politics and history of family violence.* New York: Penguin Books.

Graft, J.L. (1996, September 2). The gorilla of America's dreams. *Time*, p. 70.

Graham-Kevan, N., and Archer, J. (2003). Intimate terrorism and common couple violence: A test of Johnson's predictions in four British samples. *Journal of Interpersonal Violence, 18,* 1247–1270.

Greene, E. (1993). Religious freedom and the effect on children of viewing animal sacrifices. *American Psychological Association Monitor,* Feb., 6.

Griffiths, H. (1975). *Just a dog.* New York: Holiday House.

Guillet, C. (1904). A glimpse at a nature school. *Pedagogical Seminary, 11,* 91–98.

Gullone, E. (2003). The proposed benefits of incorporating non-human animals into preventative efforts for Conduct Disorder. *Anthrozoös, 16,* 160–174.

Gunter, B. (1999). *Pets and People.* London: Whurr Publishers.

Guymer, E.C., Mellor, D., Luk, E.S.L., and Pearse, V. (2001). The development of a screening questionnaire for childhood cruelty to animals. *Journal of Child Psychology and Psychiatry, 42,* 1057–1063.

Hall, G.S. (1883). The content of children's minds. *Princeton Review, 2,* 249–272.

Hall, G.S. (1904). *The psychology of adolescence,* vol. 2. New York: D. Appleton and Company.

Hall, G.S. (1972). The contents of children's minds on entering school at the age of six years. In W. Dennis (ed.) (pp. 119–137). *Historical readings in developmental psychology.* New York: Appleton-Century-Crofts.

Hall, K.R. (1992). *Beyond the Killing Fields.* New York: Aperture.

Hallie, P. (1997). *Tales of good and evil, help and harm.* New York: Harper Collins.

Hallie, P.P (1982). *Cruelty.* Middletown, CT: Wesleyan University Press.

Hanson, R.F., and Spratt, E.G. (2000). Reactive Attachment Disorder: What we know about the disorder and implications for treatment. *Child Maltreatment, 5,* 137–145.

Hastings, P.D., Zahn-Waxler, C., Robinson, J., Usher, B., and Bridges, D. (2000). The development of concern for others in children with behavior problems. *Developmental Psychology, 36,* 531–546.

Headey, B. (1999). Health benefits and health cost savings due to pets: Preliminary estimates from an Australian national survey. *Social Indicators Research, 47,* 233–243.

Health Tips: Preventing dog bites. (2001). *Mayo Clinic Health Letter, 19,* 3.

Hewitt, S. (1990). The treatment of sexually abused preschool boys. In M. Hunter (ed.), *The sexually abused male.* Vol. 2 (pp. 225–248). New York: Lexington Books.

Hewitt, S. (1999). *Assessing allegations of sexual abuse in preschool children: Understanding small voices.* Thousand Oaks, CA: Sage.

Hickey, E. W. (1991). *Serial murderers and their victims.* Belmont, CA: Wadsworth, Inc.

Hill, S.A. (2000). The man who claimed to be a paedophile. *Journal of Medical Ethics, 26,* 137–138.

Hindman, J. (1992). *Juvenile Culpability Assessment,* 2nd ed. Ontario, OR: Alexandria Associates.

Hodge, C.F. (1899). Foundations of nature study. *Pedagogical Seminary, 6,* 536–553.

Hodge, C.F. (1900). Foundations of nature study [III]. *Pedagogical Seminary, 7,* 208–228.

Holden, C. (2000). The violence of the lambs. *Science, 289,* 580–581.

Hoover, E. (2003, September 12). Animal cruelty 101. *The Chronicle of Higher Education,* p. A33.

Horiuchi, V. (1993, July 31). Boy, 13, beats two birds to death at aviary. *Salt Lake Tribune,* p. B1.

Horn, J.C., and Meer, J. (1984). The pleasure of their company: A report on Psychology Today's survey on pets and people. *Psychology Today, Aug.,* 52–58.

Hunt, S. (1996). Battered wife is acquitted of murder. *Salt Lake Tribune,* p. B1.

Hunt, S. (1999, July 14). Account of 3-year-old's death called a 'stupid story.' *Salt Lake Tribune,* pp. C1-C2.

Hunt, S. (2000, March 18). Animal cruelty conviction preceded murder charge. *Salt Lake Tribune,* p. D2.

Hutchinson, B. (1994, June 3). Boy, 13, laughs at law after dog kill. *Boston Herald,* p. 1.

Itzin, C. (1998). Pornography and the organization of intra- and extrafamilial child sexual abuse. In G.K. Kantor and J. L. Jasinski (eds.), *Out of darkness: Contemporary perspectives on family violence* (pp. 58–79). Thousand Oaks, CA: Sage Publications.

Jacobsen, W. B. (2000). *Safe from the start: Taking action on children exposed to violence.* Washington, DC: Office of Juvenile Justice and Delinquency Prevention.

Jacobson, N., and Gottman, J. (1998). *When men batter women.* New York: Simon and Schuster.

James, P.D. (1982). *Shroud for a nightingale.* New York: Warner Books.

Jarolmen, J. (1998). A comparison of the grief reaction of children and adults: Focusing on pet loss and bereavement. *Omega, 37,* 133–150.

Jenkins, P. (1998). *Moral panic: Changing concepts of the child molester in modern America.* New Haven: Yale University Press.

Jersild, A.T. (1954). Emotional development. In L. Carmichael (ed.), *Manual of child psychology,* 2nd ed. (p. 888). New York: Wiley.

Johnson, B., and Becker, J. (1997). Natural born killers?: The development of the sexually sadistic serial killer. *Journal of the American Academy of Psychiatry and the Law, 25,* 335–348.

Jones, L., and Finkelhor, D. (2001). The decline in child sexual abuse cases. *Juvenile Justice Bulletin, January,* Office of Juvenile Justice and Delinquency Prevention.

Jory, B., and Randour, M.L. (1999). *The* AniCare *model of treatment for animal abuse.* Washington Grove, MD: Psychologists for the Ethical Treatment of Animals.

Kahn, P.H., Jr., and Kellert, S.R. (Eds.). (1994). *Children and nature: Psychological, sociocultural, and evolutionary investigations.* Cambridge, MA: MIT Press.

Katcher, A.H., and Wilkins, G.G. (2000). The Centaur's lessons: Therapeutic education through care of animals and nature study. In A. Fine (ed.), *Handbook on animal-assisted therapy: Theoretical foundations and guidelines for practice* (pp. 153–177). New York: Academic Press.

Kattolinsky. (1937). Der tierstecher in Schleswig-Holstein (The animal-stabber of Schleswig-Holstein; trans. Dr. Andre Beetz). *Kriminalistische Monatshefte, 11,* 124–128.

Katz, J. (2003). *The new work of dogs.* New York: Villard Books.

Kaufman, K.L., Hilliker, D.R., and Daleiden, E.L. (1996). Subgroup differences in the modus operandi of adolescent sexual offenders. *Child Maltreatment, 1,* 17–24.

Kazdin, A.E., and Esveldt-Dawson, K. (1986). The interview for antisocial behavior: Psychometric characteristics and concurrent validity with child psychiatric inpatients. *Journal of Psychopathology and Behavioral Assessment, 8,* 289–303.

Kellerman, J. (1999). *Savage spawn: Reflections on violent children.* New York: Ballantine Publishing.

Kellert, S.R. (1984). Attitudes toward animals: Age related development among children. In R.K. Anderson, B.J. Hart, and L.A. Hart (eds.), The *pet connection* (pp. 76–88). Minneapolis: Center to Study Human-Animal Relationships and Environments.

Kellert, S.R., and Felthous, A.R. (1985). Childhood cruelty toward animals among criminals and noncriminals. *Human Relations, 38,* 1113–1129).

Kempe, C.H., Silverman, F.N., Steele, B.F., Droegemueller, W., and Silver, H.K. (1962). The battered-child syndrome. *Journal of the American Medical Association, 181,* 105–122.

Kidd, A., and Kidd, R. (1985). Children's attitudes toward their pets. *Psychological Reports, 57,* 15–31.

Kidd, A., and Kidd, R. (1990). Social and environmental influences on children's attitudes toward pets. *Psychological Reports, 67,* 807–818.

Killer's childhood focus of 'Megan's Law' case. Witnesses say no sign Timmendequas was abused. (1997, June 17). *U.S. News (CNN).* Retrieved from the World Wide Web: http://www.cnn.com/US/9706/17/kanka/

Kogan, L.R., McConnell, S., Schoenfeld-Tacher, R., and Jansen-Lock, P. (2004). Crosstrails: A unique foster program to provide safety for pets of women in safehouses. *Violence against Women, 10,* 418–434.

Lane, S. (1997). Assessment of sexually abusive youth. In G. Ryan and S. Lane (eds.), *Juvenile sexual offending: Causes, consequences, and correction* (pp. 219–263). San Francisco: Jossey-Bass Publishers.

Langevin, R. (2003). A study of the psychosexual characteristics of sex killers: Can we identify them before it is too late? *International Journal of Offender Therapy and Comparative Criminology, 47,* 366–382.

Lantieri, L., and Patti, J. (1996). *Waging peace in our schools.* Boston, MA: Beacon Press.

Lapouse, R., and Monk, M.A. (1959). Fear and worries in a representative sample of children. *American Journal of Orthopsychiatry, 29,* 803–818.

Larzelere, R.E., Martin, J.A., and Amberson, T.G. (1989). The toddler behavior checklist: A parent-completed assessment of social-emotional characteristics of young preschoolers. *Family Relations, 38,* 418–425.

Laurent, E.L. (2000).Children, 'insects,' and play in Japan. In A.L. Podberscek, E.S. Paul, and J.A. Serpell (eds.), *Companion animals and us* (pp. 61–89). Cambridge: Cambridge University Press.

Lawrie, M. (2002). The mandatory reporting of animal abuse. *Veterinary Surgeons Board of Western Australia, Autumn issue.* Retrieved from the World Wide Web: http://vetsurgeonsboardwa.au.com/0302_02Abuse.html.

Lazoritz, S. (1989). Whatever happened to Mary Ellen? *Child Abuse and Neglect, 14,* 143–149.

Levinson, B. (1969). *Pet-oriented child psychotherapy.* Springfield, IL: Charles C. Thomas and Gerald P. Mallon.

Levinson, B. (1972). *Pets and human development.* Springfield, IL: Charles C. Thomas.

Levinson, D. (1989). *Family violence in cross-cultural perspective.* Newbury Park, CA: Sage Publications.

Lewchanin, S., and Zimmerman, E. (2000). *Clinical assessment of juvenile animal cruelty.* Brunswick, ME: Biddle Publishing Company and Audenreed Press.

Lewis, C. S. (1962). *Perelandra.* New York: Collier Books. (Original work published 1944)

Lewis, D.O. (1998). *Guilty by reason of insanity: A psychiatrist explores the minds of killers.* New York: Ballantine Publishing.

Loar, L. (1999). "I'll only help you if you have two legs" or, why human services professionals should pay attention to cases involving cruelty to animals. In F. R. Ascione and P. Arkow (eds.), *Child abuse, domestic violence, and animal abuse: Linking the circles of compassion for prevention and intervention* (pp. 120–136). West Lafayette, IN: Purdue University Press.

Locke, J. (1693). *Some Thoughts Concerning Education,* Sec. 116. J. W. Yolton and J. S. Yoltan (eds.) 1989. Oxford: Clarendon Press.

Lockwood, R. (1989). *Cruelty to animals and human violence.* Training Key No. 392. Arlington, VA: International Association of Chiefs of Police.

Lockwood, R., and Ascione, F.R. (1998). *Cruelty to Animals and Interpersonal Violence: Readings in Research and Application.* West Lafayette, IN: Purdue University Press.

Lockwood, R., and Church, A. (1996). Deadly serious: An FBI perspective on animal cruelty. *HSUS News (Fall)*, 1–4.

Lockwood, R., and. Hodge, G.R. (1986). The tangled web of animal abuse: The links between cruelty to animals and human violence. *Humane Society News, Summer.*

Loeber, R., Farrington, D.P., and Waschbusch, D.A. (1998). Serious and violent juvenile offenders. In R. Loeber and D.P. Farrington (eds.), *Serious and violent juvenile offenders: Risk factors and successful interventions* (pp. 13–29). Thousand Oaks, CA: Sage Publications.

Loeber, R., Keenan, K., Lahey, B., Green, S., and Thomas, C. (1993). Evidence for developmentally based diagnoses of oppositional defiant disorder and conduct disorder. *Journal of Abnormal Child Psychology, 21*, 377–410.

Love, M., and Overall, K. (2001). How anticipating relationships between dogs and children can help prevent disasters. *Journal of the American Veterinary Medical Association, 219*, 446–453.

Lowry, L. (1993). *The giver.* New York: Bantam Doubleday.

Luk, E.S. L., Staiger, P.K., Wong, L., and Mathai, J. (1999). Children who are cruel to animals: A revisit. *Australian and New Zealand Journal of Psychiatry, 33*, 29–36.

Lutzker, J.R. (ed.) (1998). *Handbook of child abuse research and treatment.* New York: Plenum Press.

Lyon, J.J. (1993, June 17). Educational program cuts juvenile-set fires. *Logan Herald Journal*, p. 2.

Ma, H.K., and Leung, M.C. (1991). Altruistic orientation in children: Construction and validation of the Child Altruism Inventory. *International Journal of Psychology, 26*, 745–759.

Macdonald, A. (1981). The pet dog in the home: A study of interactions. In B. Fogle (ed.), *Interrelations between people and pets* (pp. 195–206). Springfield, IL: Charles C. Thomas.

Magid, K., and McKelvey, C.A. (1987). *High risk: Children without a conscience.* New York: Bantam Books.

Mahoney, P., Williams, L.M., and West, C.M. (2001) Violence against women by intimate relationship partners. In C.M. Renzetti, J.L. Edleson, and R.K. Bergen (eds.), *Sourcebook on violence against women* (pp. 143–178). Thousand Oaks: Sage.

Man arrested after dog tossed off cliff. (1997, August 7). Newport, Oregon *Register-Guardian*, p. 3B.

Marshall, F., Kennedy, K., and Mendel, B. (Producers), and Night Shyamalan, M. (Director). (1999). *The Sixth Sense* [Motion picture]. United States: Hollywood Pictures and Spyglass Entertainment.

Martinez, P., and Richters, J.E. (1993). The NIMH Community Violence Project: II. Children's distress symptoms associated with violence exposure. *Psychiatry, 56*, 22–35.

Masson, J. (1984). *The assault on truth.* New York: Farrar, Straus, and Giroux.

Masson, J.M., and McCarthy, S. (1995). *When elephants weep: The emotional lives of animals.* New York: Delacorte Press.

McAlister Groves, B. (2002). *Children who see too much.* Boston: Beacon Press.

McClellan, J., Adams, J., Douglas, D., McCurry, C., and Storck, M. (1995). Clinical characteristics related to severity of sexual abuse: A study of seriously mentally ill youth. *Child Abuse and Neglect, 19,* 1245–1254.

McCloskey, L.A. (2001). The "Medea Complex" among men: The instrumental abuse of children to injure wives. *Victims and Violence, 16,* 19–37.

McCloskey, L.A., and Lichter, E.L. (2003). The contribution of marital violence to adolescent aggression across different relationships. *Journal of Interpersonal Violence, 18,* 390–412.

Mead, M. (1964). Cultural factors in the cause and prevention of pathological homicide. *Bulletin of the Menninger Clinic, 28,* 11–22.

Meadow, R. (1977). Munchausen syndrome by proxy: The hinterland of child abuse. *Lancet, 2,* 343–345.

Mehta, M.D. (2001). Pornography in Usenet: A study of 9,800 randomly selected images. *CyberPsychology, 4,* 695–703.

Melson, G. (1998). The role of companion animals in human development. In C.C. Wilson and D.C. Turner (eds.), *Companion animals in human health* (pp. 219–236). Thousand Oaks, CA: Sage.

Melson, G. (2001). *Why the wild things are: Animals in the lives of children.* Cambridge, MA: Harvard University Press.

Merz-Perez, L., and Heide, K.M. (2004). *Animal cruelty: Pathway to violence against people.* Walnut Creek, CA: AltaMira Press.

Merz-Perez, L., Heide, K.M., and Silvereman, I.J. (2001). Childhood cruelty to animals and subsequent violence against humans. *Journal of Offender Therapy and Comparative Criminology, 45,* 556–573.

Mewshaw, M. (1980). *Life for death.* Garden City, NY: Doubleday.

Miedzian, M. (1991). *Boys will be boys: Breaking the link between masculinity and violence.* New York: Anchor Books.

Miletski, H. (2002). *Understanding bestiality and zoophilia.* Bethesda, MD: East-West Publishing.

Milgram, S. (1975). *Obedience to authority.* New York: Harper Colophon Books.

Miller, K.S., and Knutson, J.F. (1997). Reports of severe physical punishment and exposure to animal cruelty by inmates convicted of felonies and by university students. *Child Abuse and Neglect, 21,* 59–82.

Milloy, C. (1994, January 26). Children with compassion. *Washington Post,* p. B1.

Monet, Gaby (Producer). (1990). *Child of rage* [Documentary film]. United States: HBO, Inc.

Montminy-Danna, M., and Rice, H. (1999, October 28). Children living with domestic violence and animal cruelty. Presentation at "Creating a Legacy of Hope," International Conference on Children Exposed to Domestic Violence, Vancouver, BC.

Morris, W. (1996). *My dog Skip.* New York: Vintage Books.

Munro, H. (1996). Battered pets. *Irish Veterinary Journal, 49,* 712–713.

Munro, M.H.C., and Thrusfield, M.V. (2001a). 'Battered pets' features that raise suspicion of non-accidental injury. *Journal of Small Animal Practice, 42,* 218–226.

Munro, M.H.C., and Thrusfield, M.V. (2001b). 'Battered pets': non-accidental physical injuries found in dogs and cats. *Journal of Small Animal Practice, 42,* 279–290.

Munro, M.H.C., and Thrusfield, M.V. (2001c). 'Battered pets': sexual abuse. *Journal of Small Animal Practice, 42,* 333–337.

Munro, M.H.C., and Thrusfield, M.V. (2001d). "Battered pets": Munchausen syndrome by proxy (factitious illness by proxy). *Journal of Small Animal Practice, 42,* 385–389.

Murray, B.J. (1993). I never promised you a rose garden: Compulsive self-mutilation. In. J.M. Goodwin (ed.), *Rediscovering childhood trauma* (pp. 191–199). Washington, DC: American Psychiatric Press.

Muscari, M. (2004). Juvenile animal abuse: Practice and policy implications for PNPs. *Journal of Pediatric Health Care, 18,* 15–21.

Myers, C. (1995). Speaking for the animals. *American Scientist, 83,* 558.

Myers, G. (1998). *Children and animals: Social development and our connections to other species.* Boulder, CO: Westview Press.

Myers, J.E.B., Berliner, L., Briere, J., Hendrix, C.T., Jenny, C., and Reid, T.A. (eds.). (2002). *The APSAC handbook on child maltreatment,* 2nd ed. Thousand Oaks, CA: Sage.

Nabhan, G.P., and Trimble, S. (1994). *The geography of childhood: Why children need wild places.* Boston: Beacon Press.

Nader, K., Pynoos, R., Fairbanks, L., and Fredrick, C. (1990). Children's PTSD reactions one year after a sniper attack at their school. *American Journal of Psychiatry, 147,* 1526–1530.

Naylor, P.R. (1992). *Shiloh.* New York: Bantam Doubleday Bell.

Nelson, P. (2002). *A survey of psychologists' attitudes, opinions, and clinical experiences with animal abuse.* Unpublished doctoral dissertation, Wright Graduate School of Psychology, Berkeley, CA.

Nevada spree leaves six animals dead. Four wild horses and two wild burros have been shot to death. (2000, January 7). *Salt Lake Tribune,* p. A9.

Nordheimer, J. (1993, August 19). A big-city horror in a small town. *New York Times,* Sec. 1, p. 33.

Offord, D.R., Boyle, M.H., and Racine, Y.A. (1991). The epidemiology of antisocial behavior in childhood and adolescence. In D. J. Pepler and K. H. Rubin (eds.), *The development and treatment of childhood aggression* (pp. 31–54). Hillsdale, NJ: Lawrence Erlbaum Associates.

Oliver, R. (1998, May 6). Cat kidnap goes awry. *Logan Herald Journal*, pp. 1, 7.

Ollendick, T.H., King, N.J., and Frary, R.B. (1989). Fears in children and adolescents: Reliability and generalizability across gender, age, and nationality. *Behavior Research and Therapy, 27,* 19–26.

Osofsky, J.D. (1999). The impact of violence on children. *The Future of Children, 9 No. 3,* 33–49.

Overall, K.L., and Love, M. (2001). Dog bites to humans—demography, epidemiology, injury, and risk. *Journal of the American Veterinary Medical Association, 218,* 1923–1934.

Ownby, D.R., Johnson, C.C, and Peterson, E.L. (2002). Exposure to dogs and cats in the first year of life and risk of allergic sensitization at 6 to 7 years of age. *Journal of the American Medical Association, 288,* 963–972.

Pagani, C. (2000). Perception of a common fate in human-animal relations and its relevance to our concern for animals. *Anthrozoös, 13,* 66–73.

Parker, J.L. (1997). *Animal abuse and its relationship to the attachment disorder of childhood.*

Parkinson, V. (1961). *Kindness to pets, starring Spotty the pup.* Irvington-on-Hudson, NY: Harvey House. (Original work published 1943.)

Parslow, R.A., and Jorm, A.F. (2003). The impact of pet ownership on health and health service use: Results from a community sample of Australians aged 40 to 44 years. *Anthrozoös, 16,* 43–56.

Patronek, G.J. (1999). Hoarding of animals: An under-recognized public health problem in a difficult-to-study population. *Public Health Reports, 114,* 81–87.

Patsuris, P. (1993, July 31). Idiot's delight. *TV Guide*, pp. 20–21.

Paul, E.S. (2000). Love of pets and love of people. In A.L. Podberscek, E.S. Paul, and J.A. Serpell (eds.), *Companion animals and us* (pp. 168–86). Cambridge: Cambridge University Press.

Pearse, V.A.T. (1999). *Pilot study of children with persistent behavior problems and cruelty to animals.* Master's thesis, Monash University, Melbourne, Victoria, Australia.

Peterzell, P. (1995, November 29). Teen accused of pet torture. Novato suspect described as 'budding young sociopath.' *Marin Independent Journal*, p. A1.

Pickles, A., and Angold, A. (2003). Natural categories or fundamental dimensions: On carving nature at the joints and the rearticulation of psychopathology. *Development and Psychopathology, 15,* 529–551.

Pilkington, M. (1809). *Biography for boys; or Characteristic histories calculated to impress the youthful mind with an admiration of virtuous principles, and a detestation of vicious ones.* Philadelphia, PA: Johnson and Warner.

Pickering, S.F., Jr. (1993). *Moral instruction and fiction for children, 1749–1820.* Athens, GA: University of Georgia Press.

Pincus, J.H. (2001). *Base instincts: What makes killers kill.* New York: W.W. Norton.

Police investigating animal cruelty allegation. A teenage boy has been accused of torturing his puppy before drowning the animal and burying it next to his driveway. (1996, July 23). *Ogden Standard-Examiner.*

Ponder, C., and Lockwood, R. (2000). Programs educate law enforcement on link between animal cruelty and domestic violence. *The Police Chief, 67,* 31–36.

Poresky, R. (1990). The young children's empathy measure: Reliability, validity, and effects of companion animal bonding. *Psychological Reports, 66,* 931–936.

Poresky, R. (1996). Companion animals and other factors affecting young children's development. *Anthrozoös, 9,* 159–168.

Poresky, R., and Hendrix, C. (1990). Differential effects of pet presence and pet bonding on young children. *Psychological Reports, 67,* 51–54.

Preventing Dog Bites. (2001). *American Family Physician, 63,* 1573–1574.

Pynoos, R.S., Frederick, C., Nader, K., Arroyo, W., Steinberg, A., Eth, S., et al. (1987). Life threat and posttraumatic stress in school-age children. *Archives of General Psychiatry, 44,* 1057–1063.

Quinlisk, J.A. (1999). Animal abuse and family violence. In Ascione, F.R., and Arkow, P. (eds.), *Child abuse, domestic violence, and animal abuse: Linking the circles of compassion for prevention and intervention* (pp. 168–175). West Lafayette, IN: Purdue University Press.

Raine, A. (1993). *The psychopathology of crime: Criminal behavior as a clinical disorder.* New York: Academic Press.

Randolf, E. (1999). *Manual for the Randolf Attachment Disorder Questionnaire.* Evergreen, CO: The Attachment Center Press.

Randour, M.L., Krinsk, S., and Wolf, J.L. (2002). *AniCare Child: An assessment and treatment approach for childhood animal abuse.* Washington Grove, MD: Psychologists for the Ethical Treatment of Animals.

Raphael, P., Colman, L., and Loar, L. (1999). *Teaching compassion: A guide for humane educators, teachers, and parents.* Alameda, CA: The Latham Foundation.

Reidy, T.J. (1977). The aggressive characteristics of abused and neglected children. *Journal of Clinical Psychology, 33,* 1140–1145.

Reisman, R., and Adams, C.A. (1999). Should veterinarians tell? In Ascione, F.R., and Arkow, P. (eds.), *Child abuse, domestic violence, and animal abuse: Linking the circles of compassion for prevention and intervention* (pp. 221–227). West Lafayette, IN: Purdue University Press.

Reiss A.J., Jr., and Roth, J.A. (eds.). (1993). *Understanding and preventing violence.* Washington, D.C. National Academy Press.

Renzetti, C.M. (1992). *Violent betrayal: Partner abuse in lesbian relationships.* Thousand Oaks, CA: Sage Publications.

Ressler, R.K., Burgess, A.W., and Douglas, J.E. (1988). *Sexual homicide: Patterns and motives.* Lexington, MA: Lexington Books.

Rew, L. (2000). Friends and pets as companions: Strategies for coping with loneliness among homeless youth. *Journal of Child and Adolescent Psychiatric Nursing, 13,* 125–140.

Rice, M.E., and Harris, G.T. (1996). Predicting the recidivism of mentally disordered firesetters. *Journal of Interpersonal Violence, 11,* 364–375.

Richters, J.E., and Salzman, W. (1990). *Survey of exposure to community violence.* Child and Adolescent Disorders Branch, National Institute of Mental Health.

Rigdon, J., and Tapia, F. (1977). Children who are cruel to animals—a follow-up study. *Journal of Operational Psychology, 8,* 27–36.

Robin, M., ten Bensel, R.W., Quigley, J., and Anderson, R.K. (1984). Abused children and their pets. In R.K. Anderson, B.L. Hart, and L.A. Hart (eds.), *The pet connection* (pp. 111–117). Minneapolis: Center to Study Human-Animal Relationships and Environments.

Rogeness, G.H., Amrung, S.A., Macedo, C.A., Harris, W.R., and Fisher, C. (1986). Psychopathology in abused or neglected children. *Journal of the American Academy of Child Psychiatry, 25,* 659–665.

Rohrich, R.J. (1999). Man's best friend: Who's watching the children? *Plastic and Reconstructive Surgery, 103,* 2067–2068.

Roscoe, B., Haney, S., and Peterson, K.L. (1986). Child/pet maltreatment: Adolescents' ratings of parent and owner behaviors. *Adolescence, 21,* 807–814.

Rosenberg, D. (1995). From lying to homicide: The spectrum of Munchausen Syndrome by Proxy. In A.V. Levin and M.S. Sheridan (eds.), *Munchausen Syndrome by Proxy: Issues in diagnosis and treatment* (pp. 13–37). New York: Lexington Books.

Ross, S.M. (1996). Risk of physical abuse to children of spouse abusing parents. *Child Abuse and Neglect, 20,* 589–598.

Rother, C. (1995, November 6). Authorities seek boys who tortured, killed cat. *The San Diego Union-Tribune.*

Ryan, G., and Lane, S. (Eds.) (1997). *Juvenile sexual offending: Causes, consequences, and correction.* San Francisco: Jossey-Bass Publishers.

Sacks, J.J., Sinclair, L., Gilchrist, J., Golab, G.C., and Lockwood, R. (2000). Breeds of dogs involved in fatal human attacks in the United States between 1979 and 1998. *Journal of the American Veterinary Medical Association, 217,* 836–840.

Sagan, C., and Druyan, A. (1992). *Shadows of forgotten ancestors.* New York: Random House.

Sakheim, G.A., and Osborn, E. (1994). *Firesetting children: Risk assessment and treatment.* Washington, DC: Child Welfare League of America.

Salem, D.J., and Rowan, A.N. (Eds.). *State of the animals 2000.* Washington, DC: Humane Society Press.

Salt Lake City Area Juvenile Firesetter/Arson Control and Prevention Program. (1992). Salt Lake City, UT: Salt Lake City Fire Department.

Salter, D., McMillan, D., Richards, M., Talbot, T., Hodges, J., Bentovim, A., Hastings, R., Stevenson, J., and Skuse, D. (2003). Development of sexually abusive behaviour in sexually victimized males: A longitudinal study. *Lancet, 361,* 471–476.

Salzman, L.E., Fanslow, J.L., McMahon, P.M., and Shelley, G.A. (1999). *Intimate partner violence surveillance: Uniform definitions and recommended data elements,* Version 1.0. Atlanta, GA: National Center for Injury Prevention and Control, Centers for Disease Control and Prevention.

Samenow, S.E. (1984). *Inside the criminal mind.* New York: Crown Business.

Sandnabba, N.K., Santtila, P., Nordling, N., Beetz, A., and Alison, L. (2002). Characteristics of a sample of sadomasochistically-oriented males with recent experience of sexual contact with animals. *Deviant Behavior: An Interdisciplinary Journal, 23,* 511–529.

Sandnabba, N.K., Santtila, P., Wannäs, M., and Krook, K. (2003). Age and gender specific sexual behaviors in children. *Child Abuse and Neglect, 27,* 579–605.

Saunders, B.E. (2003). Understanding children exposed to violence: Toward an integration of overlapping fields. *Journal of Interpersonal Violence, 18,* 356–376.

Saunders, M. (1922). *Beautiful Joe.* New York: A.L. Burt Company. (Original work published 1893.)

Savesky, K., and V. Malcarne. (1981). *People and animals: A humane education curriculum.* East Haddam, CT: National Association for the Advancement of Humane Education.

Sawyer, K. (1996, August 24). A humane gorilla: The cross-species drama of Binti. *Salt Lake Tribune,* p. A7.

Scarpa, A. (2001). Community violence exposure in a young adult sample. *Journal of Interpersonal Violence, 16,* 36–53.

Schiff, K., Louw, D., and Ascione, F.R. (1999). Animal relations in childhood and later violent behaviour against humans. *Acta Criminologica, 12,* 77–86.

Schlueter, S. (1999). Animal abuse and law enforcement. In F.R. Ascione and P. Arkow (eds.), *Child abuse, domestic violence, and animal abuse: Linking the circles of compassion for prevention and intervention* (pp. 316–327). West Lafayette, IN: Purdue University Press.

Sewell, A. (1965). *Black Beauty.* Racine, WI: Western Publishing Co.

Shultz, W.J. (1924/1968). *The humane movement in the United States, 1910–1922.* New York: Columbia University Press.

Sedlak, A.J. and D.D. Broadhurst. (1996). *Third national incidence study of child abuse and neglect.* Washington, DC: U.S. Department of Health and Human Services.

Seifert, K. (2003). *Care, Child and Adolescent Risk Evaluation—A measure of the risk for violent behavior.* Champaign, IL: Research Press.

Sereny, G. (1972). *The Case of Mary Bell.* New York: McGraw-Hill.

Sereny, G. (1998). *Cries unheard. Why children kill: The Story of Mary Bell.* New York: Henry Holt and Company.

Shanab, M.E., and Yahya, K.A. (1977). A behavioral study of obedience in children. *Journal of Personality and Social Psychology, 35,* 530–536.

Shelman, E.A., and Lazoritz, S. (2000). *Out of the darkness: The story of Mary Ellen Wilson.* Lake Forest, CA: Dolphin Moon Publishing.

Shepard, P. (1996). *The others: How animals made us human.* Washington, DC: Island Press.

Sheridan, C.L. and King, R.G., Jr. (1972). Obedience to authority with an authentic victim. Proceedings of the 80th Annual Convention of the American Psychological Association, 165–166.

Shesgreen, S. (1973). *Engravings by Hogarth.* New York: Dover Publications.

Shonkoff, J.P., and Phillips, D.A. (Eds.). (2000). *From neurons to neighborhoods: The science of early childhood development.* Washington, DC: National Academy Press.

Shultz, W.J. (1968). *The humane movement in the United States, 1910–1922.* New York: AMS Press. (Original work published 1924)

Slaby, R.G., Roedell, W.C., Arezzo, D., and Hendrix, K. (1995). *Early violence prevention: Tools for teachers of young children.* Washington, DC: National Association for the Education of Young Children.

Slayer of five boys is executed in Utah by injection of drugs. (1988, June 11). *New York Times,* p. 8.

Snyder, H.N., and Sickmund, M. (1999). *Juvenile offenders and victims: 1999 National Report.* Washington, DC: U.S. Department of Justice, Office of Justice Programs, Office of Juvenile Justice and Delinquency Prevention.

Spitzer, C. (1999, November 13). Study: Talbot children live in fear of violence. Easton, MD *Star Democrat,* p. 1A.

Sprafkin, J.M., Leibert, R.M., and Poulos, R.W. (1975). Effects of a prosocial televised example on children's helping. *Journal of Experimental Child Psychology, 20,* 119–126.

Strachey, Amy (Simpson) [Mrs. St. Loe Strachey]. (1940). *Borrowed children: A popular account of some evacuation problems and their remedies.* New York: The Commonwealth Fund.

Stevens, P., and Eide, M. (1990). The first chapter of children's rights. *American Heritage, July/August,* 84–91.

Stewart, M.F. (1999). *Companion animal death.* Oxford, England: Butterworth Heinemann.

Stickle, T.R., and Belechman, E.A. (2002). Aggression and fire: Antisocial behavior in firesetting and nonfiresetting juvenile offenders. *Journal of Psychopathology and Behavioral Assessment, 24,* 177–193.

Stone, R., and Kelner, K. (2000). Violence: No silver bullet. *Science, 289,* 569.

Straus, M.A. (1991). *Beating the devil out of them: Corporal punishment in American families.* New York: Lexington Books.

Summit, R. (1983). The child sexual abuse accommodation syndrome. *Child Abuse and Neglect, 7,* 177–193.

Sussman, M.B. (ed.). (1985). *Pets and the family. Marriage and family review.* New York: Haworth Press.

Swarthout, G. (1995). *Bless the beasts and the children.* New York: Simon and Schuster Pocket Books.

Tapia, F. (1971). Children who are cruel to animals. *Child Psychiatry and Human Development, 2,* 70–77.

Taylor, M. (1999). *Imaginary companions and the children who create them.* New York: Oxford University Press.

ten Bensel, R.W. (1984). Historical perspectives of human values for animals and vulnerable people. In R.K. Anderson, B.L. Hart, and L.A. Hart (eds.), *The pet connection* (pp. 2–14). Minneapolis, MN: Center to Study Human-Animal Relationships and Environments.

ten Bensel, R.W. (1987). The importance of animals and children: Their place in the family and in the world. *Anthrozoös, 1,* 137–139.

Terr, L. (1990). *Too scared to cry.* Harper and Row.

The American Humane Association. (1996). *Growing up humane in a violent world: A parent's guide.*

The National Crime Prevention Council. (2002). *50 Strategies to prevent violent domestic crimes.* Washington, DC: National Crime Prevention Council.

Thomas, C., and McIntosh, S. (2001, June 7). Exploring the links between animal abuse and family as reported by women entering shelters in Calgary communities. Presentation at Our children, our future: A call to action, International Conference on Children Exposed to Domestic Violence, London, Ontario, Canada.

Thompson, K.L., and Gullone, E. (2003). The Children's Treatment of Animals Questionnaire [CTAQ]: A psychometric investigation. *Society and Animals, 11,* 1–15.

Tingle, D., Barnard, G.W., Robbins, L., Newman, G., and Hutchinson, D. (1986). Childhood and adolescent characteristics of pedophiles and rapists. *International Journal of Law and Psychiatry, 9,* 103–116.

Tjaden, P. (1997). *The crime of stalking: How big is the problem?* NIJ Research in Brief No. NCJ 163921. Washington, DC: U.S. Department of Justice.

To kill a sweet, furry beast. Who is killing bunnies all over Japan? (1997, September 22). *Newsweek,* p.8.

Tremblay, R.E. (2003). Why socialization fails: The case of chronic physical aggression. In B.B. Lahey, T.E. Moffitt, and A. Caspi (eds.), *Causes of conduct disorder and juvenile delinquency* (pp. 182–224). New York: Guilford Press.

Triplett, N. (1903). A study of the faults of children. *Pedagogical Seminary, 10,* 200–238.

Turner, N. (2000). Animal abuse and the link to domestic violence. *The Police Chief, 67,* 28, 30.

Unti, B., and DeRosa, B. (2003). Humane education past, present, and future. In D.J. Salem and A.N. Rowan (eds.), *The state of the animals II.* Washington, DC: Humane Society Press.

Vachss, A.H. (1991). *Sacrifice.* New York: Alfred A. Knopf.

Vachss, A.H. (1993). *Another chance to get it right.* Milwaukie, OR: Dark Horse Publishing.

Vachss, A. (1993). *Sex crimes.* New York: Random House.

VanLeeuwen, J. (1981). A child psychiatrist's perspective on children and their companion animals. In B. Fogle (ed.), *Interrelations between people and pet* (pp. 175–194). Springfield, IL: Charles C. Thomas.

Verlinden, S., Hersen, M., and Thomas, J. (2000). Risk factors in school shootings. *Clinical Psychology Review, 20,* 3–56.

Vistica, G.L. (1997, November 24). A quiet war over the past. *Newsweek,* p. 41.

Walker, L.E. (1989). *Terrifying love.* New York: Harper and Row.

Walker, L.E.(1984). *The battered woman syndrome.* New York: Springer Publishing.

Waterman, J., Kelly, R.J., Oliveri, M.K., and McCord, J. (1993). *Behind the playground walls: Sexual abuse in preschools.* New York: Guilford Press.

Watson, J., and Raynor, R. (1920). Conditioned emotional reactions. *Journal of Experimental Psychology, 8,* 1–14.

Weber, C., and Ascione, F.R. (1992, July 23). Humane attitudes and human empathy: Relations in adulthood. Keynote address at the 6th International Conference on Human Animal Interactions, Montreal, Canada.

Wertsch, M. (1991). *Military brats: Legacies of childhood inside the fortress.* New York: Harmony Books.

Wheeler, E.A. (1998). *The story of Mary Ellen.* Englewood, CO: American Humane Association.

Wherry, J.N., Jolly, J.B., Feldman, J., Adam, B., and Manjanatha, S. (1995). Child Sexual Abuse Inventory scores for inpatient psychiatric boys: An exploratory study. *Journal of Child Sexual Abuse, 4,* 95–105.

Whitelaw, K. (2001, January 8). When kids go to war: Victimizers or victims? *U.S. News and World Report,* p.28.

Whitfield, C.L., Anda, R.F., Dube, S.R., and Felitti, V.J. (2003). Violent childhood experiences and the risk of intimate partner violence in adults: Assessment in a large health maintenance organization. *Journal of Interpersonal Violence, 18,* 166–185.

Widom, C.S. (1989). The cycle of violence. *Science, 244,* 160–166.

Wiegand, P., Schmidt, V., and Kleiber, M. (1999). German shepherd dog is suspected of sexually abusing a child. *International Journal of Legal Medicine, 112,* 324–325.

Wiehe , V.R. (1990). *Sibling abuse.* Lexington, MA: Lexington Books.

Wiehe, V.R. (1997a). Approaching child abuse treatment from the perspective of empathy. *Child Abuse and Neglect, 21,* 1191–1204.

Wiehe, V.R. (1997b). *Sibling abuse* (2nd ed). Thousand Oaks, CA: Sage.

Wilson, W. (1990). I had prayed to God that this thing was fiction . . . *American Heritage,* Feb., p. 49.

Wooden, W.S., and Berkey, M.L. (1984). *Children and arson: America's middle class nightmare.* New York: Plenum Press.

Worth, D., and Beck, A.M. (1981). Multiple ownership of animals in New York City. *Transactions and Studies of the College of Physicians of Philadelphia, 3,* 280–300.

Yarrow, M.R., Scott, P.N., and Waxler, C.Z. (1973). Learning concern for others. *Developmental Psychology, 8,* 240–260.

Zahn-Waxler, C., Hollenbeck, B., and Radke-Yarrow, M. (1984). The origins of empathy and altruism. In M.W. Fox and L.D. Mickley (eds.), *Advances in Animal Welfare Science.* Norwell, MA: Kluwer Academic.

Zeanah, C., Danis, B., Hirsheberg, L., Benoit, D., Miller, D., and Heller, S. (1999). Disorganized attachment associated with partner violence: A research note. *Infant Mental Health Journal, 20,* 77–86.

Zimmerman, E., and Lewchanin, S. (2000). *Community intervention in juvenile cruelty to animals.* Brunswick, ME: Biddle Publishing.

Zolondek, S.C., Abel, G.G., Northey, W.F., Jr., and Jordan, A.D. (2001). The self-reported behavior of juvenile sex offenders. *Journal of Interpersonal Violence, 16,* 73–85.

INDEX